CUSTODIANS OF THE INTERNET

CUSTODIANS OF THE INTERNET

platforms, content moderation,
and the hidden decisions that
shape social media

tarleton gillespie

Yale UNIVERSITY PRESS/NEW HAVEN & LONDON

Yale University Press books may be purchased in quantity for educational,
business, or promotional use. For information, please e-mail sales.press@yale.
edu (U.S. office) or sales@yaleup.co.uk (U.K. office).

Set in Minion type by IDS Infotech Ltd., Chandigarh, India.
Printed in the United States of America.

Library of Congress Control Number: 2017953111
ISBN 978-0-300-17313-0 (hardcover: alk. paper)

A catalogue record for this book is available from the British Library.

This paper meets the requirements of ANSI/NISO Z39.48-1992 (Permanence of
Paper).

10 9 8 7 6 5 4 3 2 1

CONTENTS

CUSTODIANS OF THE INTERNET

1

all platforms moderate

In the ideal world, I think that our job in terms of a moderating function
would be really to be able to just turn the lights on and off and sweep the
floors . . . but there are always the edge cases, that are gray.
—*personal interview, member of content policy team, YouTube*

Titled *The Terror of War* but more commonly known as "Napalm Girl," the
1972 Pulitzer Prize–winning photo by Associated Press photographer Nick
Ut is perhaps the most indelible depiction of the horrors of the Vietnam
War. You've seen it. Several children run down a barren street fleeing a napalm attack, their faces in agony, followed in the distance by Vietnamese
soldiers. The most prominent among them, Kim Phuc, naked, suffers from
napalm burns over her back, neck, and arm. The photo's status as an
iconic image of war is why Norwegian journalist Tom Egeland included it
in a September 2016 article reflecting on photos that changed the history
of warfare. And it was undoubtedly some combination of that graphic suffering and the underage nudity that led Facebook moderators to delete
Egeland's post.

After reposting the image and criticizing Facebook's decision, Egeland
was suspended twice, first for twenty-four hours, then for three additional
days.[1] Norway's daily newspaper *Aftenposten* then reported on his suspensions and included the photo; Facebook moderators subsequently instructed the newspaper to remove or pixelate the photo, then went ahead and
deleted it anyway.[2] The editor in chief of *Aftenposten* took to the newspaper's
front page to express his outrage at Facebook's decision, again publishing
the photo along with a statement directed at Facebook CEO Mark Zuckerberg.

FREDAG 9. september 2016 Uke 36 · Nr. 253 · 157. årgang · Løssalg kr 40 (Levert hjem fra kr 12. Bestill på ap.no/abo)

Facebook krever at Aftenposten fjerner dette historiske bildet fra vår Facebook-side. Her er Aftenpostens svar:

Dear Mark Zuckerberg

Aftenposten

Jeg skriver til deg for å fortelle hvorfor Aftenposten ikke vil etterkomme Facebooks krav om å fjerne eller redigere dette viktige dokumentarbildet.

Espen Egil Hansen, sjefredaktør   Lik dette   Kommenter   Del

NYHETER · DEL 1 · SIDE 2-5 · KULTUR · DEL 2 · SIDE 2-3

Front page of the Norwegian newspaper *Aftenposten*, September 8, 2016, including the "Terror of War" photograph (by Nick Ut / Associated Press) and editor in chief Espen Egil Hansen's open letter to Mark Zuckerberg, critical of Facebook's removal of Ut's photo. Newspaper used with permission from *Aftenposten*; photo used with permission from Associated Press.

In it he criticized both the decision and Facebook's undue influence on news, calling Facebook "the world's most powerful editor."[3] Many Norwegian readers, even the prime minister of Norway herself, reposted the photo to Facebook, only to have it quickly removed.[4]

More than a week after the image was first removed, after a great deal of global news coverage critical of the decision, Facebook reinstated the photo. Responding to the controversy, Facebook Vice President Justin Osofsky explained:

> These decisions aren't easy. In many cases, there's no clear line between an image of nudity or violence that carries global and historic significance and one that doesn't. Some images may be offensive in one part of the world and acceptable in another, and even with a clear standard, it's hard to screen millions of posts on a case-by-case basis every week. Still, we can do better. In this case, we tried to strike a difficult balance between enabling expression and protecting our community and ended up making a mistake. But one of the most important things about Facebook is our ability to listen to our community and evolve, and I appreciate everyone who has helped us make things right. We'll keep working to make Facebook an open platform for all ideas.[5]

It is easy to argue, and many did, that Facebook made the wrong decision. Not only is Ut's photo of great historical and emotional import, but it also has been "vetted" by Western culture for decades. And Facebook certainly could have handled the removals differently. At the same time, what a hard call to make! This is an immensely challenging image: a vital document of history, so troubling an indictment of humanity that many feel it must be seen—and a graphic and profoundly upsetting image of a fully naked child screaming in pain. Cultural and legal prohibitions against underage nudity are firm across nearly all societies, with little room for debate. And the suffering of these children is palpable and gruesome. It is important precisely because of how Kim Phuc's pain, and her nakedness, make plain the horror of chemical warfare. Its power is its violation: "the photo violates one set of norms in order to activate another; propriety is set aside for a moral purpose. It is a picture that shouldn't be shown of an event that shouldn't have happened."[6] There is no question that this image is obscenity. The question is whether it is the kind of obscenity of representation that should be kept from view, no matter how relevant, or the kind of obscenity of history that must be shown, no matter how devastating.

Much of the press coverage treated Facebook's decision to remove the image as a thoughtless one, even an automatic one. But Egeland's post was almost certainly removed by a paid, human reviewer, though it may have been flagged by automatic software or by a user.[7] Nor was it an error: in fact, Facebook had a specific policy on this specific image, which it had encountered before, many times. It was later reported by Reuters that the famous photo "had previously been used in training sessions as an example of a post that should be removed. . . . Trainers told content-monitoring staffers that the photo violated Facebook policy, despite its historical significance, because it depicted a naked child, in distress, photographed without her consent."[8] Ut's photo is a test image, literally and figuratively, a proxy with which an industry and a society draws parameters of what is acceptable.[9]

It is important to remember, however, that traditional media outlets also debated whether to publish this image, long before Facebook. In 1972 the Associated Press struggled with whether even to release it. As Barbie Zelizer tells it, "Ut took the film back to his bureau, where he and another photographer selected eight prints to be sent over the wires, among them the shot of the napalmed children. The photo at first met internal resistance at the AP, where one editor rejected it because of the girl's frontal nudity. A subsequent argument ensued in the bureau, at which point photo department head Horst Faas argued by telex with the New York office that an exception needed to be made; the two offices agreed to a compromise display by which there would be no close-up of the girl alone. Titled 'Accidental Napalm Attack,' the image went over the wires."[10] The first version of the photo the Associated Press released was lightly airbrushed to minimize the hint of Kim Phuc's pubic hair—though the untouched photo was also made available, and was what most newspapers ran the next day.[11] The New York Times was the first to publish the photo, and it too had an internal debate as to whether it could do so.[12] Though many U.S. and European newspapers published the photo, many did so after much debate, and some did not. And some readers were offended by the photo, enough to send their complaints to the newspapers: "Readers' letters labeled the display 'nauseating,' 'obscene,' and in 'poor taste,' on the one hand, and urged the photo's widespread display so as to end the war, on the other."[13]

Since the moment it was taken, this photo has been an especially hard case for Western print media—and it continues to be so for social media.[14] It was always both a document of war and a troubling object of concern itself: "Kim's suffering was captured and published movingly in a still photograph—and the still is what became the iconic image—but the photograph also immediately became a *story*."[15] At the time, commentators like Susan Sontag wrote extensively about it; U.S. President Richard Nixon mused on his secret White House recordings whether it had been faked;[16] many others have acknowledged its troubling power ever since—in articles like Egeland's.[17]

PLATFORMS MUST MODERATE, WHILE ALSO DISAVOWING IT

Social media platforms arose out of the exquisite chaos of the web. Many were designed by people who were inspired by (or at least hoping to profit from) the freedom the web promised, to host and extend all that participation, expression, and social connection.[18] But as these platforms grew, that chaos and contention quickly found its way back onto them, and for obvious reasons: if I want to say something, whether it is inspiring or reprehensible, I want to say it where others will hear me.[19] Social media platforms put more people in direct contact with one another, afford them new opportunities to speak and interact with a wider range of people, and organize them into networked publics.[20] Though the benefits of this may be obvious, and even seem utopian at times, the perils are also painfully apparent, more so every day: the pornographic, the obscene, the violent, the illegal, the abusive, and the hateful.

The fantasy of a truly "open" platform is powerful, resonating with deep, utopian notions of community and democracy—but it is just that, a fantasy.[21] There is no platform that does not impose rules, to some degree. Not to do so would simply be untenable.[22]

Platforms must, in some form or another, moderate: both to protect one user from another, or one group from its antagonists, and to remove the offensive, vile, or illegal—as well as to present their best face to new users, to their advertisers and partners, and to the public at large.

This project, content moderation, is one that the operators of these platforms take on reluctantly. Most would prefer if either the community could police itself or, even better, users never posted objectionable content in the first place. But whether they want to or not, platforms find that they must serve as setters of norms, interpreters of laws, arbiters of taste, adjudicators of disputes, and enforcers of whatever rules they choose to establish. Having in many ways taken custody of the web, they now find themselves its custodians.

The challenge for platforms, then, is exactly when, how, and why to intervene. Where they draw the line between the acceptable and the prohibited rehearses centuries-old debates about the proper boundaries of public expression, while also introducing new ones. The rules imposed by social media platforms today respond to contemporary fears (for example, sexual predation, terrorism), and they revisit traditional concerns around media and public culture (sex, obscenity, graphic violence).[23] They also revive a perennial challenge, particularly for Western media: do private information providers, having achieved a place of prominence, have an obligation to shape and sometimes restrict content? Do such obligations accompany, or run counter to, the legal promise of free speech?[24]

Moreover, the particular ways in which these platforms enforce their policies have their own consequences. Regardless of the particular rule, it matters whether the enforcement comes in the form of a warning or a removal, whether action comes before or only after someone complains, whether the platform segregates the offending content behind an age barrier or removes it completely. And, however it is enforced, moderation requires a great deal of labor and resources: complaints must be fielded, questionable content or behavior must be judged, consequences must be imposed, and appeals must be considered. For most platforms, this is now a significant portion of what they do.

The very fact of moderation shapes social media platforms as tools, as institutions, and as cultural phenomena. Across the prominent social media platforms, these rules and procedures have coalesced into functioning technical and institutional systems—sometimes fading into the background, sometimes becoming a vexing point of contention between users and platform. Users, whether they sense it or not, are swarming within, around, and sometimes against the parameters that platforms set.

The ways that platforms moderate today are slowly settling in as the familiar and accepted ways to handle user-generated content, mundane features of the digital culture landscape. Approaches battle-tested over time by many platforms are shared among them as "best practices." They are picked up by new sites looking for "what works." To the extent that regulators see such industry "self-regulation" as effective, they tend to then craft policy to complement it or give it legal teeth.

As more and more of our public discourse, cultural production, and social interactions move online, and this handful of massive, privately owned digital intermediaries continues to grow in economic and cultural power, it is crucial that we examine the choices moderators make.

Moderation is hard to examine, because it is easy to overlook—and that is intentional. Social media platforms are vocal about how much content they make available, but quiet about how much they remove. Content-sharing platforms typically present themselves as cornucopias: thousands of apps, millions of videos, billions of search results, more than you could ever consume. With so much available, it can start to seem as if nothing is unavailable. These sites also emphasize that they are merely hosting all this content, while playing down the ways in which they intervene—not only how they moderate, delete, and suspend, but how they sort content in particular ways, algorithmically highlight some posts over others, and grant their financial partners privileged real estate on the site.

This requires regularly disavowing all the ways in which platforms are much more than mere conduits: in 2016, in the face of mounting criticism, Mark Zuckerberg made a pointed statement that Facebook was not a "media company."[25] Phil Napoli and Robyn Caplan convincingly argue that this claim is both inaccurate and strategic: Zuckerberg and his colleagues do not want to be saddled with the social and legal obligations that apply to media companies.[26] Platforms offer to merely host: positioned front and center are your friends and those you follow, and all the content they share. The platform would like to fall away, become invisible beneath the rewarding social contact, the exciting content, the palpable sense of community.

When they acknowledge moderation at all, platforms generally frame themselves as open, impartial, and noninterventionist—in part because their founders fundamentally believe them to be so, and in part to avoid obligation or liability.[27] Twitter, for example, begins its posted community guidelines with: "We believe that everyone should have the power to create and share ideas and information instantly, without barriers. In order to protect the experience and safety of people who use Twitter, there are some limitations on the type of content and behavior that we allow."[28] These companies prefer to emphasize their wide-open fields of content, and then their impartial handling of it.[29]

It's also not surprising that so few users are aware of how platforms moderate, given that few users ever encounter these rules, or feel the force of their imposition. For many, using these sites as intended, there is little reason to bump up against these restrictions. It is easy to imagine these platforms as open and unregulated, if there appears to be no evidence to the contrary. Since users tend to engage with those like them and use the platform in similar ways, the lack of any sign of rules or their enforcement can be self-confirming.[30] Even some of those suffering harassment, or regularly offended by the content they're encountering, are unaware that the platforms have rules against it or remedies on offer.

On the other hand, many users—more and more every day—are all too aware of how social media platforms moderate. Believing that these platforms are wide open to all users, and that all users experience them that way, reveals some subtle cultural privilege at work. For more and more users, recurring abuse has led them to look to the platforms for some remedy. Others know the rules because they're determined to break them.[31] And others know about platform moderation because they are regularly and unfairly subjected to it. Social media platforms may present themselves as universal services suited to everyone, but when rules of propriety are crafted by small teams of people that share a particular worldview, they aren't always well suited to those with different experiences, cultures, or value systems. Put another way, I am not a pornographer or a terrorist, but I am also not a whistleblower, a drag queen, a Muslim, a lactation specialist, a sex educator, or a black antiviolence activist. So while I may experience social media platforms as wide open, international human rights activists don't; they experience them as censored, unreliable, and inhospitable to their efforts.[32] While I have never had a post deleted or my account suspended, other users with just as much legitimacy to participate as I regularly run up against the rules the platform imposes. Moderation is meant to disappear, but it does so for some more than others.

In the press, there have been growing attention to and debate about how and why platforms moderate. In the earliest days of social media, there was sporadic coverage of the moderation decisions of platforms. Most was little more than "gotcha journalism," typically criticizing a platform for a specific decision that seemed either boneheaded or hypocritical. But in recent years the press has raised deeper concerns: about the implications of platforms intervening too much, the rampant harms for which some platforms do too little, or the punishing labor that this moderation requires. In 2010, Apple was roundly criticized for removing more than five thousand apps from its App Store, because of their sexual nature. The technology press raised a collective eyebrow when Steve Jobs said the then new iPad should offer its users "freedom from porn," but the issue did help show moderation to be systemic and values-laden.[33] In 2012, for the first time but not the last, some of Facebook's moderator training documents were leaked, giving a rare, unvarnished glimpse of what Facebook does and does not want taken down.[34] Two years later the national press finally took notice of the pervasive misogyny online in the wake of #Gamergate, a dispute in the gaming community that blew up into a venomous campaign of harassment and threats targeting women in gaming, feminist critics, and just about anyone who came to their defense.[35] When private nude photos of celebrities stolen by hackers began circulating on the news aggregation platform Reddit, the site was lambasted for allowing the groups responsible to persist.[36] Late-night talk show host Jimmy Kimmel enjoyed viral success with "Mean Tweets," a recurring feature in which celebrities read aloud to the camera hateful tweets they had received. Journalists began to examine the hidden labor behind content moderation, most notably a 2014 *Wired* report by Adrian Chen documenting the experiences of Filipino workers who scrubbed U.S. social media platforms for dollars a day.[37] Cover stories about trolling and harassment moved from the online technology press to the major newspapers, weekly magazines, and national radio programs and podcasts, especially when celebrities like Ashley Judd, Zelda Williams, Leslie Jones, and Megyn Kelly were targeted.[38] Many were troubled when terrorist organization ISIS circulated gruesome videos of civilians and journalists being beheaded, and some called on YouTube, Twitter, and Facebook to remove them.[39] And in the run-up to and the aftermath of the 2016 U.S. presidential election, many drew attention to the efforts of the "alt-right" to shut down outspoken commentators and journalists through coordinated tactics of online harassment, and to the surge of "fake news," deliberately false news stories meant to mislead voters and/or make a tidy profit from the clicks of curious readers.[40]

In 2016 *Wired*, long a source of unbridled optimism about all things digital, published an open letter to the Internet, decrying not only harassment but the failure of platforms to handle this whole array of problems: "Things aren't great, Internet. Actually, scratch that: they're awful. You were supposed to be the blossoming of a million voices. We were all going to democratize access to information together. But some of your users have taken that freedom as a license to victimize others. This is not fine."[41]

MODERATION IS HARD

But before beginning to challenge platforms for their moderation policies and their responsibility for the Internet's many troubles, let's start with a simple reminder. Content moderation is hard. This should be obvious, but it is easily forgotten. Moderation is hard because it is resource intensive and relentless; because it requires making difficult and often untenable distinctions; because it is wholly unclear what the standards should be; and because one failure can incur enough public outrage to overshadow a million quiet successes.

It would be too simple to say that platforms are oblivious to the problems or too self-interested to do enough about them. Moderators do in fact want to exclude the worst atrocities and champion some basic rules of decency, while allowing everything else to flow undisrupted. Their efforts may be driven by a genuine desire to foster a hospitable community, or by a purely economic imperative not to lose users driven away by explicit content or relentless abuse, or by a fear of legal intervention if they are unable to protect their users themselves. But in speaking with representatives of the content policy teams at some of the major platforms, I found them genuinely committed to their work, and well aware of the difficulty of the task they have taken on. In some cases, it is even their job to press the seriousness of these issues back onto their own engineers, who often fail to imagine the ways their tools can be misused: as one policy manager from Flickr observed, "There have been so many different times that you think, 'Haven't you guys thought about how people are going to abuse this?' "[42]

Given the true atrocities that regularly appear on social media platforms, the question of *whether* to intervene is, for most, settled. But figuring out where and why to intervene means wading into some thorny questions: not just determining what is unacceptable, but balancing offense and importance; reconciling competing value systems; mediating when people harm one another, intentionally or otherwise; honoring the contours of political discourse and cultural taste; grappling with inequities of gender, sexuality, race, and class; extending ethical obligations across national, cultural, and linguistic boundaries; and doing all that around the hottest hot-button issues of the day.

Another way to think about it is that every well-intentioned rule has equally important exceptions. It is more complicated than simply "How bad is bad?" The blurry edges of bright line rules involve important and long-contested cultural questions: What is the difference between sexually explicit and pornographic? When is an image of the human body artistic, educational, or salacious? Are representations of fictional violence merely entertaining or psychologically harmful? Does discussing a dangerous behavior help those who suffer, or tempt them to act? Or, as in the *Terror of War* photo, does the fact that something is newsworthy supersede the fact that it is also graphic? These questions plague efforts to moderate questionable content, and they hinge not only on different values and ideologies but also on contested theories of psychological impact and competing politics of culture.

Too often the public debate about platform moderation happens at one of two extremes. Those looking to criticize social media platforms for being too permissive point to the most extreme material that can be found there: child pornography, graphic obscenities, rape threats, animal torture, racial and ethnic hatred, self-mutilation, suicide. Those looking to criticize platforms for intervening too much or for the wrong reasons point to arguably legitimate material that was nevertheless removed: the mildest of racy content, material that is frank or explicit but socially valuable, or material simply removed in error.

One of the biggest challenges platforms face is establishing and enforcing a content moderation regime that can address *both* extremes simultaneously. The rules must account for the most egregious atrocities as well as material that is questionable but defensible. Those in charge of content policy are often motivated by, and called to task for, the worst offenses, but must be careful not to ban culturally valuable material in the process. Users troubled by the most offensive content condemn it with the same passion as those who defend the material that rides the very edge of the rule. The reviewers enforcing those rules must maintain sensitive judgment about what does or does not cross a line while also being regularly exposed to— traumatized by—the worst humanity has to offer.

A second question immediately follows: according to whose criteria? We will see in later chapters how the major platforms work this out in practice, but it is a fundamentally difficult, perhaps intractable, problem. Even an online community that is self-governed faces the challenge of who should set the rules that will apply to everyone.[43] Users within that community will have competing values; the challenge only grows as the community does.

For a platform with commercial aims, run by a small team, this tends to turn into a question about either "our values" or the "values of our users." A platform is a product of the company that runs it, so there is a certain logic that it should be the company's values and interests that determine what is acceptable and what should be removed. But these values do not exist in a vacuum. Nearly all social media platforms are commercial enterprises, and must find a way to make a profit, reassure advertisers, and honor an international spectrum of laws. For social media platforms, what ends up standing as "our values" is not some moral core that exists beneath these many competing pressures. It is whatever solution can resolve those pressures—perhaps presented in a language of "the right thing to do," but already accounting for the competing economic and institutional demands these platforms face.

On the other hand, if these platforms were imagined to be "for" their users, perhaps the values of the users should be preeminent. But how can a content policy team know the "values of our users"? Platform operators have limited ways of knowing their users. Listening to those they hear from most regularly can lead to either attending too much to those who complain, or too easily dismissing them as a noisy minority. It can also lend credence to the assumption that those who do not complain represent a "silent majority" who have no complaints—which may or may not be the case.

In the face of all this uncertainty, or sometimes in total disregard of it, designers and managers often assume their users are "just like us."[44] But platform operators are hardly a cross-section of their user base. Currently, the full-time employees of most social media platforms are overwhelmingly white, overwhelmingly male, overwhelmingly educated, overwhelmingly liberal or libertarian, and overwhelmingly technological in skill and worldview.[45] This can lead these teams to overlook minority perspectives, and only worsens as a user base grows and diversifies. And it explodes when those platforms born in northern California open up to international user communities.[46] As soon as these sites expand beyond the United States, platforms "face a world where the First Amendment is merely a local ordinance."[47] Their distinctly American assumptions about free speech, civil discourse, and healthy community are being subtly (and sometimes knowingly) imposed on an international user base with very different values.

All this means that platforms simply cannot "get it right," in some simple or universal sense. Moderation policies are, at best, reasonable compromises—between users with different values and expectations, as well as between the demands of users and the demands of profit. I am not suggesting that platforms are beyond reproach or that their efforts should not be criticized. They aren't, and they should. Users who feel wronged by the interventions, even when made on their behalf, have every right to challenge a particular decision, policy, or platform. But I'm convinced that most of the challenges are structural, that even the missteps are endemic to how the problem is approached.

The hard questions being asked now, about freedom of expression and virulent misogyny and trolling and breastfeeding and pro-anorexia and terrorism and fake news, are all part of a fundamental reconsideration of social media platforms. To move this reconsideration forward, we need to examine the moderation apparatus that has been built over the past decade: the policies of content moderation, the sociotechnical mechanisms for its enforcement, the business expectations it must serve, the justifications articulated to support it. We need to look into why this apparatus is straining under the messiness of real uses, note the harms that have been made apparent, and document the growing pressure to address them. And finally, we must ask: If moderation should not be conducted the way it has, what should take its place?

But the reason to study moderation on social media platforms goes beyond preventing harm or improving enforcement. Moderation is a prism for understanding what platforms *are,* and the ways they subtly torque public life. Our understanding of platforms, both specific ones and as a conceptual category, has largely accepted the terms in which they are sold and celebrated by their own managers: open, impartial, connective, progressive, transformative. This view of platforms has limited our ability to ask questions about their impact, even as their impact has grown and/or concern about them has expanded.

In this celebratory vision of platforms, content moderation is treated as peripheral to what they do—a custodial task, like turning the lights on and off and sweeping the floors. It is occasionally championed in response to criticism, but otherwise it is obscured, minimized, and disavowed. I propose turning this understanding of platforms on its head. What if moderation is central to what platforms do, not peripheral? Moderation is an enormous part of the work of running a platform, in terms of people, time, and cost. And the work of policing all this caustic content and abuse haunts what they think their platforms are and what they must accomplish.

And moderation is, in many ways, *the* commodity that platforms offer. Though part of the web, social media platforms promise to rise above it, by offering a better experience of all this information and sociality: curated, organized, archived, and moderated. Consider two details, the first from Julia Angwin's history of the now nearly forgotten social media platform MySpace. Tila Tequila, since disgraced for her association with white supremacists, in 2003 was becoming one of the first online celebrities for the flirty, revealing photos she posted on Friendster. But Friendster had repeatedly deleted her profile for violating their policy, and after each deletion she had to re-create her list of followers. After a fifth deletion, she decided to move to the fledgling MySpace—and brought her forty thousand followers with her. Traffic spiked the day she arrived. Her choice, between two regimes of moderation, helped buoy the new site in its transition from spyware provider to social media giant, at a moment when its future was far from certain.[48] Second: in 2016, Twitter was in negotiations with the likes of Google, Salesforce, and Disney to be acquired, but all three passed on the deal. Some in the financial press wondered whether Twitter could not be sold, might not even survive, because it had become a toxic environment marred by harassment and misogyny.[49] In one instance, the promise of lenient moderation may have saved that platform for another week, or month, or year; in another, insufficient moderation may have rendered a billion-dollar company toxic to potential buyers.

By understanding moderation not just as an occasional act platforms must engage in but as a fundamental aspect of their service and a fundamental part of their place in public discourse, we can reconsider what platforms are, and ask new questions about their power in society. A focus on moderation slices through the myth that they are neutral conduits, to reveal their inner workings, their animating logics, their economic imperatives, and the actual footprint they leave on the dynamics of sociality and public discourse. It allows us to question their claim of deserving certain legal rights and obligations, and of being free of others. It helps reveal the real and often hidden investments platforms require, including the human, technical, and financial resources necessary, and it helps make sense of their responses to growing criticism from users and the press. It highlights the solutions platform managers prefer in the face of intractable social problems, like how to reconcile competing value systems within the same community, or how to uphold consistent policies in the face of competing societal expectations. And it can help us understand our commitment to platforms, and the ramifications of that cultural shift.

WHAT IS A PLATFORM?

We talk so much about platforms these days, it is easy to forget that they are still surrounded by the "world wide web" of home pages, personal blogs, news sites, oddball discussion spaces, corporate sites, games, porn, 404 error pages, file listings, and forgotten ephemera.[50] Over the course of more than a decade, the kinds of encounters with information and people that were once scattered across the web have been largely gathered up by a small set of companies onto a handful of social media platforms. Today we are, by and large, speaking from platforms. In fact, when these platforms are compared with their less regulated counterparts, it is to Reddit or 4chan—big platforms compared with smaller ones, mainstream platforms compared with marginal ones—not with the open web, not any more.

The dream of the open web emphasized new, expanded, and untrammeled opportunities for knowledge and sociality. Access to the public would no longer be mediated by the publishers and broadcasters that played such powerful gatekeeper roles in the previous century. The power to speak would be more widely distributed, with more opportunity to respond and deliberate and critique and mock and contribute.[51] This participatory culture, many hoped, would be more egalitarian, more global, more creative, and more inclusive. Communities could be based not on shared kinship or location but on shared interest, and those communities could set their own rules and priorities, by any manner of democratic consensus. The web itself was to be the "platform."[52] It would finally provide an unmediated public sphere, a natural gathering of the wisdom of the crowd, and a limitless cultural landscape.

Soon, new services began offering to facilitate, host, and profit from this participation. This began with the commercial provision of space for hosting web pages, offered first by Internet service providers (ISPs) themselves, and increasingly by web-hosting services like Tripod, Angelfire, and Geocities. Yet these still required knowledge of web design, HTML programming, and file management. The earliest content platforms—MP3.com, SixDegrees, Livejournal, Blogger, Cyworld, Friendster, LinkedIn, MySpace, Delicious, Orkut, Flickr, Dodgeball, YouTube—often began by trying to facilitate one element of being on the web (write without needing to know HTML; keep a list of friends or fans; make content easier to find through directed search).[53] These services were meant to "solve" some of the challenges of navigating the open web. They substantially simplified the tools needed for posting, distributing, sharing, commenting; they linked users to a larger, even global audience; and they did so at an appealing price. They also had acute network effects: if you want to share and participate, you want to do so where there are people to share and participate with.

These platforms were, of course, nearly all for-profit operations. This made them quite interested in not just facilitating but also incorporating the kinds of participation that the web itself made possible.[54] Platform companies developed new ways to keep users navigating and posting, coax them into revealing their preferences and proclivities, and save all of it as personalized data, to sell to advertisers and content partners. Some pushed to become all-in-one services—combining storage, organization, connection, canvas, delivery, archive; some looked to partner with traditional media and news providers, to draw the circulation of their content onto the platforms. Some extended their services infrastructurally, building identity architectures (profiles, login mechanisms) that extend to other sites and computationally linking themselves to the rest of the web.[55] These were all strategic attempts by platforms to counter the economic risks of being mere intermediaries, by turning themselves into ecosystems that keep users using their services and make data collection more comprehensive and more valuable.

In other words, to be free of intermediaries, we accepted new intermediaries. Platforms answer the question of distribution differently from the early web or traditional media. But they do offer the same basic deal: we'll handle distribution for you—but terms and conditions will apply. These terms may be fewer and less imposing, though you may be asked to do more of the labor of posting, removing, maintaining, tagging, and so on. But the platform still acts as a provider.[56]

Many content moderators and site managers came to these roles because they themselves were active users of the early Internet. Some of today's platforms, particularly the ones that began as startups rather than as projects of large corporations, grew out of that participatory culture. The fundamental mythos of the open web was extended to the earliest platforms: they often characterize themselves as open to all; in their promotion they often suggest that they merely facilitate public expression, that they are impartial and hands-off hosts with an "information will be free" ethos, and that being so is central to their mission.[57] Unfettered speech and participation on one's own terms, they believed, meant that rough consensus would emerge and democratic values would flourish.

On the other hand, early adopters of the web were also enamored with the possibility of "virtual community": like-minded individuals, joined by interest rather than geography or social obligation, building meritocratic and progressive social structures from scratch, and achieving the kind of communitarianism that had eluded Western society thus far.[58] These champions of online communities quickly discovered that communities need care: they had to address the challenges of harm and offense, and develop forms of governance that protected their community and embodied democratic procedures that matched their values and the values of their users.[59]

Both of these were, in important ways, myths. Nevertheless, they were familiar and meaningful to many of the people who found themselves in charge of moderating early social media platforms, and remain part of the corporate culture of many of the platforms today. This has had two consequences. First, many of social media platform designers were initially caught off guard by the proliferation of obscenity and cruelty on their sites. As one content policy manager at Dreamwidth put it, "Everybody wants their site to be a place where only Good Things happen, and when someone is starting up a new user-generated content site, they have a lot of enthusiasm and, usually, a lot of naïveté. . . . They think of their own usage of social media and their friends' usage, and design their policies on the presumption that the site will be used by people in good faith who have the same definitions that they do as to what's unacceptable. That works for a while."[60]

Second, even as it became clear that content moderation was necessary, these two animating principles were in many ways at odds when it came to deciding how to intervene. Social media platform moderators often invoke one or even both principles when framing the values by which they moderate. But a platform committed to free speech, and comfortable with the wild and woolly Internet that early web participants were accustomed to, might install a very different form of moderation from that of a platform conceived as the protector of community, its moderators attuned to all the forces that can tear such community apart.

Still, from an economic perspective, all this talk of protecting speech and community glosses over what in the end matters to platforms more: keeping as many people on the site spending as much time as possible, interacting as much as possible. But even in this sense, platforms face a double-edged sword: too little curation, and users may leave to avoid the toxic environment that has taken hold; too much moderation, and users may still go, rejecting the platform as either too intrusive or too antiseptic. This is especially true as platforms expand their user base: platforms typically begin with users who are more homogenous, who share the goal of protecting and nurturing the platform, and who may be able to solve some tensions through informal means.[61] As their user base broadens it tends also to diversify, and platforms find themselves hosting users and whole communities with very different value systems, and who look to the platform to police content and resolve disputes.

Today, there are many social media platforms vying for our attention, but only a handful in each domain seem to enjoy the bulk of users and of the public's interest. Here is a representative but not exhaustive list of the social media platforms I think about, and that will be central to my concern in this book: social network sites like Facebook, LinkedIn, Google+, Hi5, Ning, NextDoor, and Foursquare; blogging and microblogging providers like Twitter, Tumblr, Blogger, Wordpress, and Livejournal; photo- and image-sharing sites like Instagram, Flickr, Pinterest, Photobucket, DeviantArt, and Snapchat; video-sharing sites like YouTube, Vimeo, and Dailymotion; discussion, opinion, and gossip tools like Reddit, Digg, Secret, and Whisper; dating and hookup apps like OK Cupid, Tinder, and Grindr; collaborative knowledge tools like Wikipedia, Ask, and Quora; app stores like iTunes and Google Play; live broadcasting apps like Facebook Live and Periscope.[62]

To those I would add a second set that, while they do not neatly fit the definition of platform, grapple with many of the same challenges of content moderation in platformlike ways: recommendation and rating sites like Yelp and TripAdvisor; exchange platforms that help share goods, services, funds, or labor, like Etsy, Kickstarter, Craigslist, Airbnb, and Uber; video game worlds like League of Legends, Second Life, and Minecraft; search engines like Google, Bing, and Yahoo.

At this point I should define the term that I have already relied on a great deal. *Platform* is a slippery term, in part because its meaning has changed over time, in part because it equates things that nevertheless differ in important and sometimes striking ways, and in part because it gets deployed strategically, by both stakeholders and critics.[63] As a shorthand, "platform" too easily equates a site with the company that offers it, it implies that social media companies act with one mind, and it downplays the people involved. Platforms are sociotechnical assemblages and complex institutions; they're not even all commercial, and the commercial ones are commercial in different ways. At the same time, "platform" is a widely used term, including by the companies themselves. And when assigning responsibility and liability (legal and otherwise) we often refer to institutions as singular entities, and for good reason.

For my purposes, platforms are: online sites and services that

a) host, organize, and circulate users' shared content or social interactions for them,

b) without having produced or commissioned (the bulk of) that content,

c) built on an infrastructure, beneath that circulation of information, for processing data for customer service, advertising, and profit.

For the most part, platforms don't make the content; but they do make important choices about it.[64] While the early platforms merely made user contributions available and searchable, increasingly they determine what users can distribute and to whom, how they will connect users and broker their interactions, and what they will refuse. This means that a platform must negotiate any tensions between the aims of independent content providers who want their work to appear on a public forum and the platform's own economic and political imperative to survive and flourish.[65] And it must do so without having produced or commissioned the content. This means that platform managers by and large cannot oversee content through more traditional media industry relations such as salary, contract, or professional norms. For traditional media, employment arrangements and shared norms were key means of prohibiting illicit content. Platforms must find other ways.

Most platforms still depend on ad revenue, extending the monetization strategy common to amateur home pages, online magazines, and web portals. Advertising still powerfully drives their design and policy decisions. But most social media companies have discovered that there is more revenue to be had by gathering and mining user data—the content users post, the profiles they build, the search queries they enter, the traces of their activity through the site and beyond, the preferences they indicate along the way, and the "social graph" they build through their participation with others. This data can be used to better target all that advertising, and can be sold to customers and data brokers. This means platforms are oriented toward data collection and retention; toward eliciting more data, and more kinds of data, from its users; and toward finding new ways to draw users to the platform, and to follow users off the platform wherever they may go.[66]

And now, for the fine print. Some would argue that I am using the term *platform* incorrectly. It has a more specific computational meaning, where it means a programmable infrastructure upon which other software can be built and run, like the operating systems in our computers and gaming consoles, or information services that allow developers to design additional layers of functionality.[67] Some have suggested that the term should be constrained to this meaning—that Facebook, for example, is not a platform because it hosts our updates and photos, it is a platform only in that it provides an application programming interface (API) for software developers to design extensions and games atop it.[68] The distinction is convincing, but at this point, it's simply too late: *platform* has been widely embraced in its new sense—by users, by the press, by regulators, and by the platform providers themselves.

I may also be using the term too broadly. Platforms vary, in ways that matter both for the influence they can assert over users and for how they should be governed. It is deceptively easy in public debates, and in scholarship, to simply point in the direction of Facebook and move on, without acknowledging the variety of purpose, scope, membership, economics, and design across different platforms. For instance, YouTube has developed a program for paying some of its users, which changes the dynamics between platform and those users significantly. A live-streaming platform like Periscope faces different challenges moderating content in real time.

I may also be using the term too narrowly. First, my location and limited proficiency in languages limits my analysis to platforms based in the West and functioning largely in English. This overlooks massive platforms in other countries and languages, like Sina Weibo in China, VK in Russia, and, until 2014, Google's Orkut in South America. However, many of the platforms I consider have a global reach and influence, mattering a great deal across many parts of the world. While this does not make my analysis universal, it does extend it beyond the specific platforms I focus on.

The platforms I spend the most time discussing are the largest, the most widely used, the best known. These are, of course, all good reasons to pay particular attention to them. It matters how Facebook sets and enforces rules, even if you're not on Facebook. And it is harder and harder to not be on Facebook, even if you are uncomfortable with its oversight. But there are dozens of other platforms competing with these to be national or global services, and there are many thousands of smaller sites, with no such ambitions, more focused on specific regions or interests. All face many of the same moderation challenges, though on a smaller scale and with substantially less public scrutiny and criticism. Smaller sites may even be breeding grounds for innovative approaches and solutions to the challenges all platforms face. And there are also plenty of social media sites that are long dead, or nearly so—Friendster, MySpace, Orkut, Revver, Veoh, Chatroulette, Ping, Delicious, Xanga, Airtime, Diaspora, Vine, Yik Yak—that also faced the challenges of moderation, and can still be illuminating examples.

I did not include messaging services, which are hugely popular competitors to the platforms mentioned above. Millions regularly use WhatsApp, Facebook Messenger, QZone, WeChat, Kik, Line, Google Hangout, and

Skype to communicate and congregate online. Because they are generally person-to-person or group-to-group, and overwhelmingly between known contacts, they sidestep many of the problems that plague platforms that offer public visibility and contact with strangers. But they too engage in their own forms of moderation.

Finally, there is a broader set of information sites and services that, while I would not lump them into this category, face similar questions about user activity and their responsibility for it: online discussion forums, unmoderated social spaces online, gaming worlds that allow for player-to-player interaction, amateur porn platforms, comment threads on blogs, news sites, and inside e-commerce sites.

PLATFORMS ARE NOT PLATFORMS WITHOUT MODERATION

To the definition of platforms, I would like this book to add a fourth element:

d) platforms do, and must, moderate the content and activity of users, using some logistics of detection, review, and enforcement.

Moderation is not an ancillary aspect of what platforms do. It is essential, constitutional, definitional. Not only can platforms not survive without moderation, they are not platforms without it. Moderation is there from the beginning, and always; yet it must be largely disavowed, hidden, in part to maintain the illusion of an open platform and in part to avoid legal and cultural responsibility. Platforms face what may be an irreconcilable contradiction: they are represented as mere conduits *and* they are premised on making choices for what users see and say.

Looking at moderation in this way should shift our view of what social media platforms really do: from transmitting what we post, to constituting what we see. There is no position of impartiality. Platform moderators pick and choose all the time, in all sorts of ways. Excluding porn or threats or violence or terrorism is just one way platforms constitute the social media product they are generating for the audience.

The persistent belief that platforms are open, impartial, and unregulated is an odd one, considering that *everything* on a platform is designed and orchestrated. Economists know this: like with any "multisided market," a platform company is a broker, profiting by bringing together sellers and buyers, producers and audiences, or those in charge of tasks and those with the necessary skills to accomplish them.[69] So, if Uber profits by bringing independent drivers to interested passengers, coordinating and insuring their interaction, and taking a fee from the exchange, Twitter does much the same: it brings together independent speakers with interested listeners, coordinates their interaction, and takes a fee from the exchange—in the form of valuable user data.

It is a position that can be, for a few, extremely lucrative: as John Herrman notes, "If successful, a platform creates its own marketplace; if extremely successful, it ends up controlling something closer to an entire economy."[70] And it depends on platforms not only bringing independent parties together but completely structuring every aspect of the exchange. YouTube connects videomakers with viewers, but also sets the terms: the required technical standards, what counts as a commodity, what is measured as value, how long content is kept, and the depth and duration of the relationship. YouTube can offer established videomakers a share of the advertising revenue or not, and it gets to decide how much, to whom, and under what conditions. And like any market, game world, or information exchange that invites users to participate according to their own interests, this requires excluding some to serve others: those who provide unwanted goods, those who game the system, those who disrupt the entire arrangement.

How platforms are designed and governed not only makes possible social activity, it calls it into being, gives it shape, and affirms its basic legitimacy as a public contribution. Platforms don't just mediate public discourse, they constitute it.[71] As José van Dijck observes, "Sociality is not simply 'rendered technological' by moving to an online space; rather, coded structures are profoundly altering the nature of our connections, creations, and interactions."[72] They are designed so as to invite and shape our participation toward particular ends. This includes how profiles and interactions are structured; how social exchanges are preserved; how access is priced or paid for; and how information is organized algorithmically, privileging some content over others, in opaque ways. These "social media logics" are the repertoires of expression and action that social media platforms trade in.[73] Put simply, if Twitter were designed and managed in fundamentally different ways, that would have some effect on what users could and would do with it. This includes what is prohibited, and how that prohibition is enforced.[74]

On the other hand, it is also easy to overstate the influence platforms have as straightforward and muscular—either facilitating participation in powerful ways or constraining and exploiting it in powerful ways. Users don't simply walk the paths laid out by social media platforms. They push against them, swarm over them, commandeer them, and imbue them with new meanings. The instant a social media platform offers its service publicly, it is forever lashed to a ceaseless flow of information and activity that it cannot quite contain. So yes, Facebook tweaks its newsfeed algorithm and suspends users for breaking the rules. But it also hosts the regular participation of more than a billion people, who use the platform for countless different activities. This torrent of participation never stops, and is shaped much more by its own needs and tactics.[75] Whatever structure a platform attempts to introduce may cause its own little eddies and detours, but they are minor compared to the massive perturbations endemic to public discourse: shifting sentiments, political flare-ups, communal and national rhythms, and the recursive loops of how forms of participation emerge and propagate, then are superseded. Platform managers may want to support and expand this ceaseless flow, but they also remain in constant fear of it turning sour or criminal, or simply drying up. While platforms structure user activity, users also have power over platforms—maybe less so as mere individuals or groups, but more in the aggregate, the slow, unrelenting shifts in what people seem to want to do.

This is not to say that platforms are of no consequence. I simply mean that we must examine their role, without painting them as either all-powerful or merely instrumental. We must recognize their attenuated influence over the public participation they host and the complex dynamics of that influence, while not overstating their ability to control it. Examining moderation and how it works slices these questions open for scrutiny.

Platforms may not shape public discourse by themselves, but they do shape the shape of public discourse. And they know it.

2

the myth of the neutral platform

> We suck at dealing with abuse and trolls on the platform and we've sucked at
> it for years. It's no secret and the rest of the world talks about it every day. . . .
> We're going to start kicking these people off right and left and making sure
> that when they issue their ridiculous attacks, nobody hears them.
>
> *Dick Costolo, CEO, speaking internally at Twitter,*
> *leaked to the Verge, February 2015*

It was a revealing statement, and a welcome one. For years Twitter had been criticized for allowing a culture of harassment to fester largely unchecked on its service, particularly targeting women, but also the LGBTQ community, racial and ethnic minorities, participants of various subcultures, and public figures. This was more than just harsh talk or personal insults. These were misogyny and hate speech, explicit threats of rape and violence, concerted and relentless attacks targeting particular individuals, and doxxing (posting the victim's private information as a veiled threat, or an invitation to others to threaten).[1] The attacks had grown more vicious, more brazen, and more visible in the midst of the 2014 #Gamergate controversy. As a result, Twitter had come under increasing criticism for failing to recognize the scope of the problem and provide the procedural and technical mechanisms victims needed.

Costolo's comment was leaked to the Verge and became the banner headline in the tech press in the days that followed. In a more carefully crafted op-ed for the *Washington Post* two months later, Twitter's general counsel Vitaya Gadde promised changes to the site and its policies, navigating a more nuanced path between freedom of expression and the protection of users than Costolo had. "Balancing both aspects of this belief—welcoming diverse perspectives while protecting our users—requires vigilance, and a willingness to make hard choices. . . . Freedom of expression means little as our underlying philosophy if we continue to allow voices to be silenced because they are afraid to speak up."[2] Here freedom of expression was positioned not as counter to restriction but as its outcome: "Protection from threats and abuse will allow users to remain and opinions to flourish, expanding diversity and debate."

Many agreed with Costolo's assessment. In fact, it may have been leaked deliberately, as a way to convince frustrated users that Twitter was finally getting get serious about the problem (and signal the same to companies who might be interested in acquiring the company). Costolo himself stepped down just a few months later. But without absolving Twitter of responsibility, it's not just that Twitter "sucked" at content moderation. Twitter was grappling with the legacy of a particular configuration of rights and responsibilities, or a relative absence of responsibilities, that was already two decades in the making, mapped out long before Twitter existed. Social media platforms, especially in the United States, had been offered a framework in which they faced little liability for what users might do across their service; they could moderate content as they wished but were under no obligation to do so. According to the principles that animated the early web, they were to a certain degree expected *not* to intervene. By 2015, the public concern and cultural tone had changed, but this legacy was hard to give up.

So how did we get here?

REGULATION OF SPEECH ON THE INTERNET (BEFORE PLATFORMS)

While scholars have long discussed the legal and political dynamics of speech online, much of that discussion preceded the dramatic move of so much of that speech onto social media platforms.[3] Twenty years ago, questions emerged about the implications of the Internet, both positive and negative, for public expression. Would the Internet be an unbounded venue for all voices and opinions, the open forum that free-speech advocates had sought all along? What might prevent this from occurring? What should be done about harmful speech online, without hobbling this fragile new venue for communication, knowledge, and community?

The optimistic view was that the web was unregulated and unregulatable, that it permitted no possibility of censorship of any kind.[4] In 1992, science fiction author Bruce Sterling captured this sentiment: "Why do people want to be 'on the Internet'? One of the main reasons is simple freedom. The Internet is a rare example of a true, modern, functional anarchy. There is no 'Internet Inc.' There are no official censors, no bosses, no board of directors, no stockholders."[5] Critics and scholars who did worry about the extension of control into online environments worried most about the power of the state. What would the legal standards for speech be online? How would local jurisdictions and community norms apply on a network that seemed to exceed geography? How would the openness of American forums play in countries that impose tighter restrictions and harsher consequences on political or explicit speech? Could governments use the worst content on the Internet to justify clumsy, overreaching, or politically motivated interventions?[6]

In the United States, though there were incidents involving defamation, the posting of private documents, and hate speech, pornography dominated the public debate about online expression.[7] In the mid-1990s, policy makers in the United States and elsewhere became aware of the proliferation of explicit sexual content on the web, fueled by panic among the popular press about a flood of "cyberporn"—a concern not unwarranted, but wildly overstated.[8] Some called for its criminalization; the U.S. government would spend the next few years passing laws prohibiting the distribution of obscenity to minors, only to have most of those laws ruled unconstitutional by the Supreme Court. Other proposals imagined control mechanisms for the entire Internet: filtering software that blocked illicit content from specific users, already available to consumers, might be applied more broadly; perhaps pornography could be "zoned" away, behind credit card–patrolled paywalls or in a ".xxx" dedicated domain easily walled off from kids.[9] Policy makers struggled, and not just because they did not yet understand the Internet as a technical and cultural phenomenon. They were having to work out the appropriate balance between protecting speech and preventing harm, in a new, dispersed, global, amorphous, and networked communication environment.

But amid the cyberporn panic, few were raising questions about the regulation of speech *by* intermediaries, be they providers of Internet access or makers of web publishing tools. Home pages were first hand-coded with simple text-editing tools, then later with the help of free-standing web design software. Bulletin board system (BBS) operators by and large embraced a hands-off approach to what users were saying and sharing, supported by a political stance that they should not be interfering. The largest ISPs, like Compuserve and Delphi, prohibited abusive, profane, and offensive content, though it is not clear how often they enforced those rules. Most of the smaller ISPs had loose rules, if any, about what sites they hosted; they were more concerned with how much traffic a site generated and the bandwidth it consumed than what it said. As web-hosting services like Angelfire and Tripod and community spaces like Geocities emerged, many did have "community guidelines" or terms of service that prohibited certain kinds of content: typically pornography, hate speech, obscenity, and illegal activity. But even as these platforms grew, they were hardly an oligopoly; website hosting services were not geographically bound, so there was nearly infinite competition.[10] If one host proved too tame, a user could simply find another willing to cater to more illicit materials.

The more pressing worry about BBSs, website-hosting services, and ISPs was not that they would restrict speech on their own accord but that they could be obligated to impose restrictions on behalf of courts or governments, or pressured to impose them to avoid liability for the content they made available.[11] Policy makers, litigants, the courts, and police were discovering how difficult it is to directly pursue online "publishers" for their illegal behavior or illicit content—particularly when they were individuals, usually amateurs, sometimes anonymous, hard to locate and identify, and often in a different jurisdiction from the complainant.

A handful of late-1990s lawsuits regarding online defamation or the dissemination of illicit content were aimed not at the individual user but at the ISP or content provider.[12] In 2000, the French government sued Yahoo for allowing Nazi memorabilia to be sold through its auction site; while U.S. courts held that the First Amendment protected Yahoo from liability, French courts later required Yahoo to block French users from accessing Nazi-related auctions.[13] In general, these lawsuits did not imply that the ISP or site operator was to blame for the offending content. Liability here was something more like a question of convenience: intermediaries were in the position to know the true identity of someone speaking or publishing online, and in a position to remove that speech or ban that speaker.

If cyberporn was first to provoke questions about the responsibilities of online intermediaries, the battle over copyright and online piracy was where these questions of responsibility would play out over the next half decade, establishing many of the fundamental arrangements that platforms would inherit. Again, the questions focused first on the users, who were making unauthorized copies of music and software available on home pages, Usenet groups, bulletin boards, and online forums. As early as 1993, copyright holders began suing individuals, most notably *Playboy* for the unauthorized circulation of photos from its magazines.[14] But the issue soon shifted to music, beginning again on websites and online forums, but exploding with the development of peer-to-peer (p2p) file-sharing software like Limewire, Kazaa, and Napster.

In 1997, in response to online software piracy, the U.S. Congress passed the No Electronic Theft (NET) Act, criminalizing the unauthorized circulation of copyrighted materials online, even in cases where no money changed hands. But the law made no reference to intermediaries or their liability. That soon changed, however, as copyright holders began targeting intermediaries for the infringing material they helped make available. The Church of Scientology, for example, attempted to shut down an entire Usenet newsgroup for circulating its secret church documents, and unsuccessfully sued the operator of a BBS and the ISP it used.[15] This same logic triumphed in the court decision rendered against Napster.[16] Despite being a decentralized network, Napster was both more appealing to users and more vulnerable to legal action than other p2p software because it served as an intermediary for the illicit sharing of music. Unlike its competitors, Napster compiled the lists of all files available from its many users into a searchable index it hosted—in this, it shared some of the DNA of contemporary platforms. And as an intermediary, it was a convenient point of intervention for the courts to interrupt the millions of unauthorized user transactions it made possible. And even more than pornography sites, Napster was also publicly framed as the bad guy: knowing, smirking, and complicit in the act of piracy. It was with copyright, first, that the United States began to extend liability to intermediaries in a significant way—and not just because intermediaries are an effective point at which to intervene, but also because their prosecution functions as an assertion of their ethical and financial responsibility.

Pornography and piracy were the biggest public stories about what users were getting away with on the new medium. They overshadowed a quieter but no less pressing concern, the increasing prevalence of verbal attacks and harassment online, often with racist or misogynistic motivations. Usenet moderators, webmasters, and the managers of online forums were discovering that their healthy communities and lively discussions some-times devolved into name calling, flame wars, and personal attacks.[17] AOL "community action teams" moderated chatrooms and even email on the system.[18] Sites differed, of course, and the tone of a community could depend a great deal on its topic, its membership, and its management. But online forums could be rough-and-tumble environments; some blamed the abil-ity to speak anonymously or under cover of a pseudonym, while others saw it as the product of the particular cultural norms of the earliest adopters of the Internet.[19]

This tendency for political discussions to devolve into insults was so commonplace that it even had an axiom, known as Godwin's Law: "If an online discussion (regardless of topic or scope) goes on long enough, sooner or later someone will compare someone or something to Hitler."[20] But this shrug of acceptance belied darker forms of online vitriol: hate speech, homophobia, violence toward women, and white supremacy all seemed to be finding a foothold in environments that, at their best, aspired to a utopia of participation and community unmarked by bias or hierarchy.[21] A 1993 essay by Julian Dibbell in the *Village Voice* documented a startling incident in which an unwelcome intruder in a long-standing online discussion space began harassing the other participants verbally, then went farther. He had the technical skill to instruct the forum software to narrate virtual actions of other players, making it appear that they were assaulting each other or themselves. This "rape in cyberspace" was not the first incident of its kind, and it would not be the last.[22]

For the most part, concerns about harassment and hate speech online did not rise to the level of public or policy debates, though organizations dedicated to eradicating hate speech were raising the alarm about its growing prevalence.[23] While harassment and flaming seemed to matter a great deal to users in the moment, the question of what to do about it rubbed uncomfortably against competing ideas about who should regulate speech and how.[24] Most proposed solutions remained within the purview of the site or forum in question. Dibbell's essay, for example, went on to document the difficult debates that the forum leaders and participants had about how to respond to the attack: whether to ban the offender, what rules of participation to establish, how to enforce them in the future. The incident shook a community that had hoped, believed, that it could function happily without oversight, but learned the hard way that it needed a system of governance.

SAFE HARBOR

The U.S. Congress crafted its first legislative response to online pornography, the Communications Decency Act (CDA), as part of a massive telecommunications bill. Passed in 1996, the CDA made it a criminal act, punishable by fines and/or up to two years in prison, to display or distribute "obscene or indecent" material online to anyone under age eighteen.[25] (It also imposed similar penalties for harassing or threatening someone online.) During the legislation process, the House of Representatives added a bipartisan amendment drafted by Christopher Cox and Ron Wyden, largely as a response to early lawsuits trying to hold ISPs and web-hosting services liable for defamation by their users. It carved out a safe harbor for ISPs, search engines, and "interactive computer service providers": so long as they only provided access to the Internet or conveyed information, they could not be held liable for the content of that speech.[26]

The Communications Decency Act was short-lived; less than a year later the U.S. Supreme Court judged it unconstitutional.[27] While the justices recognized the concerns motivating the bill, the court ruled that CDA overreached in terms of what content was prohibited (indecent, not just obscene), it extended its protection of minors to the content available to adults, and it did not deal with the question of whose community norms should be the barometer for a network that spans communities. However, because the safe harbor amendment was not at issue in the Supreme Court decision, it survived the ruling.[28]

Now known as Section 230 of U.S. telecommunication law, this safe harbor has two parts.[29] The first ensures that intermediaries that merely provide access to the Internet or other network services cannot be held liable for the speech of their users; these intermediaries will not be considered "publishers" of their users' content in the legal sense. The implication is that, like the telephone company, intermediaries do not need to police what their users say and do. The second, less familiar part adds a twist. If an intermediary *does* police what its users say or do, it does not lose its safe harbor protection by doing so. In other words, choosing to delete some content does not suddenly turn the intermediary into a "publisher," nor does it require the service provider to meet any standard of effective policing. As Milton Mueller writes, Section 230 "was intended both to immunize [online service providers] who did nothing to restrict or censor their users' communications, and to immunize OSPs who took some effort to discourage or restrict online pornography and other forms of undesirable content.

Intermediaries who did nothing were immunized in order to promote freedom of expression and diversity online; intermediaries who were more active in managing user-generated content were immunized in order to enhance their ability to delete or otherwise monitor 'bad' content."[30] This second half was crafted so that the safe harbor would not create legal jeopardy for intermediaries that chose to moderate in good faith, by making them more liable for it than if they had simply turned a blind eye.[31]

These competing impulses, between allowing intermediaries to stay out of the way and encouraging them to intervene, continue to shape the way we think about the role and responsibility of all Internet intermediaries, and has extended to how we regulate social media platforms. From a legal standpoint, broad and conditional safe harbors are profoundly advantageous for Internet intermediaries. As Rebecca Tushnet put it, "Current law often allows Internet intermediaries to have their free speech and everyone else's too."[32] It also provided ISPs and search engines with the framework upon which they depended for the next fifteen years: intervening on the terms they choose, while proclaiming their neutrality as a way to avoid obligations they prefer not to meet.

In a phrase common to their terms of service agreements (and many advantageous legal contracts), social media platforms can claim "the right but not the responsibility" to remove users and delete content. This is classic legal language, designed to protect a provider from as much liability as possible while ensuring it the most discretionary power.[33] But the phrase captures the enviable position that the Section 230 safe harbor offers. And it is an apt description for the legal and cultural standing that platforms have enjoyed since, particularly in the United States.

Section 230 extends a legislative distinction common to U.S. telecommunication law between publishers that provide information (and therefore can be held liable for it) and distributors that merely circulate the information of others (and thus should not be held liable)—known as the "content/conduit" distinction.[34] Since ISPs offered "access" to the Internet, and did not produce the content they help circulate, the law prioritized the free movement of information, and limited ISPs' liability for the content users circulated through them.[35] As with telephone systems, holding an intermediary liable for what users say or do might be an incentive to monitor users proactively and shut down anything that looked risky. This would be not only practically impossible and financially unbearable but also politically undesirable.[36] Legislators and technologists feared that this might also discourage innovation, as new ISPs or interactive computer services might not dare enter the market if the immediate legal risks were too costly.[37]

Robert Horwitz reminds us that the U.S. approach toward media and telecommunication regulation has been markedly consistent, despite having historically regulated print, broadcasting, and telecommunications industries under separate regimes.[38] First, U.S. regulation struggles to balance individualistic and collectivist interpretations of the First Amendment. The individualistic interpretation takes the First Amendment literally: speakers have the right to speak, a right that should not be abridged. If speakers speak, they should not be prevented from doing so based on who they are or what they have to say. The collectivist interpretation takes into account that, in practical terms, not everyone gets to speak with the same visibility. The obligation of policy is to cultivate a speech environment in which a diversity of speakers and perspectives is represented: this sometimes means ensuring the individual right to speak, but it can also mean regulating the medium or its stakeholders so as to produce the conditions for a robust marketplace of ideas. U.S. policy has shifted in emphasis, striking a different balance for broadcasting, print, and telecommunications, but always it is some version of this tension.

Second, U.S. policy makers seem to privilege the rights of providers over the public interest at issue. This has a great deal to do with the general friendliness of U.S. policy toward the market and market actors in general,[39] and because publishers and broadcasters have successfully played up the fact that they are both facilitators of speech and speakers themselves.[40] As Horwitz documents, U.S. courts and the Federal Communications Commission seem to privilege providers even when they're imposing obligations on them. The now-defunct Fairness Doctrine, which obligated broadcasters to provide air time to opposing political candidates and viewpoints, was a strong swing toward a collectivist notion of speech protection, and put a significant obligation on broadcasters. But even within this obligation, broadcasters were in practice given a great deal of freedom to determine how they met it. Broadcasters could decide who represented the opposing viewpoint, and had a great deal of latitude in scheduling it.

Section 230 similarly tries to balance the individualistic and collectivist interpretations of freedom of expression doctrine, and similarly errs on the side of intermediaries. Offering ISPs and search engines the protection afforded to "conduits" like the telephone companies granted them a powerful safe harbor—with no matching obligation to serve the public in any specific way. Offering them indemnity even if they do intervene meant that they could pick and choose how and when to do so, without even being held to account as "publishers," or for meeting any particular standards for how they do so.

This is the regulatory framework, at least in the United States, that platforms inherited. Outside of the United States, few nations offer the robust safe harbor provided in Section 230. Rebecca MacKinnon and her research team dub the U.S. approach "broad immunity," the most lenient of three intermediary liability regimes they identify.[41] Most of the European Union nations, as well as Russia and most South American nations, offer intermediaries "conditional liability," which is more akin to the U.S. rules for copyright: platforms are not liable for what their users post or distribute, as long as they have no "actual knowledge" of, and did not produce or initiate, the illegal or illicit material; they must respond to requests from the state or the courts to remove illicit third-party content. China and many of the nations in the Middle East impose "strict liability," requiring Internet intermediaries to actively prevent the circulation of illicit or unlawful content. This generally means proactively removing or censoring, often in direct cooperation with the government. Without a regulatory bulwark against state intervention, these private actors are much more beholden to government demands. Finally, some nations, for example in sub-Saharan Africa, have not instituted laws articulating the responsibilities of Internet intermediaries in any form, leaving intermediaries there uncertain about what they might or might not be liable for.

PLATFORMS ARE GROWING OUT OF SAFE HARBOR

While safe harbor provisions have held up for two decades, three distinct challenges are helping reveal their limitations, and in some cases are fueling calls for their reconsideration.

First and perhaps most obvious, most of these laws were not designed with social media platforms in mind, though platforms have managed to enjoy them anyway. Most of the policies that currently apply to social media platforms were intended for a broader category of online services and access providers. When Section 230 was being crafted, few such platforms existed. U.S. lawmakers were regulating a web largely populated by ISPs and amateur web "publishers"—amateurs posting personal pages, companies designing stand-alone websites, and online communities having discussions. Besides the ISPs that provided access to the network, the only intermediaries at the time were those ISPs that doubled as content "portals," like AOL and Prodigy; the earliest search engines, like Altavista and Yahoo; and operators of BBS systems, chatrooms, and newsgroups. The law predates not just Facebook but MySpace, Friendster, and Livejournal; not just YouTube but Veoh and Metacafe; not just Soundcloud but Last.fm and Lala, as well as Napster and its peer-to-peer brethren; even Google. Blogging was in its infancy, well before the invention of large-scale blog-hosting services like Blogspot and Wordpress; eBay, Craigslist, and Match.com were less than a year old; and the ability to comment on a web page had not yet been modularized into a plug-in.

Although they were not included in or anticipated by the law, social media platforms have generally claimed that they enjoy its safe harbor.[42] Section 230, designed to apply to online services and access providers, included a third category awkwardly called "access software providers" to capture these early sites that hosted content provided by users.[43] Such a site is defined as "a provider of software (including client or server software), or enabling tools that do any one or more of the following: (a) filter, screen, allow, or disallow content; (b) pick, choose, analyze, or digest content; or (c) transmit, receive, display, forward, cache, search, subset, organize, reorganize, or translate content." Contemporary social media platforms fit this category, but they also complicate it. This definition might capture YouTube's ability to host, sort, and queue up user-submitted videos, but it is an ill fit for YouTube's ContentID techniques for identifying and monetizing copyrighted material. It may approximate some of what Facebook offers, but it could hardly have anticipated Facebook's NewsFeed algorithm.

Social media platforms are eager to hold on to the safe harbor protections enshrined in Section 230, shielding them from liability for nearly anything that their users might say or do. But all of them also take advantage of the second half of its protection: nearly all platforms impose their own rules and police their sites for offending content and behavior themselves. In most cases their ceaseless and systematic policing cuts much, much deeper than the law requires. In terms of impact on public discourse and the lived experience of users, the rules these platforms impose probably matter more than the legal restrictions under which they function.

Safe harbor gives platforms room to choose when, to what degree, and why to claim responsibility for the material that they host—beyond what is legally required. They have reasons to be reluctant to take on this task, but they also have reasons to take it on. These are mostly economic reasons, though not exclusively so. Most social media platforms, if they have a functioning business model at all, depend on either advertising, on the data their users generate, or both. Troubling content can scare off wary advertisers, who are not eager to see their products paired with an X-rated video or a xenophobic rant. Platforms fear that users will leave if the site is overwhelmed by porn or trolls. No matter how successful or established or near-monopolistic, platform operators all fear users flocking en masse to a competitor. While the major platforms have developed clever ways to keep users within their ecosystem, they remain haunted by the fact that alternatives are "just one click away." A graveyard of past social media services like MySpace and Digg linger in their discussions as cautionary tales of how a successful platform can collapse when users decide that it is not serving their interests or that a better alternative exists. And to be fair, these economic considerations are intertwined with other kinds: the deeply felt commitment of the platform operators to nurture a community or encourage the best creative output of their users; a sense of public obligation, especially as a platform grows and exerts greater influence on the public landscape; and the day-to-day need to respond to criticisms leveled by angry users, journalists, or activists.

Racy or unpleasant content and behavior, even if users are fine with it, does not always fit neatly with a platform's effort to protect its public brand. This concern certainly motivated Apple's 2010 efforts to purge not only sex apps but also badly designed apps as well—this policy represented two forms of quality control more than a moral or legal imperative. YouTube may want everyone to post, but it also partners with professional content producers and offers incentives to high-quality and popular amateurs. Patrolling its platforms for the gruesome and the obscene is part of tending to its public image and protecting its advertising revenue.

A second challenge is that while these intermediary liability regimes are bound by nation or region, platforms often are not. An ISP is almost exclusively located in the nation in which regulation is imposed and enforced, in terms of the (physical and legal) location of the company, its material infrastructure, and its users. This is not the case for the likes of Twitter, Instagram, or Wikipedia. Most of the major social media platforms today are, as corporate and legal entities, based in the United States, where they enjoy the broadest safe harbor, but they serve millions of users living in nations that impose much stricter liability, or have specific requirements about responding to state or court requests to remove content.

Major social media platforms have had to develop their own policies on how to respond to requests from foreign governments to remove content. Google famously pulled out of China rather than filter its search results according to Chinese dictates (although there was certainly a variety of motivations for the move).[44] LinkedIn remained by honoring the Chinese government's policies and seeking financial investment from Chinese firms.[45] Twitter will remove tweets in response to government requests, but does so only for users in that nation (rather than removing them from the entire service) and makes clear what has been removed and at whose behest.[46] Many of the major platforms publish data on the number of removal requests they receive, by country and by category of request.[47]

Because Western platforms have sometimes been reluctant to honor removal requests from foreign governments, some nations have threatened to block content they deem illegal or offensive. China and the Islamic nations of the Middle East and North Africa have been most aggressive with this tactic. This typically involves providing local ISPs with a "blacklist" of pages deemed criminal or otherwise unacceptable. This is more complicated, of course, on massive platforms where the offending post or video is just one element of a complex and constantly changing archive. This can lead to "overfiltering," where a nation ends up blocking not just a single YouTube video or Facebook user, but YouTube or Facebook in its entirety.[48] What often follows is a high-stakes game of chicken: platforms do not relish being blocked from an entire nation of users; at the same time, doing so is risky for the government as well, as the policy may have costs in terms of public sentiment. For countries with a stronger commitment to freedom of expression or independent telecommunications, this tendency to block legitimate content along with the offensive is an unpalatable one, but others may justify it as a bulwark against an unwelcome intrusion of Western culture and values.

Third, a slow reconsideration of platform responsibility has been spurred by categories of content particularly abhorrent to users and governments. Public and policy concerns around illicit content, at first largely focused on sexually explicit and graphically violent images, have expanded in recent years to include hate speech, self-harm, and extremism; and to deal with the enormous problem of user behavior targeting other users, including misogynistic, racist, and homophobic attacks, trolling, harassment, and threats of violence. These hesitations are growing in all corners of the world: even U.S. policy, with the broadest safe harbor, has shifted in the face of specific concerns.

Most pressing has been, unsurprisingly, the issue of terrorism. Certainly, terrorist organizations have grown increasingly savvy in the use of social media platforms.[49] At the same time, terrorism offers a compelling rationale for the imposition of policies that may have other aims as well.[50] Even in the United States, where the First Amendment provides intermediaries a powerful shield against government intrusion, inhibiting terrorism can be a convincing counterargument. But as ISIS and other extremist groups have distributed gruesome beheading videos and glossy recruitment propaganda on YouTube and Twitter, and more quietly coordinated with supporters and radicalized the disaffected, pressure from Western governments on social media companies to "crack down" on terrorist organizations has grown.

In Europe, this has meant an increasing expectation that platforms, once informed of terrorist content, must remove it quickly. Under the U.K. Terrorism Act of 2006, platforms have only two days to comply with a takedown request; otherwise, they are deemed to have "endorsed" the terrorist content.[51] Others have called for imposing fines on platforms for failing to remove terrorist materials, compelling them to cooperate more readily with police investigating terrorist incidents, and requiring them to share data with counterterrorist investigators.[52] Several governments in the Middle East have instituted new antiterrorism laws (or attempted to) that affect platforms. In Egypt, for example, a law drafted in 2014 gave authorities much wider latitude to intervene in and surveil online communication for suspected terrorist activity. Similar laws have been passed in Jordan, Qatar, and Saudi Arabia.[53] In the United States, several lawsuits have been brought by the families of victims of terrorist attacks against Twitter or Facebook for providing "material support" to terrorist organizations, though none has succeeded thus far.[54]

Hate speech and racial violence have also fueled debates about the obligations of social media platforms, particularly in Europe.[55] Germany and France both have laws prohibiting the promotion of Nazism, anti-Semitism, and white supremacy. As we saw, the French law produced one of the earliest online content cases, in which Yahoo was compelled to prevent French users from accessing online auctions of Nazi memorabilia.[56] More recently, when anti-Semitic comments began appearing on Twitter under the hashtag #unbonjuif, or "a good Jew," French courts pressed Twitter to turn over the user data behind the offending tweets.[57] In 2016, European lawmakers persuaded the four largest tech companies to commit to a "code of conduct" regarding hate speech, promising to develop more rigorous review and to respond to takedown requests within twenty-four hours. Similar concerns have emerged in other parts of the world. An addition to Argentinean antidiscrimination law was considered that would require intermediaries to proactively monitor their sites and remove comments that were racist or discriminatory, and would even encourage them to do away with the comment features of their sites entirely.[58]

Nations that do not share the American version of freedom of expression have been more willing to criminalize speech that criticizes the government or upsets public order. Some nations are limiting press freedoms for bloggers and even amateur speech on social media platforms. Laws that curtail the press online have appeared in Egypt, Iran, Pakistan, Tunisia, and the United Arab Emirates.[59] In other nations, including Kuwait and Lebanon, laws that prohibit the disruption of public order have been applied to political activists.[60] Some countries prohibit speech that directly criticizes their leaders, and in some cases these rules have been extended to social media platforms. In 2012, authorities in Brazil arrested the head of Google Brazil for refusing to remove YouTube videos that targeted Brazilian political candidates,[61] and Facebook now complies with Turkish law criminalizing defamation of the country's founder, Mustafa Kemal Atatürk, or the burning of the Turkish flag, by removing any such content flagged by users.[62] Facebook works with Pakistan to remove online blasphemy, with Vietnam to remove antigovernment content, and with Thailand to remove criticism of the royal family.[63]

Other countries have used laws that purportedly combat cybercrime, protect children, or prohibit terrorist content as ways to pressure platforms to remove politically contentious materials. Russia has been the innovator in this regard. In 2009, Russian law held that website owners are responsible for what users post in the comments on their site. In 2012, Russia developed a "blacklist" of sites that include "forbidden information"—on, for example, illicit drugs, porn, and suicide—and required Russian ISPs to block these sites. ISPs were forced to respond to requests not only from the court or state regulatory authorities but also from regular citizens, including the Media Guard youth group, which was targeting gay teen forums and Ukrainian political organizations.[64] In 2014, the Russian government took a bolder step: a new dictate would require any foreign platforms that have Russian users to store those users' data on servers located physically in Russia; otherwise the whole platform would be blocked nationwide.[65] The revelations of U.S. National Security Agency surveillance by Edward Snowden were Russia's nominal justification, but many suspected that housing the data within Russia's borders would make it easier for the government to access that data and squelch political speech. As of this writing, the (mostly U.S.-based) platforms have refused, and Russia has extended the deadline for compliance. In addition, in 2015 Russia decreed that bloggers with more than three thousand page views per day must register as media organizations and follow Russian media laws. Though terms of the requirement are unclear, it seems also to include users with more than three thousand daily visitors on Twitter or Facebook.[66]

The United States has by and large held to the safe harbor protections first offered to online intermediaries. But growing concerns about terrorism and extremist content, harassment and cyber bullying, and the distribution of nonconsensual pornography (commonly known as "revenge porn") have tested this commitment. Some critics suggest that Section 230 supports a marketplace-of-ideas approach to free speech, but that "so much deference to the content policies of private technology platforms in fact causes a unique brand of reputational and psychological indignity."[67] A number of platforms have developed specific policies prohibiting revenge porn, modeled on the notice-and-takedown arrangements in copyright law: platforms are not obligated to proactively look for violations but will respond to requests to remove them.[68] This can involve the kind of adjudicating platform moderators prefer to avoid: determining whether a complainant (who may not even be a user of that platform) is in fact the subject of the video or photo, whether the material was posted with or without the subject's consent, who owns the imagery and thus the right to circulate it. In early 2016, the Obama administration urged U.S. tech companies to develop new strategies for identifying extremist content, either to remove it or to report it to national security authorities.[69] In response to harassment, pressure is coming from users, particularly women and racial minorities, who argue that the abuses have become so unbearable that platforms have an obligation to intervene.[70] Together, these calls to hold platforms liable for specific kinds of abhorrent content or behavior are undercutting the once sturdy principle of safe harbor articulated in Section 230.

PLATFORMS ARE NOT LIKE TRADITIONAL INTERMEDIARIES

The early logic of content moderation, and particularly the robust safe harbor protections offered to intermediaries by U.S. law, makes sense in the context of the early ideals of the open web, fueled by naïve optimism, a pervasive faith in technology, and single-minded entrepreneurial zeal. Even in the face of long-standing and growing recognition of harms and problems, this logic persists. Only a platform defined as a mere service, bought and paid for by its users (through fees or attention to advertising), could launch without giving much thought of community guidelines, could respond with surprise when unanticipated, reprehensible, or criminal uses emerged, and could lean back on a simplistic rendition of the First Amendment. Like the Internet itself, these sites often began with small, like-minded user communities who wanted to see them succeed as much as the developers; much conflict could be handled interpersonally, or through appeals to the "community"—which to this smaller group looked like a singular and recognizable entity, more or less like the developers themselves. Only inside of this logic could a platform provider propose neutrality as a policy, could liken itself to ISPs as mere conduits, and could thus claim protection from legal liability and cultural obligation—a protection that network providers, fully aware of the long debates about telecommunications, had fought hard to assert. The promise of openness, neutrality, meritocracy, and community was powerful and seductive, resonating deeply with the ideals of network culture and much older dreams of a truly democratic information society.[71]

But if such a utopia ever existed in the smaller enclaves of online community, it most certainly could not as these platforms grew larger, more visible, more global, and more commercial. As social media platforms multiply in form and purpose, become more and more central to how and where users encounter one another online, and involve themselves in the circulation not just of words and images but of goods, money, services, and labor, the safe harbor afforded to Internet providers seems more and more problematic.

Social media platforms *are* intermediaries, in the sense that they mediate between users who speak and users who might want to hear them, or speak back. This makes them similar not only to search engines and ISPs but also to all forms of traditional media and telecommunications.[72] Media industries of all kinds face some kind of regulatory framework designed to oversee how they mediate between producers and audiences, speakers and listeners, the individual and the collective. But social media do violate the century-old distinction deeply embedded in how we think about media and communication. On the one hand, we have "trusted interpersonal information conduits"—the telephone companies, the post office. Users give them information aimed for others and trust them to deliver it. We expect them not to curate or even monitor that content; in fact we made it illegal to do so. We expect that our communication will be delivered, for a fee, and we understand that the service is the commodity, not the information it conveys. On the other hand, we have "media content producers"—radio, film, magazines, newspapers, television, video games—that make entertainment for us, entertainment that feels like the commodity we pay for (sometimes with money, sometimes with our attention to ads), and is designed to speak to us as an audience. We understand that the public obligation of these providers is to produce information and entertainment for public consumption, and we task them in that role with moderating away the kinds of communication harms we worry about most: sexual and graphic content, violence and cruelty, dangerous kinds of information and knowledge. And we debate the values of those public media, as a way to debate about our values as a people.

I believe we are now dealing with a third category: a hybrid of the two, perhaps, or something new emerging from it. Social media platforms promise to connect users person to person, entrusted with messages to be delivered to a select audience (sometimes one person, sometimes a friend list, sometimes all users who might want to find it). But as a part of their service, these platforms host that content, they organize that content, they make it searchable, and in some cases they even algorithmically select some subset of it to deliver as front-page offerings, news feeds, subscribed channels, or personalized recommendations. In a way, those *choices* are the commodity, meant to draw users in and keep them on the platform, paid for with attention to advertising and in exchange for ever more personal data. Users entrust to them their interpersonal "tele" communication, but those contributions then serve as the raw material for the platforms to produce an emotionally engaging flow, more like a "broadcast."

This makes them distinctly neither conduit nor content, not only network or only media, but a hybrid that has not been anticipated by information law or public debate. It is not surprising that users mistakenly expect them to be one or the other, and are taken aback when they find they are something altogether different.[73] And social media platforms have been complicit in this confusion, as they often present themselves as trusted information conduits, and have been oblique about the way they shape our contributions into their commodities. It takes a while—years, decades—for a culture to adjust itself to the subtle workings of a new information system, and to stop expecting from it what traditional systems provided. This shift, not just in the size and prominence of platforms but in their purpose and practice when it comes to mediating our content, may warrant a full reconsideration of what we expect of them in this regard.

The promise that platforms are impartial is a powerful one, and it is easy to embrace that promise, at two levels: that social media platforms are impartial in that they do not intervene, and that social media platforms are impartial in the way that they intervene. The two halves of Section 230 support this twinned mythology. But the principle of impartiality is a distraction. Even the early web tools, used only to help design a page or run a blog, shaped how people communicate; even the ISPs that served as "mere conduits" had an influence on what we did over them. But the moment that social media platforms introduced profiles, the moment they added comment threads, the moment they added ways to tag or sort or search or categorize what users posted, the moment they indicated what was trending or popular or featured—the moment they did anything other than list users' contributions in reverse chronological order—they moved from delivering content for the person posting it to constituting it for the person accessing it.

And this makes a great deal of economic sense: for a business that built itself on the hope of advertising revenue, social media platforms had to face their audience, and treat those who produce content as laborers. This is true if the platform is largely a one-way affair, but it is true even if users are just as often posting as they are reading: in the moment a user posts, that contribution becomes raw material for the platform to construct a news feed, a channel, a category, a trend list, constituted for the benefit of the users it is then delivered to. The commitment to advertising revenue and, more recently, the value of compiling user data, push social media away from providing a service for content producers and closer to providing that amateur content for audiences.

There are many who, even now, strongly defend Section 230. The "permissionless innovation" it provides arguably made the development of the web, and contemporary Silicon Valley, possible; some see it as essential for that to continue.[74] As David Post remarked, "No other sentence in the U.S. Code, I would assert, has been responsible for the creation of more value than that one."[75] But among defenders of Section 230, there is a tendency to paint even the smallest reconsideration as if it would lead to the shuttering of the Internet, the end of digital culture, and the collapse of the sharing economy. Without Section 230 in place, some say, the risk of liability will drive platforms to either remove everything that seems the slightest bit risky, or turn a blind eye. Entrepreneurs will shy away from investing in new platform services because the legal risk would appear too costly.

I am sympathetic to these concerns, but there is a whole lot of room between all and nothing. If social media platforms are neither conduit nor content, then legal arrangements premised on those categories may be insufficient. One possibility would be to recommit to, even double down on, Section 230, but with a sober and unflinching eye for which platforms, or aspects of platforms, warrant it and which exceed it. If a platform offers to connect you to friends or followers, and deliver what they say to you and what you say to them, then it is a conduit. This would enjoy Section 230 safe harbor, and could include the good faith moderation that safe harbor anticipated. But the moment that a platform begins to select some content over others, based not on a judgment of relevance to a search query but in the spirit of enhancing the value of the experience and keeping users on the site, it has become a hybrid. As soon as Facebook changed from delivering a reverse chronological list of materials that users posted on their walls to curating an algorithmically selected subset of those posts in order to generate a News Feed, it moved from delivering information to producing a media commodity out of it. If that is a profitable move for Facebook, terrific, but its administrators must weigh that against the idea that the shift makes them more accountable, more liable, for the content they assemble— even though it is entirely composed out of the content of others.[76] And this would absolutely include the marketplace services that present themselves as social media platforms, like Airbnb, Etsy, and Uber: though as part of their services they do host and distribute users' speech (profiles, comments, reviews, and so on), and to that degree should enjoy protection from liability, they are also new kinds of employers and brokers, and should not get to use 230's protection to avoid laws ensuring fair employment, fair housing, antidiscrimination, or fair pricing.[77]

A second possibility would be to redress a missed opportunity when Section 230 was first drafted. Intermediaries were granted safe harbor, including the right to moderate in good faith, but this double protection came with no concomitant expectations. The gift of safe harbor could have come with obligations, just as the grant of monopoly to the telephone company came with the obligation to serve all users, or the awarding of a broadcasting license comes with obligations about providing news or weather alerts or educational programming. Platform moderation could be required to meet some minimum standards, or commit to some degree of transparency, or provide specific structures for appeal and redress. But until intermediary liability law is rethought, social media platforms will continue to enjoy the two sides of safe harbor, the "right but not the responsibility" to police their sites as they see fit.

3

community guidelines, or the sound of no

> Some parts of the Internet lack rules. This isn't one of them. . . . Medium is a
> free and open platform for anyone to write their views and opinions. . . . We
> believe free expression deserves a lot of leeway, so we generally think the best
> response to bad ideas is good ideas, not censorship. However, Medium *is* a
> shared space. We want many different kinds of ideas and people to thrive here.
> Some types of speech tend to stop good conversation from ever happening
> rather than advancing it. . . . So, we need a few ground rules.
>
> *Medium Rules*

Explaining the rules is just one part of platform moderation—a small part,
perhaps. Few users read them, many don't even know they exist. And while
they often get invoked the moment they are imposed, the rules as stated
may or may not have a close correlation with how they're actually enforced.

Still, *how* they are articulated is of enormous importance. For practical
reasons, social media platforms need rules that can be followed, that make
sense to users, that give their policy team a reasonably clear guide for deciding what to remove, that leave enough breathing room for questionable
content they might want to retain, that can change over time, and that will
provide a satisfactory justification for removals if they're disputed, whether
by users themselves or in the glare of public scrutiny. More than that, articulating the rules is the clearest opportunity for the platforms to justify
their moderation efforts as legitimate. The rules are their most deliberate
and carefully crafted statement of principles—not just of what is or is not
permitted, but why. Less an instruction manual for how to moderate, the
community guidelines are what remains after moderation, like a constitution,

documenting the principles as they have been forged over routine encounters with users and occasional skirmishes with the public.

Most platforms present users with the rules through two main documents. The "terms of service" is the more legal of the two, a contract that spells out the terms under which user and platform interact, the obligations users must accept as a condition of their participation, and the proper means of resolving a dispute should one arise. It addresses not just appropriate content and behavior but also liability, intellectual property, arbitration, and other disclaimers. It is arguably written with an eye toward avoiding future litigation, often indemnifying the company as broadly as possible against any liability for users' actions.[1]

Its partner document, called "community guidelines" or by some similar title, is the one users are more likely to read if they have a question about the proper use of the site, or find themselves facing content or users that offend them. In deliberately plainspoken language, this document lays out the platform's expectations of what is appropriate and what is not. It also announces the platform's principles, and lists prohibitions, with varying degrees of explanation and justification.

It is quite possible to use social media platforms for years without ever reading these guidelines or running afoul of them. But to understand the project of moderation, it's worth becoming acquainted with them: what they say, how they sound, and what they hope to accomplish. It's soothing to hear calls to protect freedom of speech and self-expression, and jarring to realize that these platforms need rules against rape and pedophilia. But reading just one is not enough. Looking at dozens of them, across a variety of platforms, helps highlight what is common to all, and what is specific to just a few.[2]

One might dismiss these guidelines as mere window dressing—performances of principles, ringing so clear and reasonable, that do not in fact have much to do with the actual enforcement of policy, which in practice can be more slapdash, strategic, or hypocritical. I find it more convincing to say that these are statements of both policy and principle—struggled over by the platform operators at some moments and ignored at others, deployed when they are helpful and sidestepped when they are constraining. And they do important discursive work, performing but also revealing how platform companies see themselves as ambivalent arbiters of public propriety.

Legible in these guidelines are the immense challenges involved in overseeing massive, global social media platforms. They reveal how social media platform administrators try to make sense of and assert their authority over users in the first place. They attempt to provide users with suitably clear definitions of what is unacceptable, even as such definitions are necessarily subjective and shifting and incomplete. They buttress these definitions with an array of logical principles and borrowed value systems, to legitimate their imposition and to support later interventions that, while arguably necessary, are immensely difficult to impose to everyone's satisfaction. And they are scarred by the controversies that each platform has faced, and the bumpy road that all social media have traveled together over the past decade.

The guidelines also make clear the central contradiction of moderation that platform creators must attempt to reconcile, but never quite can. If social media platforms were ever intended to embody the freedom of the web, then constraints of any kind run counter to these ideals, and moderation must be constantly disavowed. Yet if platforms are supposed to offer anything better than the chaos of the open web, then oversight is central to that offer—moderation is the key commodity, and must be advertised in the most appealing terms.

HOW THEY SOUND

These guidelines are discursive performances, first and foremost. While platform moderators do point to them when they remove content or suspend users, the terms of service matter more when a decision is actually disputed. The primary purpose of the community guidelines is not arbitration. Instead, they constitute a gesture: to users, that the platform will honor and protect online speech and at the same time shield them from offense and abuse; to advertisers, that the platform is an environment friendly to their commercial appeals; and to lawmakers, to assure them of the platform's diligence, such that no further regulation is necessary. They articulate the "ethos" of the site, not only to lure and keep participants, but also to satisfy the platform's founders, managers, and employees, who want to believe that the platform is in keeping with their own aims and values. So these guidelines are revealing not just for where they come down on a particular issue but also as performances that make legible the anxieties and assumptions of the platform providers, and the challenges they face as they find themselves becoming curators of (often contentious) public speech.

What is immediately striking is the distinctly casual tone of the community guidelines, compared with the denser legal language of the terms of service. As the guidelines represent one of the first opportunities for a platform to set expectations or intervene in a problem, most adopt a "firm but fair" tone. But within those limits, there is a range of registers on display: fussy schoolteacher, stern parent, committed fellow artist, easygoing friend.

The particular voice is typically consistent with the character of the site—though it is more accurate to say that that character is a platformwide performance, of which the rules are a part. YouTube, for example, asks users to "Respect the YouTube Community: We're not asking for the kind of respect reserved for nuns, the elderly, and brain surgeons. Just don't abuse the site. . . . We trust you to be responsible, and millions of users respect that trust. Please be one of them." Etsy's tone is more homespun: "Please read this page with care, as it explains the dos and don'ts, the ins and outs, the ups and downs (and everything in between) of being a member of the Etsy community. These policies only apply to Etsy.com; alas, we do not control the universe, or even the rest of the Internet."[3] Foursquare is more muscular: "Be respectful of other people. Duh. Keep the Foursquare community positive! Harassing other people through photos, tips, lists, shouts or places is SO not cool. So just be nice and respectful, instead. Comprende?"

Most community guidelines begin with a preamble, offering a principled justification for both the platform itself and its need for rules. It can be an awkward dance: a proclamation of the wonders of an open platform, then a turn to explain why rules are necessary, followed by a long list of everything that is prohibited. These preambles fall into two categories, and they're not surprising, given the popular discourses about the Internet from which these platforms emerged. Some platforms position themselves as *speech machines:* their emphasis is on a commitment to free speech, self-expression, and access to information. For example: "Blogger is a free service for communication, self-expression and freedom of speech. We believe Blogger increases the availability of information, encourages healthy debate, and makes possible new connections between people. It is our belief that censoring this content is contrary to a service that bases itself on freedom of expression. However, in order to uphold these values, we need to curb abuses that threaten our ability to provide this service and the freedom of expression it encourages. As a result, there are some boundaries on the type of content that can be hosted with Blogger." Dreamwidth, Medium, Quora, Snapchat, Tumblr, and Twitter adopt similar positions. Users are declared to be largely responsible for what they say, read, or watch; the rules are reluctantly imposed, and only to the degree necessary. The understanding of users and platforms here is an individualistic, mechanistic, and liberal one: the platform must excise the bad, and the good will flourish.

The other sort of preamble, now more common, justifies platforms as *community keepers:* the platform makes possible a diverse but fragile community, one that must be guarded so as to survive. This frame shows up in the statements from Facebook, Flickr, Foursquare, Instagram, Last.fm, Nextdoor, Secret, Skype, Vimeo, and YouTube; here's Soundcloud's version: "We want SoundCloud to be a community where everyone feels respected. It's up to all of us to make that happen. This page includes important information about our expectations of you while using SoundCloud. Please take the time to carefully read through this information; we take these guidelines seriously and expect you to do the same." The emphasis is on safety, comfort, and mutual respect. Rather than the rules being a necessary intervention to prevent the inhibition of speech, they are what make healthy participation in the community possible.

These two justifications are not mutually exclusive or contradictory. Sites that highlight the protection of free expression will also at times draw on the language of community, and vice versa. They do not even map neatly onto platforms with different approaches to moderation; rather, they are two available ways to justify moderation itself. DeviantArt even makes this explicit in its preamble: "As the guiding force of this large and vibrant community we have two primary and often conflicting goals in the service we provide for you, the members of the community; the first being to ensure that members are free to express themselves within reason with as few restrictions as possible while nurturing an environment of creativity, learning, and talent and the second is to protect the members of the community, to the best of our abilities, from infringement of copyright, discrimination, harassment, and prejudice." Free expression and vibrant community have long served as the twin principles for the social web; here they again provide discursive frames not just for celebrating social media but for justifying its self-regulation.

A number of the content policy managers I spoke with expressed ambivalence about the policing they find necessary. While many like their jobs and find value in what they're doing, they don't like that it is necessary to impose such a high degree of oversight. As one Facebook manager fretted, "If you exist to make the world more 'open and connected' and you're a content-sharing platform, the critical question to answer is why you'd ever delete anything, right? Because deleting things makes things less open, on its face."[4] This ambivalence haunts the edges of these guidelines, particularly between the statement of principles that begin the document and the specific rules that follow. Some minimize their intervention. Ning demurs, "We tidy up." Kickstarter downplays, "We don't curate projects based on taste. Instead, we do a quick check to make sure they meet these guidelines."[5] Of course, these disclaimers are cast into doubt somewhat by the lengthy lists of rules that follow. In other cases, the push and pull between intervening and not is even more clear: just as an example, after promising not to be "big brother" about reviewing user content (while retaining the right to do so when necessary), Delicious states, "We are also not your mother, but we do want you to be careful crossing the Internet." There is a thorny contradiction in these guidelines, between the wish not to moderate and the compulsion to. My point here is not that these sites are hypocritical, but that moderation as a project is fueled by this contradiction: an ambivalence about intervening, and a fear of not intervening.

This ambivalence comes through in other ways. Though these documents are basically lists of prohibitions, they are often wrapped in more positive statements. It is as if the sites can't fully embrace the policing role they must play without reminding the reader of what the platform has to offer, in a language more suited to promotional material. Some simply preface the rules with a fluffy reminder of the platform's value: "At Pinterest, our mission is to help you discover and do what you love. To make sure everyone has a great experience, we have a few guidelines and rules." Others litter their guidelines with exclamation marks like an eager tween: "Welcome to the new Tagged Community! We want this to be a great place for you to find answers to any question you have about Tagged! We've established some guidelines that we hope will make this a great place for engaging discussions and insightful posts. Please read them before posting!"[6] Again, Foursquare is the most blunt: "Here's the thing: Foursquare is great. Help us keep it that way by following a simple set of House Rules developed for (and by!) our community."

One common way to temper the stern tone of these prohibitions is to frame them as "do's and don'ts." Versions of this approach have appeared in the guidelines for Flickr, Foursquare, Instagram, Reddit, Soundcloud, Tagged, Tumblr, and Yahoo Search. This approach forces some platforms into grammatical pretzels, as when Instagram's managers felt the need to repeat the same prohibitions in both positive and negative terms—"Do share photos and videos that are safe for people of all ages," and later, "Don't share photos or videos that show nudity or mature content"—or to concoct some "do" platitude to balance each of the "don'ts" they need to cover, like "Do have meaningful and genuine interactions" as a counterpoint to rules against harassment.[7] Etsy titled its guidelines document "Dos and Don'ts," though the body of the document contains only prohibitions.[8] Besides harking back to the simplicity and sensibility of "things I learned in kindergarten," this desire to mix in the positive with the negative reveals a reticence to simply say no, over and over again.

Invoking a commitment to free speech or healthy community is a powerful way to justify rules that will, in practice, limit some users' speech and ban some users from that community. But these guidelines also borrow other frames of legitimacy. The law, usually U.S. law, is the most common reference point. For instance, many of the prohibitions on hate speech invoke the legal language of protected categories from U.S. antidiscrimination law: "But we don't support content that promotes or condones violence against individuals or groups based on race or ethnic origin, religion, disability, gender, age, nationality, veteran status, or sexual orientation/gender identity, or whose primary purpose is inciting hatred on the basis of these core characteristics" (Blogger). Also common is the invocation of children as warranting special protection.[9] "Be thoughtful when posting anything involving a minor. Don't post or solicit anything relating to minors that is sexually suggestive or violent. Don't bully minors, even if you are one. Being a teenager is complicated enough without the anxiety, sadness, and isolation caused by bullying" (Tumblr).

Some platforms direct users to rely on their own moral compass: Reddit urges you to "use your best judgment" when tagging posts as Not Safe For Work (NSFW), while Twitter reassures users that "For the most part, using common sense won't steer you wrong."[10] Some invoke familiar social frameworks for that common sense: "If you wouldn't show the photo or video you are thinking about uploading to a child, or your boss, or your parents, you probably shouldn't share it on Instagram."[11] Quora titled its user policy "Be nice, be respectful"—and while a great deal of further explanation follows, the title alone speaks volumes. Flickr makes a similar move, but in reverse: "Don't be creepy. You know the guy. Don't be that guy." Of course, gestures to common sense ignore the fact that these platforms serve so many communities and subcultures, across nations, languages, and cultures, each with its own notion of decency and propriety. And there is something circular about continuing to gesture to common sense on platforms where obscenity and harassment have proven so common. But individual common sense, loosed from the particulars, offers a familiar sensibility with which to explain and justify their particular rules.

WHAT THEY SAY

When it comes to the details, the guidelines at the prominent, general-purpose platforms are strikingly similar. This makes sense: these platforms encounter many of the same kinds of problematic content and behavior, they look to one another for guidance on how to address them, and they are situated together in a longer history of speech regulation that offers well-worn signposts on how and why to intervene. I want to briefly highlight what these guidelines generally cover, what kinds of exceptions are built in, and how the prohibitions in each category vary when they do. It is worth noting that beyond these common categories of illicit content and bad behavior, many platforms use the community guidelines document for their rules about privacy, intellectual property, and spam. I will not be discussing those here, though it is important to remember that these restrictions can also affect speech and participation.

Sexual Content (Nudity, Sex, and Pornography)

The short version: Some nudity is okay for Pinterest, some isn't. The longer version: Artistic, scientific or educational nude photographs are okay here, but we don't allow those (like photographs of sexual activity) that could be a bad experience for people who accidentally find them. We also allow images of paintings or statues featuring nude subjects, but may remove things like pornographic cartoons. We don't try to define art or judge the artistic merit of a particular photograph. Instead, we focus on what might make images too explicit for our community. For example, we don't allow pornography, and you can't promote escort, prostitution or other adult sexual services. We're particularly sensitive about explicit content involving minors—if we find it, we'll report it to the National Center for Missing and Exploited Children. We'll remove nude photographs of anyone who appears to be a minor (other than infants).

Pinterest

Rules addressing sexual content must cover an enormous range, from the hint of nudity to the most extreme pornography, from the self-produced to the professional, from the consensual to the abusive. They must consider visual performances of sexual acts, the incidental or accidental or partial exposure of the body, sexual language and double entendres and indecent proposals, sexual objects and fetishes. They line between the appropriate and the illicit is drawn differently in different cultures and communities. No matter where they draw the line, some users will criticize the platform as too permissive and others as too prudish.

Although they differ in the details, most platforms draw one of four lines. For a few, like Airtime, trying to re-create Chatroulette after it drowned in rampant indecent exposure, a strict policy against not just nudity but even "sexually suggestive behavior" was in order. Ask is similarly restrictive. Most platforms draw the line at nudity: Google+ originally prohibited "nudity, graphic sex acts, or sexually explicit material," but softened the rule in May 2015 to allow some nudity. Similar prohibitions appear for Instagram, MySpace, and Ning. Slightly more permissive sites do not specify nudity, and by their silence implicitly allow it, but prohibit the "sexually explicit" or pornographic—leaving it to the user and the moderator to decide what counts as explicit. LinkedIn warns that "it is not okay to share obscene images or pornography on LinkedIn's service." The guidelines for Last.fm, Kickstarter, and Pinterest are similar. And a few platforms are more permissive still: Blogger, Tumblr, and Flickr allow explicit content and pornography.

Especially for the more permissive platforms, anxieties around sexual content are evident. After allowing sexual content, Blogger immediately and vociferously prohibits "non-consensual or illegal sexual content . . . rape, incest, bestiality, or necrophilia . . . child sexual abuse imagery . . . pedophilia." Most of the more permissive platforms also have robust systems for separating adult content from children, and from adult users who prefer not to encounter it: Reddit, Flickr, and Tumblr use a rating system and lets users exclude adult content from their searches. And on Blogger, users can post sexual content but cannot profit from it: Blogger prohibits advertising on "adult" blogs, or substantial linking to commercial porn sites. The very pillar of Blogger's business model, banner ads placed through Google AdSense, must be upended when the content is explicitly sexual.

Many platforms make some categorical exceptions, such as artistic representations of the human body, frank images and comment in the service of sexual health or education, and the exposure of one's own body during specific life moments like birth and breastfeeding. Pinterest's rule quoted above, which the platform expanded in 2014 from an otherwise bright-line rule against all "sexually explicit or pornographic" images, is a contortionist's trick that tries to account for the aims of the person posting, the effect on the viewer, aesthetic judgment, community values, historic traditions of art and representation, the intrusion of commerce, and the protection of children. The site has since added visual examples clarifying exceptions for breastfeeding, nonsexual poses, and artistic works—re-presenting the very images that, were it not for the exception, would violate the site's rules. In these contortions are visible a microcosm of the legal debates about pornography for the past century.

While the public is more likely to hear about whether a platform accidentally removed a photo of a naked statue, content policy teams spend more time on much more troubling issues: the distribution of nonconsensual pornography (revenge porn), sex trafficking, and the grooming of minors for sexual exploitation. Finally, all platforms are legally required to prohibit child pornography. U.S. law imposes clear and special obligations on content and social media platforms, under which suspected content and users must be immediately reported to the National Center for Missing and Exploited Children (NCMEC). The law offers no safe harbor for child pornography, but it is an obligation all platforms are eager to honor.

Graphic Content (Violence and Obscenity)

Crude Content: Don't post content just to be shocking or graphic. For example, collections of close-up images of gunshot wounds or accident scenes without additional context or commentary would violate this policy.

Blogger

Nearly all social media platforms prohibit the representation of violence, obscenity, and graphic content, to some degree. As is obvious from the example Blogger offers, this is more than just kick-in-the-crotch hijinks or fake-blood-spurt cartoon mayhem. These policies govern a range of troubling examples: gratuitous images of injuries, fight videos circulated by the instigators, cruelty to animals, deliberate acts of political brutality. These include everything from celebrations of violence (for example, a fan page that celebrated James Holmes, who shot and killed twelve in a Colorado movie theater in 2012)[12] to incitements to violence (a fan page titled "Zimmerman Must Die," referring to George Zimmerman, the shooter in the 2013 Trayvon Martin case in Florida).[13]

This is more than just keeping the gruesome and the horrible away from those who would find it offensive. Posting violent content on social media can be a tactic for doing further harm. A fight in a school cafeteria is recorded and posted to YouTube as a badge of honor; the next brawl might be worse than the last, in order to rack up more views. Posting a video may be a way to further torment the victim, embarrass a participant, or celebrate a victor. Prohibiting the representations of violence is seen as one way to discourage violence itself.

Similar tactics have been exploited on a much larger and more brutal scale by terrorist organizations, who circulate videos of beheadings and other images of political violence. They do so not just to send specific messages to governments that oppose them and strike fear in those who watch, but also to assert themselves as a powerful group in the public eye, to inspire people to join their cause, to goad other extremist groups to do the same, and to affirm a society in which such acts are possible. ISIS has proven particularly skilled at using social media in this way, circulating glossy recruitment magazines and videos documenting the beheadings of political prisoners and journalists, spurring a contentious discussion in the United States about the responsibility of YouTube and Twitter regarding them. Removing this content not only avoids shocking viewers, it preempts use of the platform in service of this larger aim.

Platforms differ, however, in the degree of violence needed to run afoul of the rules. As YouTube puts it, "It's not okay to post violent or gory content that's primarily intended to be shocking, sensational, or disrespectful. If posting graphic content in a news or documentary context, please be mindful to provide enough information to help people understand what's going on in the video." The platforms have settled on a few different adjectives to draw this line: prohibiting violence that is "graphic or gratuitous" (Google+, Hunch), "unnecessary" (Periscope), "gruesome" (Metacafe), or "extreme" (Vimeo). Is the implicit assumption, if graphic or gratuitous violence is not allowed, that garden-variety violence presumably is? Some sites spell out their prohibition with examples, which can read like a rogue's gallery of atrocities, presumably each of which has come up on that platform at some point: "the mutilation or torture of human beings, animals, or their remains" (Tumblr), or "realistic images of people or animals being killed, maimed, tortured, or abused" (Apple). Other platforms prefer to speak in generalities, leaving the distinctions to be made on a case-by-case basis.

Platforms that offer live video streaming, including Facebook Live, Periscope, and YouTube, face the additional challenge of moderating live violence in real time. Perpetrators have streamed their violent crimes as they committed them; bystanders have captured violent incidents as they happened; victims of racially charged and even deadly encounters with police have streamed the incidents as a form of witnessing. As Facebook has noted, "One of the most sensitive situations involves people sharing violent or graphic images of events taking place in the real world. In those situations, context and degree are everything."[14] Platforms must weigh the graphic against the significant, aware that intervening means censoring the broadcast.

Harassment (Abuse, Trolling, and Direct Threats)

Be cool and play nice. The Internet is a pretty cool place, but it also gives people the means to insult and/or harass others without taking full responsibility for their words. We request—nay, we insist!—that while you are on Vimeo you respect the people you encounter, as well as their videos. You are free to disagree and/or provide critical feedback, but please keep it respectful.

Vimeo

It has become clear that harassment is not an aberration but a condition of social media.[15] As Ellen Pao, uniquely familiar with this issue as the former CEO Reddit and a frequent target of harassment and abuse, put it, "The foundations of the Internet were laid on free expression, but the founders just did not understand how effective their creation would be for the coordination and amplification of harassing behavior. Or that the users who were the biggest bullies would be rewarded with attention for their behavior."[16] Social media platforms have become a space for, and all too hospitable to, all sorts of banal cruelty: garden-variety hatred, misogyny, and homophobia tossed at whomever is there to receive it; brutal gamesmanship of trolling public figures, especially women; intimidations and threats directed at those who dare to be feminist, progressive, or even merely outspoken; expressions of meanness and violence that pour out of already sour relationships: broken friendships, jilted exes, bullies, stalkers.[17] Groups gang up on a single target, shifting between accounts to elude platform moderators. Coordinated attacks often include planning and preparation on other platforms or in private groups, can employ automated techniques, and may even use the flagging and complaint mechanisms, meant to protect the harassed, against them. More recent tactics include revealing a person's private information, address, or location (doxxing), manipulating a person's photo in brutal ways, sending revealing information to a target's friends or coworkers, hacking and taking over a person's social media accounts, or calling the police to a victim's door on false pretenses (swatting).

Many platforms now characterize harassment as fundamentally destructive to the lofty goals of social media: this issue is now "taken very seriously" (YouTube), it rises "above all else" (Newsvine), it is approached with "zero tolerance" (Last.fm). Harassment is a broad category of problematic behaviors, and has grown both as we investigate its nuances and as harassers continue to innovate.[18] It can encompass anything from trash talk to insults to bullying to unwanted attention to threats to stalking to abuse that spills out into real-world consequences. Exactly what crosses the line as harassment varies across platforms. Foursquare draws a wide circle when it prohibits "negativity directed at another person." Skype even used to prohibit embarrassment, though I suspect this was one of those rules it did not try to enforce: "Don't . . . harass, threaten, embarrass, or do anything else to another Skype user that is unwanted." Periscope emphasizes intention: "Do not engage in dialogue or behavior that intends only to incite or engage in the targeted harassment of others." DeviantArt justifies its prohibition as avoidance of a slippery slope: "Discouraged commentary is typically considered to have the potential to escalate into an aggressive or abusive situation." Twitter, on the other hand, draws a much tighter circle around what it considers "abusive behavior" (for which the platform has long come under fire): "You may not publish or post direct, specific threats of violence against others." (This was broadened slightly in early 2016, to "You may not make threats of violence or promote violence, including threatening or promoting terrorism.")

Sometimes the harassment rules are framed as a prohibition against "trolling."[19] Reddit, a site plagued by abuse, includes it as a separate item: "Don't troll. Trolling does not contribute to the conversation." It then lists a variety of separate prohibitions of what might also count as trolling: personal attacks against others, mass downvoting of a user's posts, starting flame wars, joining in on an attack against a redditor without knowing the situation, or enlisting others to troll someone. SoundCloud even offered a pop psych theory for why people troll, when it warned, "Don't: rant, flame, troll or be an asshole. SoundCloud is a social place but it's not the place for you to act out rage from other parts of your life. Don't let a personal issue strain the rest of the community."[20] Trolls often look to game the platform itself: misusing complaint mechanisms, and wreaking havoc with machine learning algorithms behind recommendation systems and chatbots.[21]

Unfortunately, platforms must also address behavior that goes well beyond spirited debate gone overboard or the empty cruelty of trolls: directed and ongoing harassment of an individual over time, including intimidation, stalking, and direct threats of violence. This is where the prohibitions often get firm: "Never threaten to harm a person, group of people, or property" (Snapchat). Many sites point to the law as justification for their prohibitions against threats and stalking: "We remove content, disable accounts, and work with law enforcement when we believe there is a genuine risk of physical harm or direct threats to public safety" (Facebook). Identifying and discerning the credibility of such threats is of course extremely difficult. The guidelines are generally quiet on how that will be accomplished.

Hate Speech

Hateful conduct: You may not promote violence against or directly attack or threaten other people on the basis of race, ethnicity, national origin, sexual orientation, gender, gender identity, religious affiliation, age, disability, or disease. We also do not allow accounts whose primary purpose is inciting harm towards others on the basis of these categories. Examples of what we do not tolerate includes, but is not limited to behavior that harasses individuals or groups of people with: violent threats; wishes for the physical harm, death, or disease of individuals or groups; references to mass murder, violent events, or specific means of violence in which/with which such groups have been the primary targets or victims; behavior that incites fear about a protected group; repeated and/or or non-consensual slurs, epithets, racist and sexist tropes, or other content that degrades someone.

Twitter

All social media platforms prohibit hate speech; the few that don't mention it in a specific rule include it under a broader category like "personal attacks." Concerns about racial hatred, white supremacy, Holocaust denial, and sectarian conflict online date back to the early web; more recently, worry about misogyny, homophobia, and hatred directed at nearly every imaginable group have extended to social media platforms.[22] In recent years these voices have greatly expanded their reach, finding purchase in anti-immigrant and anti-Muslim sentiment in Europe and the United States, and a resurgence of nationalist and white supremacist activity, particularly around the 2016 U.S. presidential election.[23]

In most instances, platform hate speech guidelines echo U.S. legal language, particularly the list of groups to which the rule applies. This is the most obvious place where legal language overtakes the otherwise casual tone of these guidelines. As in Twitter's policy, most list the "protected classes," those groups that enjoy protection from discrimination in U.S. law, developed over time as in a series of antidiscrimination statutes, from Title VII of the Civil Rights Act of 1964 (which prohibits discrimination based on "race, color, religion, or national origin"), the Equal Pay Act of 1963 (sex), the Age Discrimination in Employment Act of 1967 (age), the Americans with Disabilities Act of 1990 (disability), and so forth.

Prohibiting hate speech is a safe position politically, and does not require hedging, balance, or exceptions.[24] In fact, unlike other rules, which can feel weighed down by the inevitable disagreements that follow, the rules against hate speech sound a clear, ethical note. Medium framed its rule as being in tension with its embrace of contentious speech: "We think free expression deserves a lot of leeway. So, we generally think the best response to hateful speech is more speech, not censorship. Still, we reserve the right to take down hateful slurs, which tend to silence others while adding little if anything."[25] But parsing the way hateful speech is used can be trickier. As one policy representative from LiveJournal put it, "Obviously a site does not want to wake up one morning and discover it has become the watering hole for Neo-Nazis and the KKK. It is, however, nearly impossible to write a policy for, since you also get (a) people using slurs in a reclaimed fashion for an 'in-group' they are part of; (b) activists documenting groups that hold those positions to 'name and shame'; (c) people who are entirely innocent of the alternate usage/history of a particular term; (d) someone saying something thoughtless or ignorant not motivated by animus; (e) people who *do* hold those opinions fully aware that they are unpopular and devising elaborate vocabularies to talk about them in code."[26]

Illegal Activity

Harmful or dangerous content: While it might not seem fair to say you can't show something because of what viewers might do in response, we draw the line at content that intends to incite violence or encourage dangerous or illegal activities that have an inherent risk of serious physical harm or death. Videos that we consider to encourage dangerous or illegal activities include instructional bomb making, choking games, hard drug use, or other acts where serious injury may result.

YouTube

Unlike the classic First Amendment categories of sex and obscenity, violence and harassment, prohibiting illegal activity and contraband goods is something traditional media do not have to worry about much: except for recurring public worry about the "glorification" of crime, broadcasters and publishers can and regularly do show illegal activity. On social media, illegal activity is much more problematic: here it may be the actual exchange of contraband, or a representation of an actual criminal act being committed. Television networks can portray fireworks, burglary tools, and black-market medical devices; Craigslist could actually facilitate their sale.

Platforms that facilitate the sale or exchange of goods and services must prohibit illegal contraband. While the platform is not selling these items themselves, it is fundamentally facilitating the transaction, and falls under the same kinds of laws that apply to the proprietor of a flea market. Craigslist, Etsy, and Kickstarter have long lists of prohibited items, including weapons, pesticides, fireworks, medical devices, used batteries, and body parts. These items may be illegal in one state but not another, or in one country but not in all; but these platforms generally prefer to avoid these regulated categories altogether, rather than deal with laws jurisdiction by jurisdiction. For example, Apple restricts in all cases apps that alert drivers to the location of DUI police checkpoints, though the apps are illegal only in some states. In other cases, such prohibitions can be good public relations, as when Facebook banned person-to-person sales of handguns, less than two months after the 2015 shootings in San Bernardino, California.[27]

In some cases, platform managers feel they must restrict the discussion of illegal activity, even though it is merely speech, if the discussion might signal or lead to illegal activity. For instance, Grindr allows "No photos or mentioning of . . . drugs or drug paraphernalia, including emoji" in user profiles and photos. This seems a strict restriction of speech; however, because Grindr combines private messaging with the identification of people geographically nearby, exploiting the platform to facilitate distribution of drugs would be easy to do and difficult to police. Mentioning drugs in a user profile would be an easy way to signal a willingness to distribute drugs privately.

Trickier still are prohibitions on the representation of illegal activity specifically out of concern for its influence on others—for example, the portrayal of drug use. YouTube's acknowledgment that it "might not seem fair to say you can't show something because of what viewers might do in response" reveals the needle being threaded here: whether representation of illegal activity amounts to encouragement of it; whether children in particular are more vulnerable to such persuasion; whether instructions are tantamount to facilitating the activity.

Self-Harm (Pro-Anorexia, Cutting, and Suicide)

Don't post content that actively promotes or glorifies self-harm. This includes content that urges or encourages readers to cut or injure themselves; embrace anorexia, bulimia, or other eating disorders; or commit suicide rather than, e.g., seeking counseling or treatment, or joining together in supportive conversation with those suffering or recovering from depression or other conditions. Dialogue about these behaviors is incredibly important and online communities can be extraordinarily helpful to people struggling with these difficult conditions. We aim to sustain Tumblr as a place that facilitates awareness, support and recovery, and to remove only those blogs that cross the line into active promotion or glorification of self-harm.

Tumblr

Some social media platforms prohibit the encouragement of self-harm. Strong calls to intervene against self-harm materials, including posts and images encouraging anorexia, cutting, and even suicide, must be balanced against the fact that many people find a great deal of support online in forums where they can discuss these challenging health issues with others.

Of all the prohibitions common to social media platforms, these may be the hardest to justify. Harassment and hate speech have victims to protect. Pornography and graphic violence offend viewers. The celebration of drug use or the selling of contraband encourages illegal activity. Users of self-harm sites are sharing and speaking freely together, expressing genuine opinions, and in some cases finding solace and community. This sounds exactly like what proponents of social media promised. But images of dangerously thin women shared by the "thinspiration" or "thinspo" community, or exhortations about the benefits of suicide make all this sharing and connecting a bit more unsettling.

Platform moderators must then justify their intervention as being on behalf of someone else who will be harmed—in this case young girls (as these are gendered concerns), presumed to be susceptible to influence. This pushes social media platforms to distinguish not between what is reasonable and what is unhealthy but between what is glorification of self-harm and what is merely support for those who struggle with it. Users are asked to not "promote or glorify" (Medium, Instagram), "encourage or instruct" (Livejournal), or "advocate" for (Quora) these activities.

Real Names

By joining Facebook, you agree to use your authentic name and identity. . . . People connect on Facebook using their authentic identities. When people stand behind their opinions and actions with their authentic name and reputation, our community is more accountable. If we discover that you have multiple personal profiles, we may ask you to close the additional profiles.

Facebook

Some platforms require users to participate using their real names. Facebook and LinkedIn have long insisted on a "real name" policy; Google+ did for its first few years, until relaxing the rule in 2014. LinkedIn also prohibits inaccurate information in user profiles.[28] In addition, platforms that facilitate the exchange of goods, money, or services often require proof of identity as part of a credit card or other payment transaction architecture, though some (like Etsy) allow that information to be obscured behind a pseudonymous profile that need not match the real name and fiduciary identity made known to the platform. And because Facebook and Google+ provide secure login mechanisms for other websites, some of the platforms using these systems have a kind of real-name policy by proxy—sometimes by design, as when Tinder requires that users link their dating profiles to their Facebook accounts.

Facebook and LinkedIn's desire to tether user profiles to real names broke from the logic of the early web, where pseudonymity was imagined to grant people the freedom to be more creative, intimate, flexible, and honest, freeing them from the burden of social markers of race, place, and gender.[29] But this freedom, many argued, also made it easier to circulate illicit content and engage in harassing behaviors, without fear of social or legal consequence or the social inhibition of being known.[30] Facebook regularly justifies its real-name policy in these terms, as an essential part of its efforts to protect users from harassment, trolling, racism, and misogyny—though in fact these problems plague Facebook anyway, even with a real-name policy in place.[31] Some critics have suggested that Facebook in fact needs to require real names for economic reasons: the massive troves of user data it collects are valuable precisely because they map to real people.[32]

Facebook has faced a series of public challenges for its dogged commitment to its real-name policy. Some feel the requirement imposes an undue burden on those who have reason to shield their identity: victims of past domestic abuse or stalking, those engaged in politically sensitive activities, or whistleblowers and activists who might fear identification or reprisals. A second challenge has come from users who want to play with their online personas, or to participate through multiple identities. This includes the kind of parody accounts that frequently appear on Twitter and elsewhere, and nonnormative communities like drag queen performers, who have personal, political, and commercial reasons for wanting to be on Facebook as their stage personas, and to manage how they engage socially both in and out of character.[33]

Most other sites (including Medium, Pinterest, Tumblr, Twitter, and YouTube) do not require users to provide real names, but some insist that users not impersonate others—typically this means in a malicious way, but in some cases even in a misleading way, as in using someone's trademark of posing as someone as a form of parody.

Commercial Activity

Don't use Flickr for unauthorized commercial activity. We offer tools for the community to license their works to others; if interested, visit our Marketplace. Flickr generally supports photographer entrepreneurs big and small, but we don't want to be a platform for your commercial activity or your business transactions, except for photos you enroll directly in our Marketplace. In your photo descriptions and on your profile page, you are welcome to link to your website or blog where you might also sell your work, but do not link directly to a shopping cart, checkout page, or pricing pages on other sites, and don't list prices on your Flickr photo descriptions.

Flickr

With the exception of exchange platforms like Etsy, Craigslist, Kickstarter, and Facebook Marketplace, most social media platforms impose some form of regulation on the commercial activity of their users. Nearly all social media platforms are themselves profit-seeking commercial entities, of course; the commercially motivated content they provide (like ads and sponsored posts) is treated as conceptually distinct from the contributions of users, which are supposed to be genuine and unsullied by commercial aims.[34] This distinction is a false one, or at least an untenable one. But to the extent that these platforms generally offer a separation from mere e-commerce as part of their purpose, commercial activity users might engage in via that platform must be curtailed.

Most of the prohibitions of commercial activity are less about maintaining some ideal about genuine participation than they are assurances that the platform will not be exploited by users or overtaxed by commercial traffic. For example, Flickr and Pinterest, each of which invites the user to gather a catalogue of images, regulates against that display's becoming an actual catalogue—a listing, that is, of products to be sold, on the platform or elsewhere. Other sites, to ensure that the integrity of user experience will not be undercut by some people's tactical efforts to accumulate friends or reputation, prohibit "self-promotion." One could argue that all participation on social media platforms is a form of self-promotion: we perform ourselves, and hope to gain something from doing so, though this gain may be in forms other than financial remuneration.[35] What these rules actually require is that users do this fairly, without taking advantage of the platform or running afoul of the spirit of the community: no asking for followers (Instagram), no deceptive means of encouraging traffic (Medium), no manipulation of rankings (Google+), no paying for positive reviews (Stumbleupon), no overposting (Craigslist).

Quality Contributions

Read over your submission for mistakes before submitting, especially the title of the submission. Comments and the content of self posts can be edited after being submitted, however, the title of a post can't be. Make sure the facts you provide are accurate to avoid any confusion down the line.

Reddit

Finally, some of the rules are designed not to limit the "wrong" kinds of content and participation but to encourage the "right" kinds. Certainly, social media platforms provide instructions elsewhere on how to use the platform properly: "about" pages that describe the service and its imagined uses, tips and tutorials that guide new users through the basic mechanisms, best practices and FAQs explaining how to use the platform properly and effectively. But this need to guide users toward the right kinds of participation bleeds into the guidelines as well.

Unlike rules against child pornography or personal attacks, where the platform stands opposed to the bad intentions of the user, these rules align the user and the platform, both (presumably) invested in producing a quality experience for all. This alignment, however, is in the service of convincing users to produce quality content and proper participation—work that benefits the platform. Many of these platforms depend to a great degree on their users producing the bulk of the content, labeling it, organizing it, and promoting it to others. This "labor" has been of growing scholarly concern, seen by many as work that goes largely unnoticed and uncompensated, while the benefits and revenue accrue to the platform.[36] As these guidelines reveal, not only do platforms need this labor, they must also manage it for quality control—to encourage engaging material and social opportunity and to deter low-quality or disruptive participation.

Some rules are meant to ensure that user participation fits the functioning of the platform, that, for example, posts be timely or regularly updated (Google Glass, Reddit, Yelp); content be correctly categorized or tagged (Craigslist, Etsy, Hi5, Newsvine); and redundancies and dead links be avoided (Apple, Google Play, Hi5, Metacafe, Microsoft Windows Live, Reddit, Tagged). Other rules urge users to produce the best kind of content within that range of activity, content that is factually accurate or carefully sourced (Wikipedia, Pinterest, Reddit, Yelp); not plagiarized (Newsvine); grammatically correct or professionally designed (Apple, Ask); artistic, beautiful, or of high-quality design (Foursquare, DeviantArt, Yelp); thoughtful or well reasoned, fair and unbiased, open to diverse opinions (Ask, Hunch, Reddit); and relevant, on-topic, and useful to the users who will find it (Apple, Ask, Craigslist, Foursquare, Google Play, Hunch, Last.fm, Newsvine, Ning, Quora, Reddit, Tagged, Yelp). This exhortation can become bizarre, since each rule is so specific to how the platform works: my favorite is from Foursquare: "Try not to add places to Foursquare that don't actually exist."

Rules about quality contributions were largely uncontroversial—until the "fake news" problem exploded around the 2016 U.S. presidential election.[37] Facebook and others were lambasted for fraudulent headlines circulating as legitimate news. Some worried that these concocted reports might have influenced voters; one story, that Hillary Clinton was involved in a child prostitution ring run at a Washington, DC, pizza shop, inspired one man to investigate the shop armed with an assault rifle.[38] Platforms first resisted the notion that they had any responsibility for such content, or any reasonable way to police it. Then Google and Facebook barred fraudulent news sites from profiting from their advertising networks.[39] Facebook also partnered with fact-checking organizations like Snopes, Politifact, and Factcheck.org to mark some stories as "disputed," and added a way for users to flag stories they believe to be false.

Though Facebook's policy was instituted in December 2016, as of October 2017, no new wording has been added to the community standards document that could reasonably refer to this change. One could argue that Facebook does not prohibit fake news, it only labels it; another possibility is that in some cases policies are instituted, but their addition to community guidelines documents lags behind.[40]

EVERY TRAFFIC LIGHT IS A TOMBSTONE

Across the social media platforms, at least the commercial, U.S.-based ones, the guidelines are generally similar, and specifically different. On the one hand, the platforms function differently, serve different audiences, and position themselves in opposition to one another. They have historically faced different challenges, and answered them in different ways. Policies develop over time, in ways specific to a platform and its economic and cultural trajectory—as the platform grows, as new user communities emerge and others depart, as it tries on new business models, as international audiences are pursued, or as particular controversies arise on that platform or on others.[41]

On the other hand, these platforms seem to be converging on a commonsense notion of what should be prohibited—or perhaps a few versions of common sense. This does not mean that they've all finally gotten it right, or that they've slowly converged on some universal norms, even just American ones. They are similar because, despite their material differences and despite any market pressure to differentiate themselves from their competitors, social media platforms structurally inhabit the same position—between many of the same competing aims, the same competing users, and between their user bases and lawmakers concerned with their behavior. They have responded to these tensions in similar ways, in part because of the similarity of position and in part because they have shared tactics, in both official and more informal ways. And they do not function in isolation, but rather they are together part of a patchwork of governance mechanisms, drawing on a commonly available cultural vocabulary.

Of course, the guidelines do change. Sometimes these are high-profile changes, made with public fanfare; more often they are smaller editorial adjustments. These platforms develop rules both in anticipation of inappropriate content or activity, and in response to it. Unanticipated kinds of content or behavior may be first spotted through the complaints of users, then formalized into new rules or written into existing ones. Most platforms have instituted a routinized internal process: content policy teams must from time to time decide how to translate a new legal obligation into an actionable rule, react to the emergence of a category of content they would like to curtail, and respond to surges of complaints from users.

Platform moderators like to think that their guidelines already represent the values of users, and are responsive to shifting norms and practices, a "living document" that moves with their user community. As a representative of Facebook told me, "I think, for the most part, we've been on the same page as our user base. I think in some ways our rules reinforce their norms, and then their norms reinforce or help tweak our rules (and our standards?). But it's kind of surprising how quickly users catch on to what our expectations are based on what they hear about (in terms of what we are policing) and then adopt them as their own."[42] What is clear, however, is that in other moments the public and its advocates find they must press platforms for change. Revisions of the guidelines often come only in response to outcries and public controversies. A content policy representative from Live-Journal pressed this point: "You know that cynical old saying 'Every traffic light is a tombstone'—i.e., traffic lights don't get put in until someone gets hurt at the intersection? Social media content policy is like that: every policy is a controversy. . . . When you look at a site's published content policies, there's a good chance that each of them represents some situation that arose, was not covered by existing policy, turned into a controversy, and resulted in a new policy afterward."[43]

In February 2012, the Huffington Post ran a lengthy and pointed essay called "The Hunger Blogs: A Secret World of Teenage 'Thinspiration.'"[44] In it, writer Carolyn Gregoire drew attention to the widespread use of social media, specifically Tumblr, by users interested in celebrating and promoting anorexia and bulimia as positive pursuits. Tumblr users (largely young women) were sharing "thinspiration" or "thinspo" photos of extremely thin women, both fashion models and amateurs, or close-ups of emaciated hips or collarbones. Alongside these, users would share motivational quotes that urged extreme dieting techniques and a single-minded focus on weight loss, document their personal food diaries and track their progress toward unhealthy target weights, and provide emotional support and encouragement for others. Together these blogs presented anorexia and other eating disorders as positive and empowering, and made space for a community of like-minded women who embrace eating disorders as a lifestyle.

This was not a new phenomenon, nor was it specific to Tumblr. Concerns for the use of the web as a supportive environment for unhealthy behaviors, particularly for eating disorders, cutting, and suicide, stretch back more than a decade. Medical and sociological researchers had documented the rise of the "pro-ana" sites, and concern had on occasion emerged in the blogosphere and the press. Pro-ana and pro-suicide sites first emerged in obscure corners of the web, a loose network of personal home pages, chatroom communities, and blog rings, and eventually migrated onto early social media sites like MySpace and Xanga.[45]

Most see this activity as harmful, sustaining and fueling those already suffering from an eating disorder and luring those who do not with a misleadingly rosy view and the support of a community. But not all agree that the causal relationship is so straightforward. Some have suggested, without dismissing the dangers, that the sites also provide the kind of belonging and support that marginalized communities often seek, both online and elsewhere.[46] And some argue that penalizing self-harm communities risks pushing them farther underground and misses an opportunity to intervene more productively.[47]

Some platform moderators were already aware of this problem, and were beginning to address it. Yahoo began removing pro-ana sites in 2001, after an episode of *Oprah* drew attention to them.[48] LiveJournal and Xanga had policies about "self-harm" as early as 2008. Also in 2008, *Newsweek* reported that pro-ana material was beginning to show up on Facebook.[49] In 2009 the Royal College of Psychiatrists in the United Kingdom called on the government to regulate sites that supported eating disorders;[50] a report in the journal *Pediatrics* in 2011 drew attention to videos on YouTube that promoted cutting and other forms of self-injury.[51]

What drew the attention of Gregoire and the Huffington Post was that pro-ana material had reached Tumblr. At the time, the image-blogging platform was enjoying a wave of new users; Tumblr had launched in 2007 but surged in popularity in 2010 and 2011.[52] What felt new was that these "thin-spo" blogs were cropping up on such a public platform in such a visible way, rather than furtively hiding out in the shadows of the web: "It is an underground phenomenon, yet it is housed on a platform that is one of the Internet's newest, burgeoning hotspots." Gregoire did not blame Tumblr, or call upon it to intervene; in fact, she included a quotation from a Tumblr representative indicating that the platform was already taking the issue seriously and looking for expertise on how to best address it. But Tumblr was the clear focus of the article, and each of the women interviewed in it was using Tumblr for her thinspo activities. More than that, Gregoire suggested that this particular thinspo activity, what she called "pro-ana 2.0," took advantage of Tumblr's specific qualities: its burgeoning popularity especially among teens, its glossy look (akin to a fashion magazine), and its combination of publicity and pseudonymity.

Just two weeks after the exposé, Tumblr announced that it would strengthen its policy against promoting or celebrating self-harm, and shared a draft of language it might add to the community guidelines. A week later it announced a partnership with the National Eating Disorders Association (NEDA). A week after that, Tumblr added a slightly revised version of the new rule to its guidelines. But the controversy was not over. In March, Jezebel ran a similar exposé, focusing this time on Pinterest (perhaps benefiting from mass migration following Tumblr's ban).[53] Pinterest quickly announced a rule similar to Tumblr's. In April, Instagram made a similar change to its policy. Facebook, which already prohibited "promoting self-harm," made some editorial tweaks to the language of its rule.

Whether these changes were effective is a matter of dispute. Tumblr seemed to have focused more on intervening in users' search habits, redirecting searches for terms like "pro-ana" or "thinspo" to a health message with emergency contact numbers and away from the content users might have been looking for—which nonetheless remained available on the site.[54] Buzzfeed asserted in January 2013 that Instagram and Tumblr had largely failed to remove the thinspo content they promised to ban.[55] Pinterest also seemed to have plenty of thinspo content, though it did seem to be blocking hashtags that might otherwise have directed users to it. Facebook, according to the article, was doing better than the others.

It is worth noting that Buzzfeed examined these four platforms and no others, probably because they were the four noted in the Huffington Post and Jezebel exposés, and the ones that had made the most public statements about addressing the issue. Other platforms seemed to evade scrutiny on this issue, not just in the original articles but in the broader conversation that followed. Few others added any direct mention of self-harm to their guidelines, either just after the controversy or in the years since. In the platform guidelines I looked at, only Livejournal and Medium specifically referenced self-harm behaviors as the four targeted platforms had; only Etsy and Quora included reference to harming oneself in their prohibitions of other harmful activities, as Pinterest had. There were no other mentions of self-harm across the other platform guidelines.[56]

The way that Tumblr, Instagram, and Pinterest developed their rules against self-harm suggests that these guidelines are open to outside pressure, whether from within the user community, from the press or other public criticism, or from other institutions. The fact that these restrictions not only emerged on these sites but were so thoroughly articulated there may have to do with the prevalence of thinspo materials on their platforms; their broader popularity with women compared with some other social media platforms; or the fit between the design of the platforms and the norms of the thinspo communities that found their way to them. But these are not robust explanations. Thinspo content can be found on other platforms that do not have these deeply articulated rules, and the tendencies of these sites that might suit thinspo are neither unique to those platforms nor essential to the practice—it may be that Tumblr and Pinterest currently borrow a "look" from fashion magazines and make it easy to post images and short quotations, but it is hard to argue that Blogger doesn't as well.

The guidelines now in place for these particular platforms have been imprinted onto the public imagination, because those platforms were drawn into the specific controversy in 2012 and their managers felt compelled to respond. But it is too simple even to say that the Huffington Post exposé led to new rules on these four platforms. No single explanation can fully account for why the guidelines of the social media platforms have turned out as they have. This kind of public controversy, shining an unwanted light on specific platforms, may push managers of those platforms to introduce a new rule; or perhaps it gives them permission to enact a change they already aspired to make. But there are as many cases in which platforms dragged their feet or were silent in the face of public criticism. Guidelines may be constitutional statements of principle, but they are also retrofitted, polished, and vacated, masking real economic imperatives. Yet they are not without momentum and teeth once laid down.

WHY THESE GUIDELINES MATTER

While these community guidelines documents may to some degree be strategic, self-serving window dressing, they are articulated as principled expressions. Perhaps they are deeply felt principles, reflective of a corporate mission, the aims of founders, the best instincts of Silicon Valley culture. I don't mean to suggest that they are *mere* performance, just hollow words. But they are performances. Genuine or not, they work to legitimate the platform's right to impose rules—not just these particular rules, but the right to impose rules at all. At the same time, they reveal little about the foundational values on which the rules were crafted, nor do they say anything about what happens when they are enforced.[57] We should approach these stated guidelines as, inevitably, provisional lines drawn in shifting sands, the residue of past tensions, and best efforts at workable compromises. But even as compromises, they do forge principles—and they must appear to users as principled.

These guidelines matter. Of course, they matter a great deal in the specific moments of use. They may to some degree guide what users choose to share, what they dare to do, and what they decide not to say. Self-censorship is an important component of the contours of public discourse, and a difficult one to assess. There are presumably absences of discourse, in the shadow cast by each of these rules, things people believe they should not or cannot say. The rules are also invoked by the platforms when content is removed or a user is suspended, which means at that moment they may be part of the way a user makes sense of the platform's intervention. And they become points around which aggrieved users or communities can challenge such decisions, or question the right of a platform to make them.

The rules established by the biggest social media platforms matter especially, and not only because they apply to such an enormous number of users. Platforms adjust their guidelines in relation to one another, and smaller sites look to larger ones for guidance, sometimes borrowing language and policies wholesale. Startups, short on personnel and expertise, often begin by tweaking the terms of service and community guidelines from the biggest player in their sector—Instagram's first community guidelines, just as an example, were copied directly from Flickr's. Sometimes guidelines travel along with personnel: Twitter was begun by the founders of Blogger, and the core of Twitter's approach to moderation was forged there.[58] Smaller platforms serving niche communities or attached to particular institutions borrow guidelines from their established and gargantuan counterparts, which they presume to be well crafted and battle-tested. Drop half a sentence from the guidelines of any major platform into a search engine and you will see a handful, even dozens, of smaller sites that evidently lifted the whole document and swapped their platform's name in. This kind of institutional plagiarism is fine, but it means that if we think not about the sixty biggest platforms but about the next six thousand smaller ones, the consistencies would be much more striking than the differences.

What is true about this complex tapestry of similarities and differences, echoes and innovations, is that there seems to be a small set of relatively stable *orientations,* not toward specific rules but toward frameworks of permissiveness and obligation. Together these policies, these orientations, are becoming industry standards.

It's also important to recognize that some platforms depend on other platforms to exist, and must align their rules with those they are obliged to honor. For example, platforms that depend heavily on mobile use need their apps to pass Apple's review. This means that the Instagram user is governed by rules established by Instagram, itself owned and influenced by Facebook, but those rules must be shaped to abide by Apple's standards as well.[59] Tinder can require users to link to their Facebook accounts, which means Tinder users are bound by two overlapping sets of rules. Different technological and institutional layers get tethered together to extend rules down the line—creating a self-reinforcing circle of prohibition and justification.

Beyond the specific interventions and disputes, these guidelines also matter more broadly for the values they articulate. These platforms reach an immense number of people, touch an immense number of interactions. What they allow and what they prohibit, and how they explain why, have both practical and rhetorical impact. Part of a democratic public culture is semiotic: the ability to represent oneself in the public dialogue, and to nominate both problems and solutions for debate.[60] The extent to which some people or perspectives are constrained or excluded by the guidelines designated by private platforms matters. This is not to suggest that platforms should have no rules at all. But it does highlight these guidelines and policies as texts into which we must peer closely, to see what values they represent and upon what theories of governance and rights they are premised.[61]

Still, in the end, the written guidelines simply aren't the whole story: there are real differences between the rules these companies post and the decisions they end up making, case by case, in practice. No guideline can be stable, clean, or incontrovertible; no way of saying it can preempt competing interpretations, by users and by the platform. Categorical terms like "sexually explicit" or "vulgar or obscene" do not close down contestation, they proliferate it: what counts as explicit? vulgar to whom? All the caveats and clarifications in the world cannot make assessment any clearer; in truth, they merely multiply the blurry lines that must be anticipated now and adjudicated later. This is an exhausting and unwinnable game to play for those who moderate these platforms, as every rule immediately appears restrictive to some and lax to others, or appears either too finicky to follow or too blunt to do justice to the range of human aims to which questionable content is put.

Looking only at the guidelines also overlooks the much messier process of enforcement, with its mistakes, overreactions, and biases. The tensions are not going to be around the easy case: something that is clearly child pornography will be easily removed for violating a widely accepted rule. The difficulty is at the edges: between racy and unacceptable, between relevant and prurient, between informing and inciting. These guidelines not only map the current terrain for what is acceptable and what is prohibited, they reveal the parameters and tensions faced by private curators of public speech. Whatever lines platforms draw, it is along those lines that adjudications must be made, and that disputes can, probably will, arise.

4

three imperfect solutions to
the problem of scale

Given the scale that Twitter is at, a one-in-a-million chance happens 500 times a day. It's the same for other companies dealing at this sort of scale. For us, edge cases, those rare situations that are unlikely to occur, are more like norms. Say 99.999 percent of tweets pose no risk to anyone. There's no threat involved. . . . After you take out that 99.999 percent, that tiny percentage of tweets remaining works out to roughly 150,000 per month. The sheer scale of what we're dealing with makes for a challenge.

> *Del Harvey, vice president of Trust and Safety, Twitter, in a TED talk,*
> *"Protecting Twitter Users (Sometimes from Themselves)," March 2014*

The problem of moderation is not new. Broadcasters, booksellers, publishers, and music labels have all grappled with the problem of being in the middle: not just between producer and audience, but between providing and restricting, between audience preference and public propriety. They have all had to set and enforce rules about what they will and will not make available.[1] Moderation is not new to the web either. From the earliest days, in threaded discussions, IRC channels, AOL chat rooms, and MUDs and MOOs, users disagreed about what these spaces were for, someone always wanted to circulate porn, someone always looked for ways to harass others, and some parameters of proper content and behavior were necessary. What is different for today's social media platforms is that they host and oversee an unprecedented amount of content and an unprecedented number of people, and must moderate on a qualitatively different scale.[2]

The most obvious difference is the sheer number of users, the sheer amount of content, and the relentless pace at which they circulate. It was once difficult to imagine how traditional media could review, rate, and police all of the U.S. television programming running twenty-four hours a day across multiple channels. That was a small challenge compared to what social media platforms must now do. As one policy manager at Flickr put it, "the scale is just unfathomable."[3]

Unfortunately, there's very little data about how large a task platform moderation really is; Jillian York is correct in her critique that, though some of the major platforms publish "transparency reports," these report only takedown requests from governments and companies; they say nothing about how much material is flagged by users, how many posts or images or videos are removed, how many users do the bulk of the flagging, and so on.[4] We can gather some rough clues at best. In May 2017, Mark Zuckerberg noted that Facebook receives "millions" of complaints per week.[5] *S/Z* reported that German contractors doing moderation work for Facebook handled one thousand to three thousand "tickets" a day. Twitter's March 2017 transparency report noted that the service had suspended more than 636,000 user accounts since the middle of 2015 just for terrorist-related activity.[6] Extrapolate from these few data points—across multiple categories, multiple reviewers, and multiple platforms—and we have at least a fuzzy sense of the enormity of this undertaking.

At this size, certain approaches to content moderation are practically impossible. For instance, there is simply too much content and activity to conduct proactive review, in which a moderator would examine each contribution before it appeared. Apple is a notable exception, in that it reviews every iPhone app before making it available in its store. But Apple fields hundreds of submissions a day, not hundreds of thousands. Nearly all platforms have embraced a "publish-then-filter" approach: user posts are immediately public, without review, and platforms can remove questionable content only after the fact.[7]

This means that everything, no matter how reprehensible or illegal, can be posted to these platforms and will be available until it is noticed and removed. Vile or criminal behavior may occur, and have its intended impact, before anything is done in response. Another way to think about it is that there is always something on a social media platform that violates the rules, and typically lots and lots of it. Someone is being harassed right now. Plenty of porn, graphic violence, animal cruelty, and hate speech are available as you read this. They will remain there for hours, days, or years, because of the challenges of policing platforms as immense as these. Because social media platforms operate at this scale, we as a society are being asked to tolerate the fact that even content as universally abhorred and clearly illegal as child pornography can be and is available on our favorite platforms, if only briefly. At such a scale, the problem of detection becomes pivotal, and perhaps impossible.

But the question of scale is more than just sheer number of users. Social media platforms are not just big; at this scale they become fundamentally different than they once were. They are qualitatively more complex; while these platforms may speak to their online "community," singular, at two billion active users there simply can be no such thing. Platforms must manage multiple and shifting communities, across multiple nations and cultures and religions, each participating for different reasons, often with incommensurable values and aims. And communities do not independently coexist on a platform, they overlap and intermingle—by proximity, and by design. Some Reddit users may be devoted to just one or a handful of particular subreddit groups, and Reddit is in many ways built to suit that—yet Reddit is also designed to algorithmically collect the most popular posts from nearly all of the subreddits, throw them together onto a front page, then pour the subsequent attention from users back into the subreddits from which they came. This collision of content and of users means that, almost by definition and almost unavoidably, any social norms that might emerge as common to a subreddit group will soon be destabilized as a viable means of governance, as newbies constantly roll in.

At this scale, some moderation techniques that might have fit smaller venues simply will not translate. For instance, the techniques of online community management are ill-suited to the scale of major social media platforms. Managing early online communities depended in part on community members knowing the webmaster, regulars knowing one another, and users sharing an accumulated history of interactions that provided the familiarity and trust necessary for a moderator to arbitrate when members disagreed.[8] Tough cases could be debated collectively, policies could be weighed and changed by the community. The scale of the forum made self-government possible.[9] But as these platforms have grown in scale and ambition, traditional community management has become increasingly untenable.

This means that the approaches social media platforms take, toward not just content moderation but all types of information management, are tied to this immense scale. Content is policed at scale, and most complaints are fielded at scale. More important, the ways moderators understand the problems have been formed and shaped by working at this scale. As a content policy manager from Facebook noted, "The huge scale of the platforms has robbed anyone who is at all acquainted with the torrent of reports coming in of the illusion that there was any such thing as a unique case. . . . On any sufficiently large social network everything you could possibly imagine happens every week, right? So there are no hypothetical situations, and there are no cases that are different or really edgy. There's no such thing as a true edge case. There's just more and less frequent cases, all of which happen all the time."[10] What to do with a questionable photo or a bad actor changes when you're facing not one violation but hundreds exactly like it, and thousands much like it, but slightly different in a thousand ways. This is not just a difference of size, it is fundamentally a different problem. For large-scale platforms, moderation is industrial, not artisanal.

Given the enormity of the archives they manage, social media platforms have had to develop a set of "solutions" to the challenge of detecting problematic content and behavior at scale. Some have updated approaches taken by traditional media, where the responsibility of *editorial review* remains fully in the hands of the platform; oversight is imposed before the content is made available. But this is a resource-intensive approach that is difficult to scale. Many have offloaded the first line of review to users, relying on *community flagging* to identify problematic content for further review. Doing so takes advantage of the user base by deputizing users into the moderation process, but requires a great deal of interpretation and coordination. And many are exploring computational techniques that promise *automatic detection* of specific kinds of problematic content like pornography, harassment, and hate speech. This depends on sophisticated software for matching new content with known violations, and increasingly on machine-learning algorithms evolving to recognize problematic content. These techniques promise to avoid the problems of human biases, but they threaten to introduce some of their own.

I will be discussing these three strategies as ideal types, abstract approaches to the problem of detection. In practice, these strategies overlap in messy ways, they require an immense amount of labor and resources, some decisions are more ad hoc, and the results are not always as expected. But even if the three types are unattainable ideals, it is important to consider them: for what they entail, for their priorities and presumptions, for the kinds of problems they presume to solve and the kinds of problems they introduce.

EDITORIAL REVIEW

Some platforms take it upon themselves to identify problematic content or behavior before it can cause offense or harm. Content is reviewed by someone in the employ of the platform, who approves or rejects content before it is posted. This kind of editorial review is a gargantuan undertaking, which means few of the major platforms rely on it exclusively. Still, it is worth noting what is required—both because it is a viable approach, at least in principle, and because, when a platform opts instead for more distributed or automated approaches, all of the steps and the labor involved in editorial review must be relocated somewhere, in some form.

Editorial review of platforms is most similar to the ways traditional media handle offensive content. Of course, traditional broadcast and publishing media have the advantage that they typically oversee the production of that content before it ever reaches their audience. Television shows are commissioned and produced, news articles are assigned and filed. Even independent productions, be it a television pilot or an unsigned demo recording, have to be brought to the distributor for consideration. For U.S. films, for example, the MPAA ratings board is charged (by the major studios) with imposing its ratings system on all films slated for U.S. release. It is feasible for that board to screen every film before it goes to theaters, and it has the authority to demand changes. Some films are released without a rating, but they find it hard to get major theater distribution or advertise in major newspapers.[11]

Even when schedules are tighter, editorial review is still possible for traditional media. Because editorial judgments about quality or relevance determine whether something will appear at all, in that same moment a judgment can be made as to whether it might also be offensive or harmful. Language in a magazine article can be adjusted before it goes to print, whether for clarity or propriety; a television program or prerecorded radio broadcast can be trimmed, whether for length or age appropriateness. Having possession and control of the material before it reaches an audience is fundamental to that editorial review. Live broadcasting, then, poses the biggest challenge, because there is no moment between production and distribution: news broadcasts and call-in programs cannot anticipate what might happen in front of a hot microphone. Yet even here, broadcast media have established a tiny but sufficient time lag: the seven-second delay, a technical gap between the moment happening in front of the camera and when that moment goes out to audiences. This delay reinserts the briefest opportunity for prepublication, editorial review—just long enough for a quick-fingered censor to "bleep" out profanity, or cut the feed if something truly outrageous occurs.[12]

The dream of editorial review, if not always the reality, is perfect moderation. If it is done correctly, nothing that reaches the public violates the rules. Audiences would not be offended, regulations would be honored, corporate brands would be untarnished. It is an airless vision of public culture, but it speaks to the challenges and anxieties media distributors face. The additional dream, much harder to achieve, is that the provider could toe that line between satisfying the audience's desires, which might call for titillation, shock, or ribaldry, without offending them. Striking that balance is much more challenging. Either way, the proactive review of traditional media has the benefit of never showing the audience what it *might* have seen otherwise. This avoids offense but also avoids alerting viewers to what is being excluded.

Editorial review is, in most countries, an obligation: broadcasters can be fined millions for allowing profanity or nudity to be broadcast; newspapers can be pilloried for publishing a gruesome photograph or revealing classified information. And broadcasters have actively internalized this obligation not only to avoid offending viewers but to fend off the greater intrusion or oversight from regulators. Even so, stuff slips through.[13]

The expectation of perfect enforcement has not been extended to social media platforms, which largely enjoy the safe harbor that U.S. and European law has provided for Internet intermediaries. So only certain providers have voluntarily taken on this burden. Among the largest social media platforms, Apple's App Store is the only one that has instituted a review mechanism for user-provided content that precedes the content's being made available. For Apple, this was extremely important. Ensuring the user "freedom from porn," as Steve Jobs notoriously promised, was just part of the broader promise of the iPhone and iPad.[14] Apple wanted the feel and experience of each device to seamlessly extend to the apps designed for it. Imposing a review process for third-party apps, to ensure that they meet Apple's standards of technical quality and design but also of propriety, was a way to protect the Apple brand—by extending the boundaries of the commodity itself to include not just the iPhone or iPad but a carefully moderated set of apps for them.

Reviewing apps in a timely and careful way is hard enough. But the reality is that editorial review requires Apple to impose a guiding hand along the entire path of app development, and to position the App Store as a bottleneck through which apps must pass. This bottleneck depends on a combination of technical constraints, contractual and legal obligations, and human assessment; it powerfully shapes what apps get made, how they are designed, and how Apple sells and distributes them to users.

All iPhones and iPads remain "tethered" to Apple. This means that Apple can upgrade an app or delete it remotely, can extract fees from any financial exchanges, and can collect user data from within them.[15] It also makes Apple obligatory: developers must work exclusively through Apple, using Apple software to design their apps, abiding by Apple's terms, and finally submitting apps for review.[16] Users can get only the apps that Apple approves and distributes. The scope of this highly structured bottleneck is largely invisible to most users, and can be somewhat obscure even to the developers who depend on it.

First, the Software Development Kit (SDK) designers need to create apps compliant with iOS devices is available only from Apple. That SDK structures what software app developers can use, how the app will communicate with the device, what kind of user data can be collected, and so forth. Even to get the SDK, a developer must sign a contract, which not only specifies the technical standards and economic obligations Apple demands but also requires the developer to submit any app for review.[17] All of this allows Apple to guide the development of and "certify" apps—as functionally sound, and as editorially acceptable.

Second, the App Store is the only place where Apple users can get iOS apps. Unlike Google's Android phones, iPhones will install software only from the App Store. Some users have managed to circumvent these digital protections, "jailbreaking" their iPhones, allowing them to load uncertified apps from gray-market sites.[18] Still, though jailbreaking a phone is now a legally protected exception to U.S. copyright law, many users continue to believe that jailbreaking is illegal, or at least illicit.[19] And Apple works to foil jailbreaking by closing vulnerabilities with each upgrade of its operating system. So for the overwhelming majority of iPhone and iPad users, the App Store is the only game in town. App developers must pass through this bottleneck, and users must wait at its exit for approved apps to emerge.

While this distribution system was a relatively new innovation in how users bought software, such arrangements are endemic to running a "multi-sided platform."[20] The intermediary's economic interests depend on coordinating an exchange between two or more groups (here, app developers and iPhone users). This bottleneck allows Apple to control the financial side of this exchange as well: how prices are set, how updates are delivered, how customer feedback and reviews are received and responded to.[21] Extracting rent requires some way to keep participants where rent can be extracted.[22] And Apple can direct how apps are presented to users: how apps are described and categorized, how the collection can be navigated, how new or popular apps are introduced and highlighted.

At this precise point of economic control also sits Apple's review process. Every app must pass through a review by Apple's team before appearing in the store. This allows Apple not only to ensure that the app works properly but to prevent spam and malware, prohibit specific software configurations, insist on interface design consistencies across apps, exclude apps that might undercut Apple's own services—and reject apps it deems inappropriate. Apple has constructed the marketplace, the clearinghouse, and the editor's desk, all in one place, and gets to set the terms for how they all work. Users see only those apps that satisfy all of these structures of oversight.

Apple has established itself as the "networked gatekeeper."[23] It is a position Apple wants and enjoys for a number of reasons, but it is not the only way to run an app store. Android developers can distribute their apps through the Play Store, Google's official app store, but they can also provide apps independently, can even create Android app markets of their own. Users who can't find the pornographic apps they want, for example, can go to Mikandi to get their fill. Google retains the ability to kill apps loaded on Android phones, though so far it has reserved this power for removing malware or privacy breaches. This means Google does not, and cannot, claim to enforce content standards on all Android apps, just the ones provided in the Play Store. Still, whether strict or permissive, both platforms share a sensibility that, as providers of the devices and the operating system, they are to some degree responsible for the apps that run atop them.

But Apple's approach, more than most, puts it in a precarious position, practically and politically. Requiring review must come with a promise to move apps through that review process expeditiously, an enormous challenge for a small team tasked with carefully but quickly reviewing a growing queue of apps. The bottleneck must not become a logjam; for small-scale developers, a delay or an unanticipated rejection can be costly, even devastating. A gatekeeper quickly comes under pressure to articulate guidelines that are clear enough for developers to follow, consistent enough that they can be fairly applied by reviewers, imaginative enough that they can anticipate apps that have not yet been developed, reasonable enough that they can be defended under public scrutiny, and comprehensive enough to discourage policy makers from intervening. Apple was criticized by app developers early on for guidelines deemed unclear and a review process considered capricious and opaque, and developers regularly complain about delays.[24]

Editorial review can also creep beyond its stated intentions. What may be justified as ensuring quality content, and may really be about establishing a way to extract fees, can drift into moral judgments. Having put itself in a position of apparent or actual oversight, a platform can find itself saddled with some sense of responsibility, to users and to the public at large. And when review is enacted as and presented as editorial judgment, summarily executed by and in the name of the platform, it is also open to charges of subjectivity, hypocrisy, self-interest, and conservatism.

In 2010, many were surprised to find that Apple had rejected NewsToons, an app by Mark Fiore, an independent political cartoonist whose comics regularly appeared on the online component of the *San Francisco Chronicle*. Fiore had recently been awarded the Pulitzer Prize, the first online cartoonist to win the award. Fiore's rejection notice stated that his app, which included comics that poked fun at Presidents Bush and Obama and other U.S. political figures, had been rejected "because it contains content that ridicules public figures and is in violation of Section 3.3.12 from the iPhone SDK Agreement which states: 'Applications must not contain any obscene, pornographic, offensive or defamatory content or materials of any kind (text, graphics, images, photographs, etc.), or other content or materials that in Apple's reasonable judgement may be found objectionable by iPhone or iPod touch users' "—a policy at odds with a long U.S. tradition protecting satire of public figures, especially political ones, from charges of defamation.[25]

After being criticized by the press, Apple quickly encouraged Fiore to resubmit his app, and it was accepted. But NewsToons was not the only political satire app to be rejected, only the most prominent. In 2008, several apps making light of President Bush were rejected, including Bushisms and Freedom Time.[26] The election of President Obama was followed by a rash of apps poking fun of the new president that Apple also rejected, including Bobblicious, Obama!, Obama Trampoline, OutOfOffice!, You Lie Mr. President, BidensTeeth, and Bobble Rep.[27] Apple also rejected iSinglePayer, an app advocating the "single-payer" approach to health care, by comparing the costs for the user of a single-payer plan to the user's own.[28]

When the developer of Freedom Time, an app that simply counted down the days until President Bush would leave office, asked Steve Jobs by email why it had been rejected, Jobs responded, "Even though my personal political leanings are democratic, I think this app will be offensive to roughly half our customers. What's the point?"[29]

Apple has since dropped the specific rule against "content that ridicules public figures," and many rejected apps were subsequently approved.[30] But apps continue to be rejected or removed for their political content. An unofficial WikiLeaks app was removed in 2010, just after WikiLeaks released its trove of U.S. diplomatic cables; while the app was not designed or sponsored by WikiLeaks, it streamlined access to WikiLeaks documents and donated part of the price of the app to WikiLeaks, as a proxy user donation.[31] Apple executives (like those at other companies at the time, including Amazon, PayPal, and Mastercard) worried that supporting the app and donations would open the company to criminal liability. In 2012 Apple rejected Drones+, an app that tracked U.S. drone strikes based on news reports. Two years later it was accepted—but without the drone-tracking feature and with a new name, Metadata+. The designers then restored the drone-tracking feature to the app after it was in the store.[32]

Other apps ran afoul of content prohibitions for profanity, nudity, and violence. Apple was roundly criticized for censoring news publications and fashion magazines: apps for the *Sun* in the United Kingdom and *Stern* in Germany were both briefly removed until nude images published in their print versions had been excised.[33] The comics community cried "censorship" when Apple rejected app versions of the graphic novels *Murderdrome, Zesty,* and *Sex Criminals.*[34] Other decisions were seen as prudish, as when Apple asked developers of a comics version of James Joyce's *Ulysses* to remove a single panel that included exposed breasts, or when a comic version of Oscar Wilde's *The Importance of Being Earnest* was fitted with a black bars across images of men kissing, or when the Ninjawords dictionary app was approved only after developers removed entries for common profanities, or the Eucalyptus e-book reader was removed for including the Kama Sutra.[35]

More recently, Apple has rejected several "serious games" apps, games designed to draw critical attention to some political issue: Smuggle Truck dealt with the hazards of illegally crossing the Mexico-U.S. border; Joyful Executions criticized the North Korean dictatorship; Ferguson Firsthand offered a virtual reality walkthrough of the protests in the Missouri city; Sweatshop HD highlighted exploitative labor conditions in a factory.[36]

Apple also rejected Endgame: Syria, a battle game designed to highlight the ongoing Syrian civil war.[37] Designed by the founder of Game the News, Endgame: Syria was rejected for violating a different part of Apple's review guidelines, a fascinating restriction that, as far as I can tell, has no corollary in traditional media or in other digital environments thus far. Under Apple's rules on violence, "'Enemies' within the context of a game cannot solely target a specific race, culture, a real government or corporation, or any other real entity." In spirit, this rule is a component of their rules against hate speech.[38] However, this rule's dragnet snared apps with educational rather than xenophobic aims, including Phone Story, a game critical of Apple and its partnership with Chinese megamanufacturer FoxConn.[39] The line between personal attacks, hateful speech, and incitement to violence, on the one hand, and legitimate political debate on the other, is being navigated in these decisions, here around an emergent form of political expression.

Apple received the sharpest criticism for its February 2010 purge of more than five thousand apps, already approved by its review process and available in the App Store.[40] All of these apps were "adult": sexually explicit, though not pornographic (which would not have been approved in the first place), including bikini shots, topless images, peekaboo teasers, and double entendres. That these apps had all been approved suggested that their removal represented a change in policy, an effort to clean up the apps Apple had already made available. Though this was clearly an editorial decision, Apple VP Phil Schiller asserted publicly that Apple was responding to complaints from women and parents.[41] Given the timing, the action was probably taken in anticipation of the release of the first iPad, which had been announced a month before and hit the market just over a month after.

The press challenged this wave of removals. Some suggested that Apple was being prudish, deleting apps that were by no means illegal or even obscene, apps that, after all, some developers wanted to offer and some users wanted to use. Others charged Apple with removing apps that did not deserve to be removed, such as Simply Beach, an app that sold bathing suits. Others suggested that the move was pointless: given that the iPhone and iPad both came preloaded with the Safari web browser, any user could surf the web for content that was far more explicit. Finally, some called Apple hypocritical: somehow the *Playboy, Sports Illustrated* Swimsuit Issue, and Victoria's Secret apps survived, despite being arguably no less explicit than many of the apps that did not. Of course, Apple has the legal right to remove any app it wants, to distribute the *Playboy* app, even to be inconsistent. But the expectation from the public is that, if platforms moderate, they should do so fairly and consistently.

This was an admittedly early incident in the public life of social media platforms; Apple and its peers have since matured in their approach about how and why to intervene. And the controversy was in many ways specific to Apple's desire to control its devices and the aesthetic experience of their use, and to a moment when Apple was seeking a new and much larger audience, which might be turned off if a first visit to the app store was an unseemly one. But editorial review on social media platforms, especially of sexual content, continues to be contentious. Google banned the first porn app designed for Google Glass when that device was still imagined to be an exciting consumer market possibility.[42] Facebook has regularly been taken to task for deleting what users argue is artistic, educational, or politically relevant nudity, or isn't even nudity at all: children's dolls, Burning Man sculptures, hand-drawn cartoons, even an exposed elbow. Major publishers and cultural institutions like the *New Yorker* and the New York Academy of Art have contested Facebook's right to intervene as well as its judgment in doing so.[43] The larger point is that editorial review can quickly widen to include decisions that are morally loaded, and financially or politically motivated. In some cases there is no choice that is not political to someone.[44] Even the best-intentioned decisions can appear politically motivated; all moderation, especially when the process is so opaque, remains open to interpretation and criticism. And editorial review requires making decisions that cannot be entirely separated from the imperative to protect a community, a brand, or a valuable set of users.

The editorial moderation of sexual content has implications not just for app developers but for the sexual cultures that adopt these apps and form around them. Grindr, as an iOS app, must impose restrictions on its users designed to ensure that it abides by Apple's expectations. This includes prohibition of profile photos that even "imply nudity."[45] Apple accepted the dating app Tinder but rejected the hook-up app Bang with Friends—then accepted the same app when it was renamed Down.[46] It is unclear what motivated these particular decisions, but Apple moderators seemed to draw a distinction between admittedly seeking sexual encounters and seeking sexual encounters under the guise of dating, impressing a cultural and moral judgment onto that distinction. LinkedIn quickly removed an app called Bang with Professionals built on top of LinkedIn's application programming interface.[47] The app was meant as a goof. But before you laugh—or while you laugh—recognize that, even if you agree that it isn't appropriate for a professional social networking tool to include a hook-up service, its rejection is nevertheless a judgment about the edges of propriety for professional interactions, and it's being made by a small team of California millennials working at LinkedIn.

The biggest challenge is how to scale such a review process. The resources required for a full-scale, proactive review are immense, and grow exponentially with the platform. For Apple, this is challenge enough, but Apple is more like traditional media in two ways: with apps, there is much less material to review, and every submission can conceivably be examined before it is posted without creating too great a delay for the developer. This is still a large-scale undertaking, as Apple employees must review hundreds of apps a day, including minor revisions to existing apps, and must figure out not only whether they abide by Apple content rules but whether they work as claimed and are free of harmful errors or malware. App developers have complained about delays, but so far the system has not collapsed. But for, say, all the images posted to Instagram, or the flood of tweets constantly moving through Twitter, Apple's review bottleneck would simply be unworkable. Second, apps are developed by software developers. Even if many are independent amateurs, they are more likely to share a set of quasi-professional norms, which shape how they think of software, what they know to be expected, and why it makes sense to honor the platform's expectations.

Apple is not alone in imposing proactive review, however. Many online news organizations tried proactive moderation, at least at first, queueing user comments for review before they were posted. This approach was controversial: many news sites felt that comment threads were public spaces and should be unmoderated, while others felt that the journalistic commitment to high-quality information should apply to all the material available on a site, and worried that ill-informed or offensive comments would be perceived to be part of the article and diminish its journalistic quality and integrity (and profit).[48] But it was the practical limits that eventually proved insurmountable: proactive review is workable when comments are trickling in, but when the articles that drew the most attention received a flood of comments, review teams were quickly overwhelmed. Many sites that began with proactive review either shifted to moderating comments

after they appeared, gave readers tools to hide comments they found personally offensive, or outsourced the comment space altogether to third-party
plug-in tools, partner discussion sites, or major social networking platforms
like Facebook and Twitter.[49]

COMMUNITY FLAGGING

For most social media platforms, the amount of material is so immense and
relentless, and the expectation of users that their content should appear
immediately is so established, that prepublication editorial review is impossible.[50] Few sites attempt to moderate user content before it appears online.
Detection, then, shifts from previewing everything beforehand to scouring
what is already posted and available. It is in fact a mistake to think of platforms as filters, or even as gatekeepers in the traditional sense of the meta-
phor, when it comes to content moderation. Platforms are filters only in the
way that trawler fishing boats "filter" the ocean: they do not monitor what
goes into the ocean, they can only sift through small parts at a time, and
they cannot guarantee that they are catching everything, or that they aren't
filtering out what should stay. This also means that even the most heinous
content gets published, at least briefly, and the most criminal of behavior
occurs and can have the impact it intended, before anything might be done
in response. Content that violates site guidelines can remain for days, or
years, in these wide oceans.

Most platforms turn largely or exclusively to their user base to help
identify offensive content and behavior. This usually means a "flagging"
mechanism that allows users to alert the platform to objectionable content.
In this sense it is not unlike when television viewers write in to a network
or to a regulatory body complaining about offensive material, though in
practice it has more in common with the logic of customer service. But flags
also hand over policing in part to the community, deputizing users as a first
line of detection.

Using the users is practically convenient in that it divides this enormous
task among many, and puts the task of identifying offensive content right at
the point when someone comes into contact with it. Moreover, relying on
the community grants the platform legitimacy and cover. The flagging
mechanism itself clearly signals that the platform is listening to its users and
providing avenues for them to express offense or seek help when they're
being harmed. As a policy manager at Flickr noted, "This whole idea of having a site where anyone in the world can use it because they have a similar

interest . . . having this whole community of people who are interested in the site's purpose, who kind of have some—ownership is the wrong word, because they don't have an actual financial stake, but they have a say in how the site works."[51] Giving users a "say" in moderation may appear more democratic than Apple's concentration of editorial power. In reality, it allows platforms to retain the very same power to moderate as they see fit, as if it's done at the users' behest. Changes made to guidelines can be framed as "what users want." Some complaints can be taken seriously, while others can be dismissed as users misapplying the rules or gaming the system. Liability for offensive content can be rewritten as a responsibility only to respond to complaints, a lesser requirement.

This can still require enormous resources on the part of the platform: Facebook, for example, claims that it receives "millions" of reports to review each day.[52] And there are problems inherent in asking a community to police itself—more so, in fact, when that "community" is not a community at all, but a user base in the millions or billions, spanning the globe, speaking different languages, with beliefs that are antagonistic to one another, and sometimes counter to the aims of the platform itself. Like a neighborhood watch, its animating principles may be good; but a great deal can go wrong in the implementation. An anonymous volunteer police force from within the community is not always a neat fit when the platform hosts users with competing cultural or political values, discussing contentious political topics.[53] (The fact that the user "community" is being invoked partly to structure the policing of that community, poses a challenge to the way the scholarship about new media has traditionally thought about online community.)[54]

When YouTube added a flagging mechanism to its videos back in August 2005, introduced in the same blog post as the ability to share videos and put them into channels, it was a substantive change to the site.[55] Before allowing users to "flag as inappropriate," YouTube had only a generic "contact us" email link in the footer of the site; it was intended primarily for technical support and job inquiries.[56] Since YouTube set the precedent, most platforms have introduced some way of flagging content where it is; Twitter was notably late to the game, adding a "report" link next to every tweet in 2013, after much criticism.

The specific implementation of flagging differs between platforms. Some sites position a flag alongside every bit of content, some allow flagging of a particular user or channel, some provide sitewide feedback mechanisms, and some do all of the above. In some sites, a flag constitutes a single bit of

Report ✕

Help us understand the problem. What is going on with this Tweet?

◉ I'm not interested in this Tweet

○ It's spam

○ It's abusive or harmful

Learn more about reporting violations of our rules.

Next

Twitter, flagging pop-up window (2017)

expression. For example, the (short-lived) short video service Vine offered users the ability to "report a post." Click, and the offending video was immediately reported. There was no space to articulate the reason why the video was being reported, what rule it violated, or how egregious the user found it. There was no way to "unreport" that video once it was selected. This is the simplest expression of complaint: a digital flicker saying, "I object."

Other platforms offer more expressive vocabularies by which complaints about content may be articulated, increasingly so over the years. YouTube's first flag was extremely simple, a single click. Since then, YouTube has gone the farthest in expanding its flagging vocabulary: clicking the flag leads to a menu of choices, each with a submenu, allowing/requiring users to specify the nature of the concern. In 2013, YouTube added a way to indicate the time code where the offending material appears in the video, and a text box for the user to "please provide additional details about" the offending content—though limited to just five hundred characters. These classifications channel user reports into the categories YouTube prefers,

Report this video

What is the issue?*

◉ Sexual content ❓

[Graphic sexual activity ▾]

○ Violent or repulsive content ❓

○ Promotes terrorism ❓

○ Hateful or abusive content ❓

○ Harmful dangerous acts ❓

○ Child abuse ❓

○ Spam or misleading ❓

○ Infringes my rights ❓

○ Captions issue

Timestamp selected:

[0] : [00]

Please provide additional details about:
Sexual content > Graphic sexual activity

[   ]

500 characters remaining

Flagged videos and users are reviewed by YouTube staff 24 hours a day, seven days a week to determine whether they violate Community Guidelines. Accounts are penalized for Community Guidelines violations, and serious or repeated violations can lead to account termination. Report a channel.

* Required   [Submit]

YouTube, flagging pop-up window (2017)

which it then uses to streamline its moderation process. For instance, some categories (for example, "sexual content: content involving minors") are reviewed immediately, as platforms have strict legal obligations to report child pornography. The rest can be queued up in order of importance: videos flagged as "sexual content: graphic sexual nudity" might be prioritized over those flagged as "harmful dangerous acts: pharmaceutical or drug abuse," as YouTube sees fit.

Most platforms offer little indication of what happens after something has been flagged. On some, a short message appears indicating that the report was received, or thanking the user for her feedback, in the well-worn language of customer service. But how a flag is received, sorted, attended to, and resolved remains completely opaque to users. In terms of process transparency, Facebook has gone the farthest to date. Facebook's flagging apparatus is intricate, in part because the service handles so many different kinds of user content, and in part because it has historically taken a more interventionist approach to moderation. Currently, once a report is made, a "support dashboard" allows the user to monitor the status of the complaints she has registered.

Still, flags are a thin form of expression: they provide little room to express degree of concern, or contextualize the complaint, or take issue with the rules. The vocabulary they do offer belongs to the platform, prefigured in the terms in which the site thinks about inappropriate content. Categories are not only powerful in the way they leave out things that do not fit; they also embody the structural logics of a system classification.[57] YouTube's submenus organize bad content into genres; Flickr's distinguish degrees of raciness; for Vine, the only question was to report or not to report.

But even in the most complex systems, flags articulate only a narrow vocabulary of complaint. A flag, in its purest form, is an objection. There is not, for example, a flag to indicate that something is, while perhaps troubling, nonetheless worth preserving. The vocabulary of complaint offers no way to express wanting to defend something that may be offensive, but is also necessary from a civic perspective. Nor do complaints account for the many complex reasons why people might choose to flag content for reasons other than being offended. This means that platform operators cannot glean much about the particular nature of the user's objection from just a single flag. One might imagine a flag as meaning "I have judged this to have violated the posted community guidelines"—but platform moderators know that this would be naïve. Users may not know the guidelines even exist, they may not understand them, care about them, or agree with them. It is somewhat safer to assume that a flag means something more like "I feel this does not belong here." A complaint could be fueled by the deepest sense of moral outrage, or the flimsiest urge of puerile chicanery, and it is nearly impossible to tell the difference. With this kind of ambiguity, platform managers can only take the objection into account, as a less-than-fully formed utterance, and interpret it themselves, against the community guidelines they crafted.

While these sites are full of talk about "community," the flag is a fundamentally individualized mechanism of complaint, and is received as such. But that does not mean it is used that way. Flagging can and does get used in fundamentally social ways. First, flags are sometimes deployed amid an ongoing relationship. This is most apparent in cases of harassment and bullying, where participants may know each other offline. This is not to say that the complaint is any less real or genuinely felt; but it can be a step within a longer social engagement, one the platform is not entirely privy to. This may be the case even when content is reported as offensive. Flags can be a playful prank between friends, part of a skirmish between professional competitors or rival YouTubers, or retribution for a social offense that happened elsewhere. Flagging may even help generate interest in and publicity around racy content, as in the cases where YouTube has put music videos behind age barriers, and their promoters have subsequently decried the "censorship" with mock outrage, all to drum up excitement and views. The fact that flagging is some-times a social tactic not only undercuts its value as a "genuine" expression of offense, it fundamentally undercuts its legibility as an accurate read of the community's moral temperature.

Flagging systems can also be gamed, weaponized to accomplish social and political ends. There is evidence that strategic flagging has occurred, and suspicion that it has occurred widely. Users will flag things that offend them politically, or that they disagree with; whether a particular site guide-line has been violated can be irrelevant. The hope is that enough flags might persuade platform moderators to remove it. Even if a platform is diligent about vindicating content that's flagged inappropriately, some content may still be removed incorrectly, some accounts may be suspended.

Organized flagging is generally managed surreptitiously; while only a few sites prohibit it explicitly, most see it as an unseemly use of the site's re-porting tools. But evidence of this kind of coordination can be found. This is most striking not in flagging but downvoting, on sites like Reddit and Digg, where users try to push "good" content up or downvote it into oblivion.[58] There have been instances of coordination to systematically game these downvoting mechanisms for political ends. But in a similar example, it was YouTube's flag that served as the lever for political gamesmanship. As Brit-tany Fiore-Silfvast describes, a group of bloggers angered by pro-Muslim content on YouTube began an effort called Operation Smackdown.[59] Launched in 2007 and active through at least 2011, the campaign coordinated supporters to flag specific YouTube videos as terrorism, provided step-by-step instructions on how to do so, set up playlists on YouTube of videos they were targeting, and eventually added a Twitter feed announcing a video to be targeted that day. Participating bloggers would celebrate the number of tar-geted videos that YouTube removed and would lambast YouTube and Google for allowing others to remain. Also, in 2012, accusations swirled around a conservative group called Truth4Time, that it was coordinating its prominent membership to flag gay rights groups on Facebook. One of the group's administrators claimed that this accusation was untrue—and that the group had in fact formed in response to pro-gay activists flagging its antigay posts. Either way, it seems that surreptitious, organized flagging occurred.[60] These flags are of a very different sort, not expressing individual and spontaneous concern for obscene content, though that may be part, but a social and co-ordinated proclamation of collective, political indignation—a kind of "user-generated warfare"—all through the tiny fulcrum that is the flag.[61]

There is an inherent paradox in looking to a community to police itself. The user population of Facebook or YouTube is enormous and heterogeneous; there is no one community but rather a variety of users, just as there are in other public forums, with different and sometimes competing aims and norms. These platforms are home to many communities, and some disagree—not just with one another politically, but also in their understanding of the platform and what it is for. On top of that, we know from research into online communities and collaborative projects like Wikipedia that usually only a relatively small but quite devoted percentage of users is committed enough to the community to do volunteer work, police bad behavior, clean up errors, educate new users, and so on.[62] Most people will use the platform as they see fit, but will not take on this same sense of ownership; for them the platform is instrumental, a way to distribute their videos or find their friends or discuss the news. And some sliver of participants will seek to cause mayhem of varying degrees, either because the platform lets them target someone they want to bother, or because they want to undermine the platform itself, or because they simply like to undo others' best laid plans. Not only must platforms turn to moderation strategies that can function at this scale; social media are also susceptible to the kind of information warfare tactics that take advantage of this scale. Community flagging offers a mechanism for some users to hijack the very procedures of governance.

Even more, as these platforms begin to stand in for the public itself, people no longer see them as a specific and shared project, to be joined and contributed to. Some users patrol the platform as their own form of expression: "I think this post is unacceptable, and I will use the flagging mechanism to make my feelings known." For some, the complaint may be genuine, a belief that their political views *do* constitute an appropriate code of ethics, and one shared by the platform; for others it can be quite tactical, a convenient tool by which to silence others. Most likely, it's somewhere between. And because the flagging mechanism does not reveal those who use it, and turns their complaints into legitimate and legitimized data for the platform, their aims are obscured. From this ambiguous cacophony, the platform must detect and adjudicate the content and users it should remove or keep.

In 2014, Facebook began suspending accounts of drag queens for violating their real name policy. Hundreds of drag queens who had created profiles under their stage names rather than their legal ones found themselves closed out of their accounts, or received requests from Facebook to provide identification proving that the names they chose were their legal ones.[63] The affected drag queens, especially in San Francisco, and members of the LGBT community who supported them, published angry op-eds, planned a protest, and met with Facebook representatives. After two weeks of bad press, Facebook relented, apologizing to the community and clarifying (though not substantially changing) its rule, so that the "authentic name they used in real life" would be sufficient.[64]

In the apology, the Facebook representative revealed that a single user had been entirely responsible for this rash of flagging: "The way this happened took us off guard. An individual on Facebook decided to report several hundred of these accounts as fake. These reports were among the several hundred thousand fake name reports we process every single week, 99 percent of which are bad actors doing bad things: impersonation, bullying, trolling, domestic violence, scams, hate speech, and more—so we didn't notice the pattern."[65]

The Daily Dot investigated and found the person its reporter believed to be singularly responsible.[66] Though representatives of Facebook told the Daily Dot that they did not believe the user (posting as @RealNamePolice on Twitter and Tumblr) was specifically targeting drag queens or LGBT users, evidence from his Twitter accounts and Tumblr blog suggested that his flagging was deliberate: he was aware that he was flagging (and angering) drag queens, and cited Romans 13.2[67] to explain why he was delivering God's punishment to the "perverts and sodomites."[68] Clearly, he was not offended by the use of stage names per se, given that he proudly announced this effort on Twitter using a pseudonymous Twitter handle that did not reveal his "authentic name."

Twitter and Tumblr were important to this effort, because @RealNamePolice not only flagged accounts he believed were using fake names, he tweeted out those names to encourage others to do so as well.[69] Others, possibly from within the irate community of San Francisco drag queens, even flagged @RealNamePolice's Twitter account—again, not necessarily for a specific violation of Twitter's rules but as an expression of offense about his politics, a form of retribution, and perhaps an attempt to inhibit his efforts. Twitter in fact suspended his account, though it appears he quickly established a new one as @RealNamesBack. He claimed that over the course of a month, he had flagged thousands of Facebook accounts for using fake names.

This user was politically motivated, and Facebook's flag offered him a way to enact his politics, under the guise of community moderation. He was quoted in the Daily Dot as saying, "Their names violated the Real Name Policy as it stood. The accounts which I reported initially would be removed and new names in their place the next day. Except on the weekends when it appeared no one was working on processing reports. On Monday morning the second week hundreds dropped like flies."[70] This flagging vigilante settled into the flagging mechanism, even becoming familiar with its mundane workings—so much so that, according to Facebook's apology, his flags had blended in with the other complaints coming in, and were handled according to procedure rather than being recognized as a concerted effort.

Facebook's apology and policy change notwithstanding, the paradox here is that while @RealNamePolice's motivations may have been political, and to some reprehensible, he did flag "appropriately": he did understand the policy correctly, and he did identify names that violated it. Was this a misuse of the flagging system, then, or exactly what it was designed for? Is flagging supposed to aggregate all the single users troubled by single bits of content, expressing their offense, from which Facebook forms an aggregate a map of potentially offensive content to scrub away? Or is it meant to deputize volunteer police, who take on the job of systematically scanning the archive for violations on the platform's behalf? @RealNamePolice clearly engaged in the second function. And by tweeting out profiles he believed were fake he, just like Facebook, called on others to share the labor. Either way, handing the tools of policing to the community opens them to a variety of "uses" that move well beyond the kind of purpose-consistent efforts to "tidy up" that a platform might want to undertake, under a more editorial approach.

It would be easy to see the thinness of the flag as either a design flaw, an institutional oversight, or an unavoidable limitation. Perhaps, in managing the millions of complaints they receive from users, social media platforms can process them only in their leanest form. But another possibility is that the thinness of the flagging mechanism may be of strategic value, at least accidentally so, to the platforms that employ it.

Unlike Apple's editorial review, offloading the work of identifying offensive content and behavior onto users allows platforms to appear more hands-off. In some cases, this is an important claim to be able to make. YouTube has publicly stated that it does not proactively look for inappropriate content, that it reviews only content that has been flagged.[71] This is in part because it also faced a years-long legal battle with Viacom over copyright infringement, in which YouTube claimed to be unable to proactively identify copyright violations. Acknowledging an ability to proactively identify pornography or hate speech would undercut the argument YouTube needed in the copyright case, that such "editorial review" was impossible.[72]

But turning to the community to police the platform and identify violations is not, in fact, a hands-off approach. It requires both articulating the norms and aiming the community toward them, fielding and responding to the complaints, and sometimes overriding the community and carefully justifying doing so. The ambiguity of the flag and its vocabulary is, in many ways, an asset to the platform, leaving it room to honor flags in some cases and overrule them in others.

This amounts to an arms-length form of oversight—in which platforms can retain the right to moderate, while also shifting justification and responsibility to users. Users flag, but the platform adjudicates those flags; the platform has "the right but not the responsibility" to respond. Flagging helps articulate community norms, but expressed in a language provided by the platform. A platform can defend any decision in terms of the users: either that it listened to the community, or that the content was too important to the community to remove. Users can advocate for changes to these guidelines, but any changes come from the platform. Users can criticize the platform for its decisions, but the platform can point to how it "listens to the community" as justification for those decisions.

Regulating contentious user content is in fact an invariably messy process, fraught with the vagaries of human interpretation and shaped by competing institutional pressures. It benefits social media platforms to retain the ability to make judgments on content removal based on ad hoc, context-specific, and often self-interested assessments of the case at hand. It also benefits social media platforms that this process is opaque, and is not explicitly constrained by the flagging and other feedback they receive from users. And it benefits social media platforms that they receive user complaints in the form of flags, which remain open to interpretation; this allows platforms to invoke that feedback when it helps legitimate a decision, or explain it away when the site wants to make a different decision.

AUTOMATIC DETECTION

In May 2016, TechCrunch reported a significant milestone in how Facebook handles moderation: "Facebook's artificial intelligence systems now report more offensive photos than humans do."[73] This does not mean that Facebook is using automatic techniques to *remove* photos, as some of the press coverage that followed incorrectly assumed. The platform's automatic detection software is designed to detect nudity, hate speech, and the like—to identify it and "flag" it for human review. Still, the fact that the majority of what is reviewed is there because software spotted it speaks to how important automated techniques for moderation are becoming. In many ways they fulfill the fantasy of moderation better than editorial oversight or flagging by the community.

So is AI the answer? Artificial intelligence techniques offer, first, to solve the problem of scale. Particularly for sites that are too vast, like YouTube, or that emphasize real-time communication, like Twitter, platform moderators would like to have moderation techniques that do not depend on direct and real-time human oversight, that can immediately and automatically identify unacceptable content. There is enormous pressure to find solutions of similar scale. Ideally, these automated detection techniques could be paired with automated interventions: algorithmically identified porn or hate speech would be instantly removed or withheld from some users, "a system so advanced that it wouldn't need a human backstop."[74]

In addition, these tools promise to solve the problem of subjectivity: what if automated mechanisms could identify and remove content fairly, without human bias, in any language? This is a more pervasive dream that surfaces whenever algorithmic techniques are meant to automate human judgments, whether they're determining who deserves to be removed from a platform for harassing other users, or who deserves a home loan, acceptance to a university, an expensive medical treatment, or parole.[75] Our anxiety about how humans may make such decisions in biased ways fuels the faith in technical solutions. This faith is, sadly, misplaced, in that even automated tools and complex algorithms are designed and tested by people, enacted and maintained by people, and deployed or overridden by people.[76] What automation really does is detach human judgment from the encounter with the specific user, interaction, or content and shift it to the analysis of predictive patterns and categories for what counts as a violation, what counts as harm, and what counts as an exception.

These systems are also just not very good yet. This is not to diminish the accomplishments of those developing these tools. Automated detection is just not an easy task—arguably it's an impossible one, given that offense depends so critically on both interpretation and context. State-of-the-art detection algorithms have a difficult time discerning offensive content or behavior even when they know precisely what they are looking for, when they can compare an image to a database of known violations or can scan for specific profanities or racial slurs. But detection grows vastly more complicated when platforms are trying to identify whether something is pornography or hate speech, without being able to match it to a corpus of examples. Machine-learning techniques have been applied to this problem of identification and categorization of offensive social media content, but there are fundamental limitations that may be impossible to overcome: the lack of context, the evasive tactics of users, and the fluid nature of offense. Without solving these problems, automatic detection produces too many false positives; in light of this, some platforms and third parties are pairing automatic detection with editorial oversight, in ways that must give up some of the dreams of automating content moderation but can come closer to addressing the challenge of scale.

The most effective automatic detection techniques are the ones that know what they're looking for beforehand. Word filters, designed to automatically spot text-based profanity, obscenity, or racial slurs, have been around as long as the web and have been used in a range of ways by social media platforms. The software is relatively simple: compare the user's inputted text against an existing "blacklist" of offensive words, either set by the platform, built into the tool by its third-party developer, added by the user, or through some combination of all three. There is some complicated computational work going on beneath this simple matching task, such as how to identify a string of characters as a word, how to deal with variations or misspellings, and how to deal with multiword phrases. But the upside is that detection does not require paying any attention to meaning or intention; it is simply matching—data-intensive, but computationally simple.

Word filters embody the same underlying logic as the filtering software that emerged in the 1990s, which allowed parents and employers to block access to inappropriate websites, by comparing them to a blacklist of URLs identified and updated by the provider. In 2009, YouTube introduced a profanity filter called "Filter W*rds" as an option for the comment threads below every video, in response to a widely shared sense that online comment spaces in general and YouTube's comments in particular were rife with coarse language.[77] Terms that were considered offensive could be redacted, x-ed out, leaving the comment otherwise intact.[78] The same logic animates some spam filters, and some of the "moderation bots" that automatically manage discussions on sites like Reddit and Slack.[79] The same approach has since been extended to address harassment: in 2016, Instagram introduced the ability to automatically block comments based on the presence of "offensive or inappropriate words," based on a list Instagram provided, which the user could customize.[80]

There are obvious limits to automatic detection, even when it is simply matching against a database of examples. First, these tools cannot identify content that has not already been identified. The blacklist provider must keep up with new instances: emergent profanity and slang, context-specific racial slurs, profanity in other languages. Blacklist tools also encourage evasion techniques: for example, deliberate misdirection, such as inserted punctu@tion and furking misspellings.

But the real challenges revolve around what such tools are likely to filter incorrectly, "false positives," and what they are likely to overlook, "false negatives." Word filters have a difficult time with words that have multiple meanings, words that are associated with adult topics but can be used in other ways. There are, of course, words with two meanings—as comedian George Carlin warned, "you can prick your finger, but don't finger your prick!"—though, just as you were able to parse Carlin's sentence and get the joke, more sophisticated software can now identify the intended meaning based on the immediate linguistic context. What is trickier is the way such words, inappropriate in some contexts, can be used in other, important ways. Words for intimate parts of the body may appear in insults and come-ons, but also in sex education and scientific conversations. Some salty language spoken by a public figure may be considered newsworthy, and a journalist or activist might want to quote it without running into a restriction. Language is fluid—especially in informal and playful environments, especially when people are aiming to be daring or inflammatory or coy or harmful, and especially when they are attempting to elude identification. So while it may be easy to spot Carlin's seven dirty words, the complete list of words that might warrant detection is likely a long, shifting, and contested one. Other expressions are obscene in their meaning, without using words traditionally considered profane. Text that avoids familiar racial slurs but is easily identifiable as hate speech by a competent reader, for instance, would be difficult for an algorithmic tool to identify.

This technique has not been successfully extended much past text-based profanity and slurs (which can be based on a simple and known vocabulary). It has, however, proven successful for the automatic identification of child pornography. While child pornography is a unique case in that platforms are obligated by a strict legal requirement to police it, and one with few exceptions and zero political controversy, it nevertheless presents a similar challenge: while illegal child exploitation imagery is more likely to circulate through private channels and more obscure "dark web" sites, some does appear on major social media platforms from time to time, and must be identified and removed.[81] However, the very success of these child pornography efforts helps reveal why they are difficult to generalize to the detection of other kinds of harm or obscenity.

The automatic detection of child pornography images is largely accomplished through a tool called PhotoDNA, introduced by Microsoft in 2009 and since offered for free to major social media platforms and online content providers. PhotoDNA uses a technique called "hashing," in which a digital image is turned into a numerical string based on the sequence of colors in the image's individual pixels. This string serves as an identifier, a kind of fingerprint, as it is unique to each image, and is identifiable in copies of that image, even if they've been altered to some degree.[82] A platform can then take all images uploaded by users, compare the unique hash of each to an existing database of known child pornography images maintained by the National Center for Missing and Exploited Children (NCMEC). If the image is a match, the platform can remove it, and can alert NCMEC and possibly the authorities. Every single photo you post to Instagram, every image you pin on Pinterest, every snap on Snapchat, is quickly and automatically compared to the NCMEC database to make sure it is not child pornography.

This is, at one level, an impressive accomplishment, and an undeniably noble one. But it comes with two important caveats. First, it is more than software: the detection of child pornography also requires a particular arrangement of laws, institutions, technologies, and collaborations to make it work. The fact that child pornography is illegal, in the United States and elsewhere, establishes this as a particularly high priority for platforms.

NCMEC, an independent, nonprofit organization established by the U.S. Congress, must maintain this database of known images, and add new examples to it; this work requires partnerships with social media platforms, as well as with law enforcement and child welfare organizations. Microsoft had to develop the software, then had to recognize it as good public relations to donate it to NCMEC and share it with its competitors, and allocate space and resources on its cloud services to keep the tool functioning. So beneath a piece of software that matches images to a blacklist is a broader sociotechnical apparatus that supports its efforts.

And the second caveat: PhotoDNA is still just the most sophisticated version of blacklist tools like the rudimentary word filters from a decade before: it can identify only already *known* child pornography. It is not assessing the image in any sophisticated way; it cannot recognize some aspect of the photo that suggests that it is pornographic or involves a minor. It merely matches the image to a known database. NCMEC does add new images to that database, many of which it finds because a platform identified it and forwarded it to NCMEC to assess. But this is a human review process, not an automated one.

This hashing technique is being used to address other categories of problematic content.[83] Many platforms have developed internal tools that automatically identify copies of content they have already removed once, to speed the review process by preventing moderators from having to review the same post or image they reviewed moments or days before (and potentially come to a different conclusion). And in late 2016, Microsoft, YouTube, Facebook, and Twitter agreed to partner to develop and share a hashed database of identified terrorist content, so the partner sites could more quickly identify and possibly remove copies of the same content.[84] Again, a promising step forward, but still limited to reidentifying copies of already identified content. And unlike child pornography, which is illegal and harmful regardless of how it is used, extremist content depends on context: is it news, propaganda, recruitment, or historical artifact? Yet by this system, content identified in one context will be added to the database without a sense of that context; when that video or screed is automatically identified in a new context, the relevance of the previous context or the new one is lost, overshadowed by the certainty of having identified that same content again.[85]

The dream of AI content moderation is to be able to detect not just copies of known objectionable content and their close variants but new instances of objectionable content as well—to replace the work of human moderators. This would require automating not human recognition but human judgment, and this has proven a much more difficult task. Computer scientists are now looking to machine-learning techniques, which use large, existing datasets to train an algorithm to identify qualities within that data that might help it learn to discern different types of content. In the past decade, there have been innovations in the detection of nudity in images, extremist content in video, and hate speech and harassment in user interactions in social media. But significant hurdles remain.

Machine-learning algorithms for spotting pornography can identify telltale skin tones in the color spectrum of the image itself. Large patches of an image that are uninterrupted skin tones might very well be a naked body. This recognition, extremely easy for a human, is quite difficult for an algorithm. The computer understands an image only as a series of pixels, each with a color. But an algorithm can be trained, using a very large database of images, to recognize areas of human skin color, if they have already been labeled as such.[86] The algorithm "learns" to assign different weights to different color pixels based on their likelihood of having been identified as "skin" in the training data. Once these guesses are determined, they can be applied to new images to determine whether the most weighted colors show up in telltale ways. Recognizing that skin comes in a range of colors, the researchers train the algorithm to recognize different skin tones. Some tools also examine which skin-tone pixels represent a continuous region, drawing "bounding polygons" around areas of predominantly skin-tone pixels; then they take into account the number of these skin-tone regions, their proximity to one another, and the relative percentage of the entire image that is skin tone.[87]

You can appreciate the clever approximations these filters employ to detect what might be a typical photo of a naked body: a lot of skin-tone pixels, a large proportion of the image devoted to them, large continuous spans of the image of the same skin color. You may also begin to imagine the kinds of images that would confuse such a tool: unusual lighting conditions, clothing that interrupts areas of skin, images that are easily confused with skin tones (apparently, sunsets were a persistent challenge), and images that include naked skin but are not objectionable: portraits, babies, and beach photos.

Many of the innovations in nudity detection since have built on this basic starting point.[88] To improve on this initial technique, researchers have taught their tools to spot bodylike shapes, assuming that the recognition of color and shape together increases the probability that the image is of exposed skin.[89] Some tools learn to ignore areas of skin tone that are small and distant from these major polygons, or have too straight an edge, as more likely just elements in the background that happen to be a similar color. Some alter the contrast or luminance of the entire image first, to make detection of skin-tone areas easier; others add texture analysis, to identify areas that are too rough or smooth to be human skin.[90] Others have added facial recognition tools, both to ensure that images with large areas of flesh tones are not, in fact, portraits,[91] and to identify faces as useful sources from which to draw tell-tale skin tones.[92] Other recognition tools take into account the text surrounding the image—captions, user comments, or the name and metadata of the image file.[93] Keep in mind that with machine learning, it is not as if a tool is ticking off these various features and flagging images that fail the test; it is learning from a database in which all of these features have already been labeled, running thousands of assessments of images and noting when it has made the correct classifications, then further developing detection criteria based on those successes. In fact, it is not always clear which combination of features a tool is depending on when it manages to improve its detection rate, though it is likely that all of the dynamics play some part.[94]

Other researchers have turned to machine-learning techniques to identify hate speech and extremist content, or to improve on word filters by learning profanity on a broader scale.[95] As with nudity detection, these depend on having access to a large amount of data, comprising text that has already been identified as hateful or not, extremist or not, profanity or not, and training a machine-learning algorithm on the data until it can make the same distinction on new data at a reasonable rate. Some software emphasizes specific words, or the proximity between certain words; some pays attention to parts of speech, to benefit from clues that sentence structure might offer. For extremist content, the training data may also indicate connected accounts, user activity, profile information, and other such cues. Similar tools have been used to detect harassment, trolling, and ad hominem attacks, to better anticipate when a productive conversation is beginning to sour. These may look at users' contributions over time: for users who have been banned, what did their participation look like leading up to that point? Do their words or behavior differ from users who were never banned, in ways that an algorithm might be able to learn? Similar efforts, though less widely published or discussed, have been happening internally at platforms, particularly in gaming environments, including at Riot Games and Microsoft Xbox.[96]

These efforts are growing increasingly sophisticated, usually by adding more criteria and training on larger and larger datasets. In a recent study, a team used as training data more than 40 million posts over an eighteen-month period by 1.7 million users in discussion threads at CNN, Breitbart, and IGN, all of which were managed by the Disqus comment system.[97] The data included information about the content of the posts: the specific words, but also post length, measures of grammar and readability, number of positive and negative words, how on-topic or off-topic a post was, and more. The data also included information about the users' activity in the community—number and frequency of posts, number of posts complained about by other users—and information about how they were assessed by moderators, such as the number of posts deleted before they had been banned. From this enormous and rich dataset, the team trained its algorithm to distinguish between the activity of users who ended up banned and users who did not.

Machine-learning recognition tools typically proclaim their success in terms of a detection rate. This particular analysis of banned users achieved a 73 percent prediction rate, and on the basis of a user's first five to ten posts, more quickly than most human moderators typically intervene. The best nudity detection algorithm claims to detect nudity with a 94 percent recall and a false positive rate of 5 percent—that is, it spotted nearly all the nude images it should have while misidentifying as nude only one of every twenty nonnude images. In 2015 Twitter purchased Madbits, which promised an algorithm that could identify NSFW (not safe for work) images (including porn, violence, and gore) with 99 percent accuracy and a 7 percent false positive rate.[98]

Is 73 percent good? Ninety-four percent? Ninety-nine? It depends on what the platforms hope to do with these tools. These are, from one vantage point, phenomenal achievements. But when it comes to culture and expression, even a few false positives can be a real concern, depending on whether those errors are idiosyncratic or systemic. The stakes for false positives and false negatives differ, depending on the context and audience. For example, image technologies have historically had difficulty with race. Richard Dyer notes that over its long history, photographic technology has consistently failed to realistically represent darker skin colors.[99] Early decisions about the photochemical components of film were made with an idea of "what photos looked like"—and what photography looked like was portraiture, over-whelmingly of Caucasian faces. As a result, these technologies have continued to render white faces more clearly than black ones.[100] These inequities persist even as the technologies improve, without the people behind those improvements being cognizant of the bias the technologies still carry, because early standards and technical arrangements become instantiated in the professional knowledge around them.[101] And we continue to make the same mistake, in new contexts. In one notorious embarrassment for Google, an experimental image recognition tool added to Image Search mislabeled some black faces as "gorillas." This may be the twenty-first-century version of the error Dyer described: if the image database on which this algorithm was trained included many examples of white faces but relatively few black ones, the ability to discern white faces will be more sophisticated than for the kinds of faces it had less training on. So while marking the occasional baby photo as pornography is one kind of problem for the users involved, incorrectly identifying black skin in ways systemically different from white skin is a different kind of problem, a public problem about representation and equity rather than a consumer problem about efficiency and inconvenience.

Of course, false positives are a challenge for all kinds of detection, whether by an algorithm or a human. And humans can certainly have implicit, obscure, and persistent biases at work inside their efforts at fair judgment. But machine-learning techniques, as promising as they may be, are founded on two unresolvable paradoxes specific to an algorithmic approach, and represent limitations when used for detection and moderation.

First, machine-learning recognition techniques attempt to make a meaningful distinction without understanding meaning. These techniques, while they cannot know what a particular post means, what its author intended, or what effect it had on its recipient, are intended nevertheless to classify it as pornographic or harassing or hateful, by evaluating only its visual information. Automatic detection can assess only what it can know—that is, what can be represented as data, limited to the data it has.[102] The data it can measure serves as a proxy for the meaningful element it is trying to identify. This means that automatic detection techniques can be only as good as the proxy they employ, the measurable version of the problem.

Word filters and PhotoDNA are the exception, because there is little or no distance between what they're looking for and the proxy they can recognize: the same word as is on the list, or maybe its clever misspelling; the same image as is in the NCMEC database, or maybe a version that's been resized or had its brightness adjusted. But the machine-learning techniques being deployed to identify pornography or harassment must find the problem by looking for its measurable proxy, which is not the same. These tools aspire to identify pornography, but what they actually identify is naked bodies. Not only is this distinction often elided; their designers sometimes slip fluidly between the terms "pornography," "NSFW, and "nudity" as they describe what a tool in fact detects.[103] The fact is, there is pornography that does not include nudity and nudity that does not amount to pornography. Culturally, politically, and legally there are important differences between pornography and nudity—something we could see the platforms struggle with as they articulated their community guidelines. These tools can identify nudity, with high but not perfect accuracy, but that is not the same as identifying pornography.

In fact, commitments to the proxy can pull on the rule itself. The ability to automate the identification of nudity, especially as the tools improve, may encourage a platform to broaden a restriction on sexually explicit imagery to include all nudity, to better align what can be detected by the software. This drift toward the measurable proxy helps explain how Twitter fell behind on the issue of harassment. Twitter tried to sidestep the problems of meaning and context, by focusing instead on the informational patterns of interaction. Early on, Twitter engineers noticed that the harassment being reported looked a lot like spam: rapid sequences of repeated messages without a response between, coming from new user accounts with few followers and little other interaction with users.[104] This was something they could identify, and did in some ways represent dynamics that were fundamental to harassment. However, focusing only on spamlike harassment captures just some of the many forms that harassment takes, and may have given Twitter a false sense of assurance even as other types of harassment continued to fester. This tendency is all too common to social media platforms: to solve problems of interpretation and social conflict with computational methods that require treating them like data.

Second paradox: to develop an algorithm to identify objectionable material automatically, you need to train it on data that has already been identified. Machine learning depends on starting with a known database, a "gold standard" collection of examples, an agreed upon "ground truth" that becomes the basis upon which an algorithm can be expected to learn distinctive features. In computer science, this has either meant that researchers (or their underpaid undergrad research assistants) manually labeled data themselves, paid crowdworkers through sites like Amazon Mechanical Turk to do it, or have been in a position to get data from social media platforms willing to share it. Platforms designing their own algorithms can use the corpus of data they have already moderated. This raises two further problems.

First, just as measurable data (skin-colored pixels or spamlike activity) stands in for the problem being assessed, the training database must stand in for the judgment being automated. The detection tool being trained will inevitably approximate the kinds of judgments already made, the kinds of judgments that can be made. This means that it will probably be less prepared for novel instances that were not well represented in the training data, and it will probably carry forward any biases or assumptions that animated those prior judgments. The success of a machine-learning tool is judged on how well it makes the same distinctions that were made before; this is a fundamentally conservative and inflexible approach. A platform gathers data all the time, which means its training corpus will continue to expand. But more data is not the same as more varied data. There is no reason to assume that a social media platform eventually includes "all" examples. What is more likely is that basing the training on the kinds of distinctions the platform already makes, the activities its users already engage in, and the turbulent feedback loops between the two, will in fact confirm and extend those emphases and blind spots in ways that are difficult to detect or repair.

Furthermore, the need for training data undercuts the fundamental promise of automated detection. Machine learning is regularly hyped as certain to eventually replace human assessment, but it can be developed only based on previous human assessment. The hope of platforms, of course, is that this dependence will be temporary: a small amount of human labor now will train a tool eventually to do the same work automatically. Perhaps. But I'm skeptical, for all the reasons that the computer scientists developing these tools themselves acknowledge: the fluidity of culture, complexity of language, and adaptability of violators looking to avoid detection. Even if a gold standard database of extremist videos or hateful slurs or pornography could be collected and agreed upon, and even if an algorithm could be trained to parse new content as NSFW with 100 percent accuracy, that training data—by definition and inevitably—will not include examples that developed since it was collected. Platforms will need people to continue to detect and assess emergent forms of hate, obscenity, pornography, and harassment. Yes, the tool could then be trained on those new examples too, and maybe it would learn to distinguish these novel forms as well, but it can never eliminate the need for human oversight and adjudication.

Platforms dream of electric shepherds. But it is not clear that the human labor necessary to support such automated tools can ever go away; it can only be shifted around.[105] In the end, culture may simply be too dynamic and polyvalent for automated tools. Ascertaining whether something is offensive is an interpretive leap that contemporary algorithms are simply incapable of. What is pornographic to one viewer may be artistic to another; a naked body can be judged offensive by one viewer and deemed by another to be a cause for celebration and empowerment. Certainly, current tools are not yet reliable enough to have them automatically take action based on their assessments.

What the tools are good at is handling the easy cases, identifying instances and patterns for further investigation, and scoring users on past reports. They can be used as just one part of a moderation strategy—especially when speed is of the essence—one that still relies on human oversight. So, as we have seen, Facebook scans for images that might violate their community guidelines and flags them for human review. The content policy team at YouTube uses image recognition tools behind the scenes, so that a moderator may quickly jump to those moments in a flagged video that, according to the recognition software, *might* be nudity. Whisper uses algorithmic analysis on images and posts to identify problematic content, as well as relying on human moderation.[106] Recently, third-party "concierge" services have emerged; social media platforms can contract moderation out to these providers, which offer a basic tier of purely automatic detection and a premium tier service of supplemental human assessment. In their promotional materials, these services typically justify the extra level of service by acknowledging that, while automated tools can do a great deal, human moderation is necessary for the trickiest assessments. And it is worth remembering that automatic tools like these need not be perfect, only as good as or better than existing forms of review, before platforms will begin to seriously consider installing them and even initiating automatic removal based on their calculations.

The hope of someday automating the entire process, from detection to removal, remains seductive, even as the limitations become increasingly apparent. Platform managers find it appealing, because they want to be rid of the work that content moderation requires and because these companies are filled with engineers, who often prefer to solve social problems with smarter technology. Policy makers find automated moderation appealing as well, because it promises perfect enforcement, while eliding the vagaries of human subjectivity that plague more editorial approaches.

With each emergent horror online come renewed calls to solve the problem automatically. The latest and most pressing threat is terrorism.

Jigsaw, Google's semi-independent "big idea" unit, has recently taken on the challenge of identifying and countering extremist content, partly in response to calls from the Obama administration in early 2016 to do more about the use of social media by ISIS and other terrorist groups for propaganda and recruitment.[107] The aspiration, again, is machine learning: identifying patterns in interactions across social media that suggest terrorist planning and propagandizing, patterns in the search queries that suggest an increasingly radicalized user, patterns of association between known actors and followers—all of these, the Jigsaw team hopes, would allow their tools to spot terrorist activity before it erupts into violence, and provide an opportunity to intervene with counterspeech challenging the appeal and ideology of groups like ISIS.

But challenges, both practical and philosophical, remain. On the practical side, these techniques face the same limitations as before. It is difficult to collect sufficient training data: known terrorist actors are few, and they work very hard not to be identified, making it difficult to amass a reliable database of their search queries or tweets.[108] Classifying this content into a "gold standard" database for training is a time-consuming endeavor, with a great deal of room for interpretation: what counts as terrorist recruitment and what counts as inflammatory political speech? And there is an unavoidable risk of false positives, with high costs: how does the tool distinguish extremist content from less virulent content that employs some of the same markers? What happens to the innocent individual who is flagged by this software for making the wrong queries or interacting with the wrong people? What about antiextremist activists or journalists engaged in conversation with terrorist actors? What about innocent associates? Antiterrorist tactics in the West have been shifting: from identifying likely terrorists based on directed investigation to identifying individuals who match the data patterns of terrorists—assessments that become the basis of surveillance, arrests, and drone strikes.[109] The same logic can creep into automatic assessment of social media.

The philosophical challenge is perhaps even more worrisome. Machine-learning techniques are inherently conservative. The faith in sophisticated pattern recognition that underlies them is built on assumptions about people: that people who demonstrate similar actions or say similar things are similar, that people who have acted in a certain way in the past are likely to continue, that association suggests guilt. In contexts where people are being assessed for unethical or criminal actions, this faith in pattern recognition revives old ideas about recidivism, guilt by association, and genetics. For every project like Jigsaw there is a project like Faception: an Israeli tech startup already contracted by the NSA, that claims to be able to identify terrorists and pedophiles through face recognition tools—not from a database of known felons, but *before they have committed crimes.*[110] While this *Minority Report*–esque promise is almost certainly overstated and flawed, what is just as troubling is the presumptions it rests on—eugenics—and its promise of predetermination. What is troubling about Faception is also troubling about AI content moderation more broadly. It will always fail to anticipate cultural innovation: new words, new forms of expression, new tactics, new associations, new threats. But as we come to depend on it, the assessments it does make and the premises it does learn will harden over time.

These three approaches—editorial review, community, flagging, and automated detection—are important, not just because they are currently used by platforms, but because they are also emerging as the *ways* to handle user content online. They have been battle-tested over time by many platforms. They get picked up by new sites looking for "what works." They are taken up and internalized by users, who expect sites to work a certain way, who come to know that some things are likely to be allowed, some are likely to be forbidden, and some are likely to be overlooked. They become features of the digital culture landscape, shaping both platform policy itself and policy more broadly, as lawmakers come to assume that industry "self-regulation" is adequate for certain kinds of problems, then shaping policy to pair with it, or to offer legal teeth to those industry techniques. These normalized arrangements will matter a great deal for how we think about the shared responsibility for the health of public discourse.

5

the human labor of moderation

When you go into Chipotle and you want a burrito, and they make you the same burrito in California as in New York . . . made basically the same way, pretty much always everywhere, and they put basically the same amount in each burrito when you order it, every time, like the first time. Even though there are a bunch of people involved, but they somehow get that to happen. Right? Or it's like UPS. Facebook just delivers deletion packages to people. Right? . . . it's an operations process. It's like Disneyland—it's just that Disneyland doesn't delete your photos, it makes you see Mickey. But it's this repeated operations process at high scale, it's like that. It's just that it ends up affecting people's ability to share stuff or use platforms. But it's not a classroom, it's not a courtroom. It's UPS.

Personal interview, member of content policy team, Facebook

In May 2017, the *Guardian* published a trove of documents it dubbed "The Facebook Files." These documents instructed, over many Powerpoint slides and in unsettling detail, exactly what content moderators working on Facebook's behalf should remove, approve, or escalate to Facebook for further review. The document offers a bizarre and disheartening glimpse into a process that Facebook and other social media platforms generally keep under wraps, a mundane look at what actually doing the work of content moderation requires.

As a whole, the documents are a bit difficult to stomach. Unlike the clean principles articulated in Facebook's community standards, they are a messy and disturbing hodgepodge of parameters, decision trees, and rules of thumb for how to implement those standards in the face of real content.

They are peppered with examples that almost certainly came from actual material Facebook moderators have had to consider. They make clear that, if evil is banal, the evil available on Facebook is banal on a much, much wider scale.

For instance, in its community standards, Facebook asserts, "We don't tolerate bullying or harassment. We allow you to speak freely on matters and people of public interest, but remove content that appears to purpose-fully target private individuals with the intention of degrading or shaming them." And later, "We remove content that threatens or promotes sexual violence or exploitation."[1] But a moderator looking at hundreds of pieces of Facebook content every hour needs more specific instructions on what exactly counts as "sexual violence," so these documents provide examples like "To snap a bitch's neck, make sure to apply all your pressure to the middle of her throat"—which Facebook gives a green checkmark, meaning posts like that should stay. In a time when misogyny, sexual violence, and hatred are so clearly on the rise in our society, it is disheartening, shocking, that Facebook could be so cavalier about a statement like this. But these documents are rife with examples like it, drawing artificial lines through a culture of misogyny and hatred that deliberately slips between veiled threats and generalized expressions of cruelty, slowly making it somehow acceptable to objectify, intimidate, and exclude women. Still, given ten seconds, some posts have to go and some have to stay.

Of course, when moderation moves from principles to details, it's not likely to sound particularly noble. The content and behavior Facebook moderators have to consider (and, let's remember, what users often demand they address) are ugly, and varied, and ambiguous, and meant to evade judgment while still having impact. There's no pretty way to conduct this kind of content moderation. It requires making some unpleasant judgments, and some hard-to-defend distinctions. Lines in the sand are like that.

The document, while listing all the things that should be removed, is etched with the scratches of past controversies, the "tombstones," if you know how to look for them. Graphic, violent images should be removed, with the exception of aborted fetuses. Hate speech is prohibited, but only for protected categories of people (specific races, religions, sexualities, na-tionalities), and "migrants" constitute only a quasi-protected category, so although dehumanizing statements about them should be removed, cursing at them, calling them thieves, and urging them to leave the country do not amount to hate speech. Holocaust denial is allowed, but geo-blocked from

Contemporary Activity Primary Focus:
* Support, Praise or Representation: DELETE

A great day

Our heroes

Teaching infidels their place

USA we come for you

Follow the path of enlightment

Contemporary Activity Primary Focus:
* Condemning Commentary: IGNORE

How sad

Just wait we'll get them #downwithIS

We are not afraid

They should be out playing ☹

Like rats on a sinking ship

Among the leaked Facebook moderator training documents published by the *Guardian*, May 2017, these two pages direct reviewers how to assess images of extremist or terrorist content depending on whether the user posting it has celebrated or condemned it. (In the original, the images on the first page are outlined in red, those on the second in green, to emphasize which are to be rejected and which are to be kept.)

countries that outlaw it—not all fourteen countries with laws prohibiting Holocaust denial, just the four that have pursued the issue with Facebook explicitly.[2]

But the most important revelation of these leaked documents is no single detail within them—it is the fact that they had to be leaked (along with Facebook's content moderation guidelines leaked to *S/Z* in 2016, or Facebook's content moderation guidelines leaked to Gawker in 2012).[3] These documents were not meant ever to be seen by the public. They instruct and manage the thousands of "crowdworkers" responsible for the first line of human review of Facebook pages, posts, and photos that have been either flagged by users or identified algorithmically as possibly violating the site's guidelines. The guidance they offer, while perhaps crafted with input from experts, has not benefited from public deliberation or even reaction.

These documents are a message in a bottle from a nearly invisible community of workers, part of the human reality of turning general policies into specific decisions to remove or not. This labor is largely invisible to the user, and remains largely invisible even to critics, journalists, and academics who examine social media and their workings. Social media platforms have been relatively circumspect about how they handle this task: platform managers prefer not to draw attention either to the presence of so much obscene content on their sites, or to how regularly they impose what some deem "censorship" in response. And to be fair, users may not care to see it either: it is more comforting to just be freely sharing and connecting, disavowing that in many ways users want that sharing to be cleansed of the aspects of human social exchange they find abhorrent. These documents shine a light on one part of an otherwise opaque, complex chain of people and activities required so that Facebook may play custodian, and all the darkest corners of human sociality can be swept away.

WHY MODERATION REQUIRES PEOPLE

Behind any platform, however open and automatic it may appear, is a laborious process by which an immense amount of content must be reviewed. Facebook reached 2 billion active users in June of 2017.[4] A 2012 news article reported Facebook as having 2.5 billion pieces of content shared a day, and 300 million photos posted every day[5]—and these numbers have certainly grown enormously since then. On average, Twitter users generate 6,000 tweets every second.[6] The demands of overseeing this much content and activity strain corporate resources, and the ability of moderators to be fair and thoughtful in their oversight. Moderation at scale requires immense human resources: community managers at the platform, crowdworkers reviewing tasks farmed out to them, users who avail themselves of the complaint mechanisms provided, partner organizations enlisted to help, and, sometimes all users, on platforms that require them to rate or categorize their contributions. The labor that platforms put toward moderation, and the labor we as users are conscripted to perform as part of this project, are not just part of how platforms function, they constitute it. Platforms are made by the work that goes into content moderation, and they are not platforms without it.[7]

Of course, the resources that platforms might put toward this project are limited only by convention. The Chinese government, for instance, employs hundreds of thousands of people to scour social media for political criticism and blocks many websites and keyword searches automatically.[8] I am not suggesting that China's approach is in any way ideal, or that social media contributions should queue up for publication. I am only noting that what counts as impossible only appears so to U.S. users. Users in the West are also unwilling to accept the delay between posting content and having it appear that this uniform review would require. But these constraints are in fact movable: our expectation of instant publication is no older than the contemporary web; print, radio, even the early Internet made no such promise. But in lieu of shifting these expectations themselves, social media platforms must accomplish the work of moderation within these limits.

The mere fact of these moderation mechanisms, and the real labor they require, contains an important revelation about the significance of social media platforms.[9] But mapping out this dispersed, shifting, and interwoven labor force in more detail is difficult. Most of this work is hidden—some happens inside the corporate headquarters, some happens very, very far away from there, obscured behind the shields of third-party partners. The rest is portioned out to users in ways so woven into the mundane use of platforms that it is hard to notice at all. Even the bits that show themselves—the flags and complaint mechanisms, the ratings and age barriers, even the occasional deletion—reveal little about how they fit into the larger project of moderating an entire platform. Users who have run up against moderation decisions may find it difficult to inquire about them, seek an audience with anyone at the platform, lodge a complaint, or request an appeal. When those interactions do take place, they are cloaked in form letters and

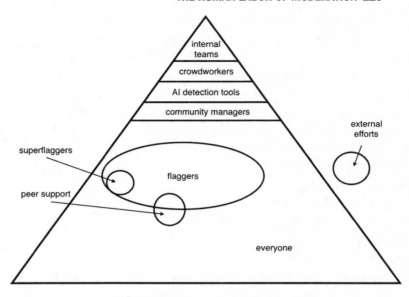

The many forms of labor involved in platform moderation

customer-support "dashboards" that continue to obscure what goes on behind the scenes. What remains are glimpses—a leaked document, an angry blog post, the occasional press exposé.

In this chapter I want to map out the general shape of the work involved, as best as I can piece it together. I will draw on examples from specific platforms, but I am mapping also what is typical across social media, the kinds of labor that are possible and commonplace. I may have missed a detail here or there—indeed, the opacity around moderation is part of the deeper problem of how platforms make these decisions and how they understand their public obligations in doing so.[10] Each platform makes different choices about how to arrange and divide out this labor, where to put different kinds of decision processes, how to reconcile challenging cases. My aim is to make generally clear what is involved: platforms currently impose moderation at scale by turning some or all users into an identification force, employing a small group of outsourced workers to do the bulk of the review, and retaining for platform management the power to set the terms.

As the epigraph for this chapter suggests, moderation at the major platforms is as much a problem of logistics as a problem of values. As much as an aggrieved user or the press can challenge what rules the platforms set and how they enforce them, and might enjoy hanging a platform out to dry for a decision that looks craven or self-interested or hypocritical, it may be more important to examine the implications of how moderation work is organized, managed, and coordinated—even, or especially, when it's working smoothly. Because this work is distributed among different labor forces, because it is unavailable to public or regulatory scrutiny, and because it is performed under high-pressure conditions, there is a great deal of room for slippage, distortion, and failure.

Internal Teams

At the top, most platforms have an internal policy team charged with overseeing moderation. The team sets the rules of that platform, oversees their enforcement, adjudicates the particularly hard cases, and crafts new policies in response. These are usually quite small, often just a handful of full-time employees. At a few platforms the team is an independent division; at others it sits under the umbrella of "trust and safety," "community outreach," customer service, or technical support. At others, setting policy and addressing hard cases is handled in a more ad hoc way, by the leadership with advice from legal counsel; an engineer may find himself asked to weigh in, in his spare time, on what counts as harassment or stalking.[11]

These teams are obscure to users, by design and policy. They are difficult for users to reach, and the statements and policies they generate are often released in the voice of the company itself. All together they are a surprisingly small community of people.[12] At the scale at which most platforms operate, these internal teams would be insufficient by themselves. Still, they have an outsized influence on where the lines are drawn, what kinds of punishments are enforced, and the philosophical approach their platforms take to governance itself.

In their earliest days, many platforms did not anticipate that content moderation would be a significant problem. Some began with relatively homogenous user populations who shared values and norms with one another and with the developers—for example, back when TheFacebook was open only to tech-savvy Ivy League university students.[13] Many of the social norms that first emerged were familiar from college life, and the diversity of opinions, values, and intentions would be attenuated by the narrow band of people who were even there in the first place. Other sites, modeled after blogging tools and searchable archives, subscribed to an "information wants to be free" ethos that was shared by designers and participants alike.[14]

Facebook User Operations team members at the main campus in Menlo Park, California, May 2012. Photo by Robyn Beck, in the AFP collection. © Robyn Beck/Getty Images. Used with permission

In fact, in the early days of a platform, it was not unusual for there to be no one in an official position to handle content moderation. Often content moderation at a platform was handled either by user support or community relations teams, generally more focused on offering users technical assistance; as a part of the legal team's operations, responding to harassment or illegal activity while also maintaining compliance with technical standards and privacy obligations; or as a side task of the team tasked with removing spam. Facebook, when it began, relied on Harvard students as volunteers, until the backlog of user complaints reached the tens of thousands; the company made its first permanent hire for content moderation in late 2005, almost eighteen months after launching.[15]

As these sites grew, so did the volume and variety of concerns coming from users. Platforms experienced these in waves, especially as a platform grew in cultural prominence, changed dramatically in its demographics, or expanded to an international audience. Some tried to address these growing concerns the way online discussion groups had, through collective deliberation and public rule making. But this was an increasingly difficult endeavor. Many of the major social media platforms found that they had to expand their internal content policy groups, first to hire full-time employees at all, then to bring in dozens of junior employees to deal with flagged content and complaints, then to seek out expertise in different languages, regions of the world, or shifting political tensions. In 2009, 150 of Facebook's then 850 employees, based in California and in Dublin, Ireland,[16] handled moderation, one click at a time; MySpace had a similar team numbering in the "hundreds."[17]

Today the teams that oversee content moderation at these platforms remain surprisingly small, as much of the front-line work handled by these once-150-strong teams has been outsourced. Again, it is difficult to know exactly how many. Because the work of content moderation is now so intertwined with legal policy, spam, privacy, the safety of children and young users, ad policies, and community outreach, it really depends on how you count. Individual employees themselves increasingly have to obscure their identities to avoid the wrath of trolls and harassers. Most of all, platforms are not forthcoming about who does this work, or how many, or how. It is not in their interest to draw attention to content moderation, or to admit how few people do it. But when a policy is reconsidered or a tricky case is discussed, such considerations are often being made by a very small group of people, before being imposed as a rule that potentially affects millions of users.

In addition, the group of people doing this kind of work is not only small, it is socially and professionally interconnected. Many of these platforms have their corporate headquarters in a tight constellation around San Francisco, which means people with this particular set of skills often move between companies professionally and circulate socially. Given its unique set of challenges, it is still a tiny group of people who have become expert in the task of large-scale platform moderation; members of this group have quickly become familiar with one another through professional conferences, changes in employment, and informal contact. As they increasingly face legal, political, and public relations implications, some platforms have begun drawing employees from outside the company to fit moderation teams with experts in sexual assault, antiterrorism, child exploitation, and so on. Still, the policies of these enormous, global platforms, and the labor crucial to their moderation efforts, are overseen by a few hundred, largely white, largely young, tech-savvy Californians who occupy a small and tight social and professional circle.

Contract worker doing content moderation for U.S. tech companies at Task Us, an American outsourcing tech company located in the Taguig district of Manila, Philippines. Photograph by Moises Saman. © Moises Saman / Magnum Photos. Used with permission

Crowdworkers

As recently as 2014, Twitter was still claiming, "Every report by a user is reviewed by a member of Twitter's Trust and Safety team."[18] Even for Twitter, which has leaner rules than similar-sized platforms, this statement is hard to believe—if what it meant was its handful of permanent employees. But Twitter, like many social media platforms, now employs a substantially larger group of people to provide a first wave of review, beneath the internal moderation team. They might be employed by the platform, at the home office, or in satellite offices located around the world in places like Dublin and Hyderabad. But more and more commonly they are hired on a contract basis: as independent contractors through third-party "temp" companies, or as on-demand labor employed through crowdwork services such as Amazon's Mechanical Turk, Upwork, Accenture, or TaskUs—or both, in a two-tiered system.[19]

The leaked 2017 documents discussed at the start of this chapter were the removal instructions provided by Facebook to its crowdworkers, to guide, harmonize, and speed their review of flagged content. Crowdworkers are now used as a first-response team, looking at flagged posts and images from users and making quick decisions about how to respond. The moderators following those leaked instructions would largely be looking at content already reported or "flagged" by Facebook users. They would either "confirm" the report (and delete the content), "unconfirm" it (the content stays), or "escalate" it, passing it up to Facebook for further review. Only the most difficult cases are passed up to the internal content team for further deliberation, though these teams would also have access to a rich flow of data on what their crowdworkers were encountering and deciding. According to a 2016 NPR report, Facebook by itself now subcontracts its content review out to "several thousand people" on three continents.[20] This number was confirmed in May 2017, when, in response to growing criticism about violent murders and suicides broadcast over the new Facebook Live feature, Mark Zuckerberg promised to add an additional three thousand moderators to the forty-five hundred they already depend on. Add that to all the other major platforms that do not handle moderation entirely in-house, and this is a significant workforce, with an unseemly task: as one moderator put it, "Think like that there is a sewer channel and all of the mess/dirt/waste/shit of the world flow towards you and you have to clean it."[21]

To cope with the immense amount of disputed content that must be reviewed, and to placate angry users and critics, platforms have increasingly promised speedy responses. Facebook currently promises some kind of response within twenty-four hours, and in 2016 all of the major platforms promised European lawmakers to ensure review of possible terrorist or extremist content within a one-day window.[22] To meet such a requirement, human review must be handled fast. "Fast" here can mean mere seconds per complaint—approve, reject, approve—and moderators are often evaluated on their speed as well as their accuracy, meaning there is reward and pressure to keep up this pace.[23] Each complaint is thus getting just a sliver of human attention, under great pressure to be responsive not just to this complaint, but to the queue of complaints behind it. To speed things along, and also for reasons of privacy, the images and posts are usually detached from their original material. Moderators are generally unaware of the identity of the user, and are provided little of the surrounding context—the back and forth of a conversation, that user's previous posts, and so on. Users expect these judgments to weigh competing values, show cultural sensitivity, and appear to the user as fair and consistent. Instead, they are being distilled from their meaningful context and compressed by the weight of this enormous and endless queue of complaints.

These crowdworkers are obscured intentionally and by circumstance. Many are in parts of the world where labor is cheap, especially the Philippines and India, far from both the platform they work for and the users they are moderating; they are also distanced from the company through contract labor arrangements and the intervening interfaces of the crowdwork platforms that employ them and organize their labor.[24] Work conditions can be grim. For a widely read 2014 *Wired* article, Adrian Chen investigated workers in the Philippines employed by crowdworker platform TaskUs to do content moderation for U.S.-based platforms, under very different working conditions from those one might find in Silicon Valley. The pay is meager: a quarter-cent per image, according to a 2012 report—or between 1 and 4 dollars per hour, according to Chen's report.[25] Kristy Milland, an outspoken activist in the Mechanical Turk community, noted, "People say to me 'Oh my god, you work at home? You're so lucky. . . . You can't tell them 'I was tagging images today—it was all ISIS screen grabs. There was a basket full of heads.' That's what I saw just a few months ago. The guy on fire, I had to tag that video. It was like 10 cents a photo."[26]

This globally dispersed and fluctuating labor force solves a series of problems these platforms face. First, a platform can assemble a response team that works twenty-four hours a day, and can draw from any geographic region, in any language.[27] And as the queue of complaints grows and shrinks, the review process can be adjusted: "Because numbers of workers can be recruited in accordance with task size, the amount of time to finish the micro-tasks does not grow or shrink with the number of tasks."[28] This is what allows the platforms to guarantee a response time, so long as the in-house team can respond quickly enough to any issues that the crowdworkers escalate to them. And the work is distanced, literally and figuratively, from the rest of the company's workers (who need not even know that some of what appears to be data processing is performed by humans). It is even separated to some degree from the internal teams that manage the labor, by the interface of the microwork platform, or by the third-party company the platform has subcontracted the work to. This helps distance this work, and all it represents, from the production of the platform and the experience its managers imagine users are having with it.

Crowdworker moderators also face a bewildering torrent of material, from harmless material flagged accidentally or incorrectly, to questionable stuff that might or might cross the line, to a blistering array of human atrocities.[29] The little press coverage available about this hidden workforce has focused primarily on the psychological toll of having to look at the worst the Internet has to offer, all day long, day in and day out. In 2010, the *New York Times* worried that content moderators, having to look at this "sewer channel" of content reported by users, were akin to "combat veterans, completely desensitized," and noted a growing call for these platforms to provide therapeutic services.[30] Chen's exposé makes this point powerfully: this is not just about deciding whether a nipple is or is not showing, it's about being compelled to look at the most gruesome, the most cruel, the most hateful that platforms users have to offer. One moderator for Google estimated looking at 15000 images a day, and grappling with the horrors he found there: child porn, beheadings, animal abuse.[31] A lawsuit was recently brought against Microsoft by two content moderators suffering from posttraumatic stress after their work reviewing gruesome images and violent posts. There is something deeply unsettling about Facebook's leaked training documents, in the way it must explain and sometimes show the horrors that Facebook users are apparently eager to share, with all the finesse of a corporate training manual.[32]

There certainly may be a psychological toll to this work. But as my colleague Mary Gray has argued, framing this labor exclusively in terms of the psychological impact may obscure the equally problematic labor politics, which is less about the shock of what workers occasionally encounter and more about the mundane realities of depending on this kind of work to provide a livelihood. For many, this is full-time work, even if cobbled together from piecemeal assignments. And while moderators do have to face true atrocities, much more of what they screen is the everyday violence, the everyday sexism and racism and homophobia, the everyday pornography, and the everyday self-harm that users share. Though some may be troubled by what they're forced to look at, more typically the worker is troubled by whether he can get enough work, whether the pay is enough to support his family, whether a bad review on one gig will block him from the best-paid tasks, whether there is any recourse for being mistreated by the company that hired him, whether he will be able to afford health insurance this month—the precariousness of the labor, more than the impact of the content.[33] Content moderation is currently one of the most common of the "human computation" tasks being handled by this growing but largely concealed workforce. And because this work is both necessary and invisible, the rights and expectations around this kind of contingent information work are just now being established, outside of public view.[34]

But why must it be so hidden? As Sarah Roberts argues, platform managers want to keep the content moderation process opaque not only to avoid helping users skirt the rules but to downplay the fact that what is available is the result of an active selection process, chosen for economic reasons.[35] When moderation is made as invisible as possible, the content we do see seems like it is simply there, a natural phenomenon—including whatever racist, homophobic, obscene, or abusive content is allowed to stay. Opacity hides not only the *fact* of selection but also the values motivating that selection, including "the palatability of that content to some imagined audience and the potential for its marketability and virality, on the one hand, and the likelihood of it causing offense and brand damage, on the other. In short it is evaluated for its potential value as commodity."[36]

There are, however, gaps in this veil of secrecy. For his 2014 exposé, Chen didn't depend on a leak: the CEO of Whisper invited him to see the way content moderation was being handled, in all likelihood to help quell concerns that Whisper was home to a troubling amount of harassment and self-harm. At the time, this process was still a secret carefully guarded by most platforms, but increasingly platform managers are sensing a need to demonstrate their commitment to content moderation. Still, platforms continue to reveal little about their process, or how big a problem it is. And third-party companies that employ these moderators are also tight-lipped, often under a contractual obligation of secrecy with their platform customers. This silence means that this work largely remains invisible, with the exception of a few reporters, activists, and academics looking to shine a light on this part of the social media industry.

Community Managers

Platforms that are designed to allow smaller subgroups to exist within the broader population of users can empower moderators to be responsible for the activity of a subgroup. These roles differ depending on the shape of the platform in question; I am thinking here of the policing power given to the admins of Facebook Groups, the "redditors" who moderate subreddits at Reddit, the administrators with enhanced editing and policing powers on Wikipedia and Quora. We could also include the moderation powers that go with operating a blog or page that has space for comments, the ways users can police their own Tumblr blogs, Instagram comments, YouTube

channels, or Facebook pages, as well as the kinds of small groups that structure some online gaming and virtual worlds, such as guilds and teams.
(I want to separate this from the power users are sometimes given to block
messages they receive or specific people that follow them; what I mean here
is the ability to remove contributions from the public or semipublic spaces
to which they are posted, not just from the user's own view.)

The community manager shares a family resemblance with some of the
figures that populated the early web: operators of bulletin board systems
(BBSs), chatroom moderators, AOL volunteers, and webmasters all performed the mundane work of keeping small communities functioning and
happy.[37] In many cases these were the same people who had set up the communities and handled the backstage technical upkeep and fielded support
questions as well. In other cases, they were users granted administrative
privileges in exchange for managing user accounts, handling disagreements,
and enforcing community norms. The amount and character of this labor
varied widely, but rested upon the manager's commitment to the community, as founder or participant. Sometimes the role shifted toward moderation in response to a shock to the community: when, for example, a troll
first disrupted a community that had simply, and perhaps naïvely, assumed
that everyone wanted the same thing, and required no governance at all.[38]
Community management has taken many forms, perhaps as many forms
as there are online communities: from the benevolent tyranny of a webmaster, to public arbitration among an entire community, to ad hoc councils
appointed to determine policies and dole out punishments.[39] As these communities grew and changed over time, new members and new conflicts
challenged these forms of governance; sometimes they adjusted, and sometimes the groups faltered and people moved on.[40]

As small-scale, commercial social media began to develop, community
managers (employed by the platform) remained important points of contact
to face the community—not exclusively for moderation, sometimes not at
all, but for troubleshooting technical problems, addressing concerns about
the community, mediating interpersonal disputes.[41] But as these platforms
grew, it became increasingly untenable to correspond directly with that
many users. On major platforms like YouTube and Twitter, users regularly
complain about how unreachable site representatives can be.

But some platforms that are designed to subdivide users into distinct
groups have retained this community manager role, in a modified form. Reddit uses volunteer "redditors" to manage individual subreddits—sometimes

a single person, sometimes a team; sometimes the person who initiated the subreddit, sometimes a user enlisted to help manage it as it expanded. The redditor is granted the technical privileges of an administrator: she has the ability to remove posts, delete comments, and suspend users from her subreddit. A subreddit can have its own code of conduct: sometimes a variation of or more articulated version of Reddit's, but in other cases with wholly new rules specific to that community.

Community moderators occupy a structurally different position from the moderation teams employed by the platforms, a difference that can be both advantageous and not. As participants in or even founders of the group, sometimes with a lengthy tenure, they may enjoy an established standing in the community. They may be enforcing rules that were generated by and consented to by the community, making enforcement easier. They are often deeply invested in the group's success, though this can be an asset or a detriment: the community manager may have a familiarity and legitimacy with the users that a distant review team does not, but he may also tend to rigidly adhere to first principles and be less willing to adapt to new members, new directions, and new challenges. Most important, a community works out its own identity and values in the very practices of developing governance that embodies its aims as a community.[42] Community managers, at their best, are well positioned to guide this process.

On the other hand, they are typically volunteers, usually uncompensated and often underappreciated.[43] Typically they do not have the authority to extend any punitive consequences beyond the groups they're responsible for—a manager can ban a user from the specific group but not from the entire platform—which significantly limits their scope and allows troublemakers to move across groups with near impunity. And because community managers are nearly always volunteers, oversight can vary widely from community to community.

But perhaps what's most challenging for community managers at larger platforms is that they are in some ways separate and yet also inextricably woven into and dependent upon that platform. A social media platform may be designed to provide specific spaces for groups to gather, but it is not franchising these community spaces to be overseen independently. The financial imperatives of subscription, advertising, and data collection drive platforms to collect and keep people rather than splintering them off, while also giving them the sensation (or illusion) of freedom of movement and the ability to organize into semi-independent communities. Platform-based groups are interwoven algorithmically: they depend on the same user profiles, their boundaries are porous, and the platforms encourage users, interactions, and data to move across and through them. This changes, and limits, what a community manager reasonably can do, and shapes the governability of the group itself. For instance, a redditor may manage a specific subreddit, one with coherent aims and stable membership. But the moment one post from within the subreddit enjoys sufficient popularity that it gets boosted to the front page, it draws attention and reaction from beyond the subreddit that the redditor cannot oversee, and may inspire a sudden influx of users who may not share the group's aims or ethos.

While groups are often able to set and enforce their own community norms, they are not free from the sitewide guidelines. A Facebook group cannot, for instance, permit pornography that the platform prohibits. (It may, of course, limit its membership to others who want pornography; if no one flags, the group might get away with it for a while. But this is different from being able to set affirmative guidelines contrary to those of the larger platform.) The reverse is also true: although the Facebook group administrator has the power to delete and suspend, all of the flagging mechanisms of the wider platform remain in place, meaning that users can easily bypass the group administrator and complain directly to Facebook.

Communities that regularly run afoul of the sitewide guidelines can become a liability for the platform, something Reddit seems to face on a regular basis. In recent years Reddit has had to ban active subreddits that were flourishing under moderators who were unconcerned about, or actively supportive of, the goings on within: subreddits dedicated to sharing stolen nude images of female celebrities, affirming white supremacist ideals and denigrating minorities, or circulating revenge porn.[44] Reddit was slow to act in many of these cases—some charged the company with studiously looking the other way until pressured to respond. But its hesitation may have also been a product of their commitment to deferring as much of the moderation as possible to redditors. Still, when a group grows too extreme or too visible, policies of the platform supersede the will of the community manager.

As J. Nathan Matias tells it, this overlapping responsibility, and the friction it can engender, was most apparent during the Reddit "blackout" of 2015.[45] Many redditors were surprised when Reddit shuttered several controversial subreddits, imposed stricter rules about revenge porn and harassment, and pressed redditors to moderate more aggressively. Some already felt constrained by the limited moderation tools Reddit provided. Their frustration came to a boil after the sudden firing of Victoria Taylor, who had been the liaison between redditors and the company. In response, many subreddits went dark as a symbolic protest, and as a way to pressure Reddit. Clearly, redditors occupy a difficult position between Reddit and their user community: beholden to both, belonging to neither. Clearly, they retain some power by being in the middle, able under some circumstances to get the attention of Reddit. But their ability to govern, as well as exactly what they are governing, is intertwined with the platform and its prevailing interests.[46]

Flaggers

Enormous platforms face an enormous moderation project, but they also have an enormous resource close at hand: users themselves. Most platforms now invite users to "flag" problematic content and behavior, generating a queue of complaints that can be fed to the platform moderators—typically, to its army of crowdworkers first—to adjudicate. Flagging is now widespread across social media platforms, and has settled in as a norm in the logic of the social media interface, alongside "favoriting" and reposting. A small icon or link beneath a post, image, or video offers the user a pull-down menu for submitting a complaint, often with submenus to specify the nature of the offense. In the earliest days of contemporary platforms, such mechanisms were nonexistent, or buried in the help pages. Platforms have since made it easier and easier to find these flags, though in some cases criticism has dogged specific platforms for the alleged inadequacy of these mechanisms.

Enlisting the crowd to police itself is now commonplace across social media platforms and, more broadly, the management of public information resources. It is increasingly seen as a necessary element of platforms, both by regulators who want platforms to be more responsive and by platform managers hoping to avoid stricter regulations. Flagging has expanded as part of the vocabulary of online interfaces, beyond alerting a platform to offense: platforms let you flag users who you fear are suicidal, or flag news or commentary that peddles falsehoods. What users are being asked to police, and the responsibility attached, is expanding.

In the previous chapter I discussed the problematic aspects of flagging as a moderation technique. Here I want to consider the population of users who actually do it. Flagging elicits and structures the work of users—transforming them into a labor force of volunteer regulators. This is part of a broader dependence on the work of users that is crucial to platforms themselves—to produce content, to like, label, review, and rank, to build networks of people and communities of interest.[47] Platforms are empty software shells; the creative and social labor of users fills those shells. Some have argued that the economic value of social media platforms is overwhelmingly built upon this labor that users give away without financial compensation, though there are arguably other forms of compensation users experience: social connection, reputation, and so forth. But wherever you stand on the question of whether this is exploitation or a fair bargain, it depends on users being enlisted to make small contributions that are aggregated for the collective benefit, and for the benefit of the platform itself. It is work, however compensated or not, however fairly arranged or not, and it takes the place of more traditional kinds of labor. User labor is a fundamental part of the social compact that platforms offer and depend upon; flagging objectionable content fits neatly into this compact, and gives rise to some of the same tensions and ambivalences.

On the one hand, flagging puts the work of review and complaint right at the point of offense, in front of those most motivated to complain. Even if moderators can't be everywhere, users can; if policy teams cannot anticipate emerging problems, users can be their sensitized nerve endings. The flagging system takes these momentary responses and aggregates them into a decentralized identification system for possible violations. Flaggers may also help a platform team to better understand the norms of the community—content that is not flagged will remain, even if members of the policy team might have worried about it had they encountered it, and they may look twice at materials they think are acceptable but that users keep flagging. As a site expands into different countries, the population of possible flaggers automatically includes people with the necessary linguistic and cultural expertise—although this is not without its own problems.

On the other hand, flagging is voluntary—which means that the users who deputize themselves to flag content are those most motivated to do so. This raises questions about the nature of that motivation. Platforms typically describe the flagging mechanism as giving an offended viewer or victim of harassment the means to alert the platform. But this is just one reason to flag, and the easiest to celebrate. There are real differences between a user complaining about harm to himself, a bystander calling out the bad behavior of others, a user serving as citizen patrol to ferret out offenses or enforce the rules, and someone gaming the flagging system to express political disdain or undercut someone else's efforts to be heard. In one analysis of harassment reports made to Twitter, a majority of the reports were found to be false, incorrect, or deliberate acts of trolling, and half of the legitimate reports came from bystanders concerned about other users being victimized, rather than from victims themselves.[48] Yet the tool is the same for all of these flaggers, and the queue of complaints they generate does not distinguish among them particularly well.

Platforms also describe flagging as an expression of the community. But are the users who flag "representative" of the larger user base, and what are the ramifications for the legitimacy of the system if they're not? Who flags, and why, is hard to know. Platforms do not report how many users flag, what percentage of those who do flag provide the most flags, how often platform moderators remove or retain flagged content, and so on. YouTube noted, in the vaguest terms, that "over 90 million people have flagged videos on YouTube since 2006—that's more than the population of Egypt—and over a third of these people have flagged more than one video."[49] We might also guess that these numbers fluctuate dramatically. Policy managers talked about surges of flags that turn out to be pranks inspired by 4chan users to disrupt the platform. Real-world events and widely shared pieces of contentious content might also lead to surges in flagging. Beyond that, it would be reasonable to guess that flagging is likely to resemble the 90/10 "power law" curves we see in participation on user-generated platforms.[50] Probably a minority of users flag, and a tiny minority of that minority does most of the flagging. But again, this is only a guess, because none of the major social media platforms has made this kind of data available.

Not all flags, or all surges of flags, are attended to in the same way. One representative of YouTube told me that the content moderation team often saw surges of flags when a new country got access to the platform. "When we actually launch in other countries, we'll see the flagging rates just completely spike, because, I think it's a combination of sort of users in those new countries don't know the rules of the road and so they're uploading anything and everything, and the community that is YouTube is actually, they can recognize the outliers pretty quickly and they sort of know what is cool for the community and what isn't, and so it's interesting to see sort of the new country absorbed into the community norms and very quickly you see that the flagging rates stabilize."[51] This struck me as an astounding assumption: a different logic would be to treat this new wave of flags as some kind of expression of values held by this new user population, to be taken *more* seriously than the rest. YouTube's approach is a reminder that while flagging can sound like an expression of the community, the platform still determines which users are "the community that is YouTube" and which need to be "absorbed."

Superflaggers, Peer Support, and External Efforts

Shifting the work of moderation to users is meant to address the problem of scale, but it gives platforms a fluid and unreliable labor force making judgments that are uneven in quality and sometimes self-interested and deceptive. As a technique, flagging privileges quantity over quality, or knowing a lot in a superficial way over knowing a little but with more certainty. But not all users are created equal, so not all users need be treated equally. Some platforms depend on subsets of users that have either the proven reliability as flaggers to be taken more seriously or the expertise to more skillfully recognize and adjudicate specific kinds of problems.

Many platform managers would like to have more high-quality flags and fewer accidental and tactical ones; there are ways to ensure this. Some platforms internally assign reputation scores to flaggers, so that subsequent flags from users who have a proven record of flagging accurately will be taken more seriously or acted upon more quickly. Others have introduced programs to encourage and reward users who flag judiciously: Microsoft's Xbox offers the Enforcement United program; YouTube began a Trusted Flagger program in 2012, then expanded it in 2016 to the YouTube Heroes program, gamifying flagging by offering points and rewards.[52] Yelp oversees the Yelp Elite Squad in which high-quality reviewers are, by invitation only, made members of a semisecret group, get invited to local parties, and are fêted as tastemakers; Yelp has since hired its community managers from this group.[53]

Similarly, some platforms have granted heightened reporting powers to "authorized reporters," organizations that have the expertise or the urgency to flag certain kinds of content quickly—police departments, health organizations, child-protection groups, fact-checking organizations, and so on. Europol formed Internet Referral Units designed to quickly forward suspected terrorist content to platforms and service providers for review and removal.[54] Again, the presumption is that flags from trusted users or expert organizations are "better intelligence" than a flag from any old user, and can be acted upon with less deliberation and delay. Who the privileged flaggers are, even the fact that these users and organizations have this power, generally remains opaque to users.

One such authorized-reporter arrangement has been discussed publicly. In November 2014, Twitter partnered with the activist organization Women Action and the Media to help field complaints regarding gendered harassment. For Twitter, this was good publicity after a particular bad news cycle, as the Gamergate controversy had been swirling for the previous six months. The experiment lasted just three weeks, but in that short time WAM was able to field hundreds of complaints of harassment; this required sorting through many that were fake or incorrect, enduring ones that were themselves harassment aimed at WAM and its volunteers, and then communicating with the victims to help WAM escalate their complaints to Twitter. This tiny glimpse—just several hundred complaints, and only those who knew to seek help through WAM—highlighted how beleaguered some of these victims were, how surprisingly complex Twitter's mechanisms were, and how they were at times ill-suited to the kinds of harassment women were experiencing. But it also helped reveal the labor required of an "authorized reporter." The work was time-consuming and emotionally exhausting, WAM drew fire from trolls and misogynists who punished it for its efforts, and the partnership between WAM and Twitter was fraught.

Other organizations do some of the support work around platforms, without partnering with them directly—particularly addressing the problems of harassment and hate speech. Heartmob was launched in 2016 by Hollaback, a group initially committed to ending the street harassment of women.[55] Heartmob was designed to encourage bystanders to become allies to victims of online harassment; volunteers made themselves available to answer a harassed user's request for advice or emotional support, help in documenting a case of online abuse, or even call a user to support her as they faced her harassers. Others, like Trollbusters and Crash Override, make similar efforts to support and advise victims of harassment outside of the official avenues Twitter provides.[56] Some of these organizations also collect data on what users are encountering and how platforms respond—data that the platforms either have or could gather, but seem reticent to make available publicly.[57]

Others have attempted to develop software that function alongside social media platforms to give users more tools for fending off unwanted content or attention. Blocking tools like Blockbot and Blocktogether are intended to aggregate the efforts of users to identify harassers and trolls, developing shared lists of offending accounts.[58] These tools represent yet another sliver of the labor of moderation: not only the labor of each user that is aggregated by these tools, but the labor that has gone into developing the tools themselves, often requiring independent and unfunded designers to work with or around the platform APIs. As Stuart Geiger notes, this labor counterbalances the "labor" of harassment itself: "The work of harassment can be efficiently distributed and decentralized, with anonymous image-boards serving as one of many key sites for the selection of targets. . . . In contrast, the work of responding to harassment is much more difficult to scale, as each of those messages must be dealt with by the recipient. . . . With blockbots, counter-harassment work can be more efficiently distributed and decentralized across a group that shares common understandings about what harassment is." Regardless of their approach or effectiveness, these independent grassroots efforts constitute another part of the labor that, in its current incarnation, supports and executes the process of content moderation.

There are moments in which platforms recognize, or are forced to acknowledge, that they need outside expertise. The array of issues platforms find themselves adjudicating are both myriad and sensitive. From time to time, and usually issue by issue and controversy by controversy, major platforms have sought the aid of existing organizations that have the expertise and legitimacy to help them address an issue with sensitivity, and shore up their legitimacy in doing so. Kate Klonick highlights these partnerships by taking a closer look at Twitter's Trust and Safety Council,[59] announced in 2016, which reveals the range of nonprofit and activist organizations Twitter had already been turning to more informally: groups with expertise in a particular kind of harm (the Anti-Defamation League, the National Domestic Violence Hotline), groups dedicated to a vulnerable population (ConnectSafely, the Family Online Safety Institute, GLAAD), and groups advocating for user rights online (the Center for Democracy and Technology, Internet Watch Foundation).[60]

Everyone

Finally, some platforms ask users to rate their own content when it is first posted, and then provide filtering mechanisms so that users can avoid content they want to avoid. Unlike flagging, this enlists every user, distributing the work more equitably and diminishing the problem that those doing the flagging do not represent the whole community. The challenge in this approach is how to get users to rate their own content fully and consistently.

Platforms don't want to introduce too many steps at the moment a user posts, worried that an unwieldy and multiclick interface will discourage participation. So any user-rating process either must be lean and depend heavily on defaults or it must happen less often. On Tumblr, for example, each user is asked to rate her entire blog, rather than each post, and the default rating is "safe." While this makes the interface quite simple, the rating can only serve as a blunt instrument: a Tumblr user who occasionally posts risqué art and a user who regularly posts pornography might have the same "Explicit" rating. Users inevitably have different interpretations of what is "adult" or "violent" or "not for children," especially regarding their own posts, leaving the platform with limited means for ensuring consistency across users.

User ratings make up an important component of the moderation of some online platforms. When Flickr first launched, it quietly encouraged uses to follow the NIPSA rule: Not in the Public Site Area. Photos considered adult by Flickr's moderators would be tagged as such, so as not to appear in search results. In 2007, Flickr shifted this to a user-assigned rating system, where users were expected to rate the photos they post as "safe," "moderate," or "restricted."[61] Flickr's moderators can change a photo's ratings if they feel it has been incorrectly assessed and can suspend a user for regularly failing to rate photos correctly. YouTube can "age-restrict" specific videos or channels; users who come across these videos are warned that they are about to see restricted content and must click through to the video. Registered users under the age of seventeen cannot click through; neither can users who have not logged in, as YouTube has no way of knowing their age. (This also benefits YouTube/Google, subtly encouraging users to sign in, which is in the company's broader financial interests.)

Just as with flagging, user ratings are invariably subjective. Ratings may vary because of differences in how the same content is assessed by different users, or because of differences in how users interpret the vocabulary of the ratings system, or both. What I might rate as "moderate," you might very much not. And when I rate my own contributions, though there may be incentives to rate accurately, I may also be subject to a perceptual bias: my own content is likely to seem acceptable to me. And because it is in the interest of a producer to be found by other users, ratings can tend to be strategic: does rating it as more acceptable than it actually is avoid its being filtered away from most people? Does rating it NSFW give it more allure than it may deserve? Finally, ratings are relative to one's own understanding of the platform and its norms, which come partly from the platform itself and partly from the encounters a user might have on that platform. For a user who regularly explores the racier side of Flickr or Tumblr, and regularly encounters other like-minded users there, the platform as a whole may seem very permissive; another person who uses the same platform to share only uncontroversial content may develop a different sense of what the platform might find acceptable. Their ratings may skew differently, relative to their perceptions of the platform.

Ratings systems on U.S. social media platforms tend to deploy one of two vocabularies: based on age, like YouTube, or on a spectrum of appropriateness, like Flickr and Tumblr. The rating systems for Hollywood film and, more recently, television, use similar vocabularies. But there is no reason why ratings must hew to these two vocabularies. Like U.S. television ratings, age appropriateness can be combined with indications of types of potentially offensive content, providing the user, parent, or filtering algorithm information to help determine whether to allow access to that content. Since digital content can convey a rich array of categorical information as "metadata," rating schemes are limited only by how much the platform is willing to ask the contributor at the moment of posting. However, the design of a rating system can have curious consequences.

Apple asks a great deal of developers when they post their apps to the App Store. Apple's rating system is not based on age or on a single spectrum of appropriateness. Instead, developers must assess the presence of ten different kinds of problematic content, such as "cartoon or fantasy violence," "horror/fear themes," or "simulated gambling," each assessed at one of three levels: "none," "infrequent/mild," or "frequent/intense"; Apple then mathematically combines these answers into a single age rating for the app, expressed in terms of age: 4+, 9+, 12+, 17+, or "No Rating."[62] These ratings matter. Without a rating, the app cannot appear in the App Store. Apps rated 17+ present the user with a warning before they can be downloaded; the other ratings are provided as information in the app store, and can be filtered out for individual accounts, presumably by parents. But the calculus behind the transformation of descriptive answers into age rating is mysterious, and largely opaque to the developers. Some have experimented to see what answers will warrant particular age ratings, and raised questions about what the difference might be between saying your app has "intense" "sexual content and nudity" or saying it has "mild" "graphic sexual content and nudity"—which end up generating different age ratings.[63]

THE LABOR AND THE LOGISTICS

Each social media platform has cobbled together a content moderation process that draws on the labor of some combination of company employees, temporary crowdworkers, outsourced review teams, legal and expert consultants, community managers, flaggers, admins, mods, superflaggers, nonprofits, activist organizations, and the entire user population. Not all platforms depend on all of these different labor forces, and no two do so in exactly the same way. What I have laid out in this chapter represents the terrain of work that together constitutes the often invisible, mundane, and embedded logistics of content moderation. Given the scope and variety of this work, it should give us pause when platforms continue to present themselves as open and frictionless flows of user participation.

Each part of this process is a kind of answer to the problem of scale: with numerous interactions, but limited resources to attend to them all. Each element provides a way for either a few people to do a great deal with limited resources, or a lot of people to each do a little, together. A generous interpretation would see these as attempts, some more successful, some less, to apportion the immense labor of content moderation to those best positioned to do it. Rating content falls to producers, who know the content best; flagging abuses falls to the victims, as they are most aware and most in need; disputes in a foreign language fall to internally employed field experts, or crowdworkers drawn from that culture or region; adjudicating the hardest cases falls to the company leadership, who can maintain consistent policies and enforcement across the site, and bear the responsibility for and consequences of a bad decision.

A less forgiving interpretation is that these are arrangements of expediency, even exploitation. Social media platforms have successfully cemented the idea that users pay for their services not with dollars but with effort: posting, commenting, liking, reviewing, forwarding. Users have accepted the notion that their microcontribution, their labor, is the fair price for whatever value and satisfaction they get from the platform. Adding rating and flagging to the user's already long list of jobs is a small ask. Crowdworkers are a cheap and flexible labor force who can perform the kind of detection and classification that machine-learning techniques can't quite do, can be flexibly moved (or hired and fired) as different kinds of user behavior wax and wane, and can absorb the psychological toll of wading through the mind-numbingly mundane and occasionally traumatic. The scope and character of that labor force remain hidden from the clean hallways and day-glo cafeterias of Silicon Valley headquarters, and from the legal protections attached to traditional employment. The crafting of the rules themselves stays nearest to the platform, where it can be aligned with and help extend the performed ethos of the company, including the promises made to advertisers, and controversy and criticism can be managed with nearby public relations and legal expertise.

I think both these interpretations have some truth to them. Media industries, new and old, have tried to balance serving the public and serving themselves. Moderators, both the internal teams and the crowdworkers, probably are motivated by a personal and institutional desire to help protect their users and affirm a moral baseline, and a belief that this division of labor between moderators and users is a good approach for doing so. But such aims cannot be disentangled from the economic imperatives that drive moderation too, especially under the pressure of this highly regimented, breakneck, and compartmentalized work process. And, whether we like the particular division of labor a platform settles on, there has to be *some* division of labor, and it undoubtedly will demand some effort from the platform and some from the users.

We can and should ask questions about judgment, self-interest, and structural constraints at any point along this chain of work. Anyone, at any level of this enormous undertaking, can make a mistake, be ill-suited to the task, or implement a partial or skewed set of values that does not match those of the users. But this intricate division of labor raises two additional challenges: the *coordination* of these efforts and the *translation* of both concerns and criteria between the different layers.

The challenge of content moderation, then, is as much about the coordination of work as it is about making judgments. First, decisions the press or disgruntled users see as mistaken or hypocritical might be the result of slippage between these divisions of labor—between what is allowed and what is flagged, between how a policy is set and how it is conveyed to a fluctuating population of crowdworkers, between how a violation is understood in different cultural climates, between what does get objected to and what should. A platform might instantiate a reasonable rule with good intentions and thoughtful criteria, but that rule may be interpreted very differently by the internal policy team, the temporary reviewers in another part of the world, the community moderator on the ground, and the offended user clicking the flag. Policy decisions made by a company may too slowly filter down to those doing the actual reviewing; shifts in users' sensibilities or surging problems may too slowly filter up to platform leadership. This is a problem for platforms that seek consistency: as one representative of Facebook put it, "The central goal of all enforcement is repeatability at the kinds of scale we're talking about, because if Facebook or Twitter or whoever can't do the policy the same way over and over again given similar cases they don't have a policy. They have some cool aspirations and then chaos, right?"[64]

Second, perhaps our concerns about what is allowed or prohibited should be paired with concerns about how platforms organize, distribute, and oversee new forms of labor—from soliciting the labor of users as a voluntary corps of flaggers, to employing thousands of crowdworkers under inequitable employment arrangements, to leaving the task of setting and articulating policy to a tiny community of San Francisco tech entrepreneurs who have been socialized and professionalized inside a very specific worldview. Spreading the work of moderation across these different labor forces, and organizing them as a computational flow of data, transforms a human and social judgment of value and harm into a logistical problem-solving exercise.[65] All these arrangements need to be scrutinized.

The challenges of coordinating the distributed and decentralized work of moderation are probably most acute at the points of contact. Between flaggers and crowdworkers, and between crowdworkers and policy teams, are membranes across which must flow both expressions of principle in one direction and expressions of concern in the other. At these points of contact, these expressions get rewritten, translated into a new form that is meant to both retain the meaning and fit it to the work that will respond to it. These translations can introduce distortions, ambiguities, and even new meanings.

For instance, enlisting the crowd to police itself can work at this scale only if the concerns of users can be transformed into manageable bits of data.[66] When a user flags some problematic content, the character of his concern must be reduced to fit the data entry format provided: the flag itself, its particular submenus, time codes, and so on. This takes an affective, socially loaded, and meaningful expression of a user, scrubs it of emotion and detail, and restates it in desiccated terms. What may have been "Ugh! That's terrible!" becomes "flag :: hateful or abusive content :: promotes hatred and violence :: 5:40." The data subsumes and comes to stand in for the users and their objections.[67] Something is lost, and something is added.

Similarly, when policy teams craft specific guidance for crowdworkers, as in the leaked documents that began this chapter, they must translate the platform's community guidelines into instructions that will suit the modular, rapid work of the reviewers. But these two documents are not congruent in their spirit, emphasis, or detail. One is a performance of principle, the other combines a restatement of those principles with internal rules not shared with users, ad hoc tactics harvested from the moderation work itself, and the scars of past incidents and external pressures. Again, much is lost and much is added.

Many of the problems with these systems of platform moderation lie in the uncertainties of this distributed system of work, and they breed in the shadow of an apparatus that remains distinctly opaque to public scrutiny. Platforms do an injustice, both to effective moderation and to the workers involved at every level, when they hide the character and arrangements of this labor. This makes it extremely difficult to understand why particular decisions are made, why certain rules are inconsistently enforced, and how the review process can be improved—not only for the user who might want to dispute a decision, and not only for the public who should have a better understanding of these inner workings, but even for the operators of the platform themselves.

Some content policy managers are hoping that more sophisticated data collection and analysis will help them better address the logistical challenges of content moderation. Platforms manage themselves through the gathering of data, and they gather an immense amount of it. This is no less true for the procedures of content moderation, for which platforms also now collect data. But data is never definitive; it always requires interpretation. Imagine that the data on our platform suggests that a great deal more nudity was removed this week. Was more being posted? Were flaggers being more sensitive? Were community managers in revolt? Was a new population of crowdworkers implementing the criteria differently? Did a policy change or a high-profile piece of viral content subtly shift what users think is acceptable to post, or what they think they can get away with? It is extremely difficult to parse the fluctuations with logistics this complex and distributed, workers differently situated and motivated, and the whole system constantly in flux.

With more clarity, this work could be better managed, more effectively audited and researched, and perhaps more trusted. Users might not immediately assume that the platform is being hypocritical, self-interested, or spineless, when in fact a decision might be coming from somewhere along this chain of labor that does not align with the stated policy. This does not mean that content moderation must all be performed publicly, or that it must be flawless. It means that platforms must stand accountable for constructing this chain of labor, for making cogent decisions about how this work should be done and by whom, for articulating why moderation should be parceled out in this particular way, and for articulating clearly and publicly how they plan to make their moderation effective and responsive while also protecting the labor rights and the emotional and social investments of everyone involved. And while it may be too much to ask, these statements of accountability would be stronger and more persuasive if they came not just from each platform individually, but from all the platforms together as industry-wide commitment.

6

facebook, breastfeeding, and
living in suspension

Last year, . . . while you were entertaining the virtual masses, I (along with millions of other women around the world!) was busy creating and nourishing human life. Not just one life, but two. That's right, Facebook. I grew two tiny people inside my womb, birthed them, almost died in the process. . . . Why am I sending this to you, Facebook? Last week, I posted a picture of myself breastfeeding my newborn twins using my Facebook account. I posted this picture to a pro-breastfeeding fan page, to help encourage other mothers. . . . But you took that picture down. You took hundreds of pictures down. You told me my picture is offensive. Inappropriate for children. . . . I spent this last year putting forth every effort of my being to make this world a better place. I contributed two beautiful children. My first and last priority in life is helping them become amazing and happy people in every way I know how. And so, Facebook, I wonder. I really wonder. What did you do last year?

April Purinton, "An Open Letter to Facebook," February 2010

Social media platforms struggle with a fundamental tension. No matter how they handle content moderation, what their politics and premises are, what tactics they choose, it must happen at a *data scale*. Such massive platforms must treat users as data points, subpopulations, and statistics, and their interventions must be semiautomated so as to keep up with the relentless pace of both violations and complaints. This is not customer service or community management but logistics—where the content, and the users, and the concerns, must be distributed and addressed procedurally.

However, the user who is the target of harassment and the user who is summarily suspended experience moderation very differently. The experience of harm and of content moderation is at an *intimate scale,* even if that user knows, intellectually, that moderation is an industrial-sized effort.[1] "This is happening to me; I am under attack; I feel unsafe. Why won't someone do something about this?" Or "that's my post you deleted; my account you suspended. What did I do that was so wrong?" The press also tends to cover moderation at this intimate scale: it challenges the actions of a behemoth company by pointing out a single violation and shows the people who were misunderstood or harmed by it. Compelling, human-sized stories fit the journalistic frame well, but they are orthogonal to the scale at which social media platforms process intervention.

It may be that this gulf can be bridged. Users may become more aware of this sociotechnical apparatus and their place in it; social media platforms might better recognize that impersonal interventions make users feel personally judged or silenced. On the other hand, it may be that these scales are simply irreconcilable, that interventions made at a data scale will always run up against the lived experience of those interventions, felt intimately by individuals.

Thus far, this book has focused on the platforms, and the platform managers: how they think of their role as moderators, what they do, what problems they encounter, how they justify themselves in the face of criticism. But content moderation is also a lived experience. Every deletion or suspension involves specific users; every rule draws a line through a community, that then adjusts around it. In this chapter I want to consider moderation from the user's perspective, not just in the moment of being harassed or flagging content or having a post removed, but as a lived and ongoing negotiation with the platform—sometimes a negotiation with the interface, sometimes a negotiation with the company itself, and sometimes a public reckoning about our shared values.

Social media platform managers are certainly aware of and attentive to the users they serve and, sometimes, must also police. But those users are so numerous that they typically can be known only either as data or as a composite type—rarely as individuals, and only in the briefest exchanges. However, around a small set of contentious issues, platforms have been forced to confront the ways their rules affect people and communities, and to recognize that some users understand some content and behavior in very different ways than does the platform's management. And at times, that management has found it necessary to interact with and even collaborate with members of that community, to shape fairer policies.

Undoubtedly, every kind of platform intervention has rubbed someone the wrong way. But the battles that have cropped up, between social media platforms and specific user communities that contest their rules and their right to impose them typically do so because the issues involved strike a broader cultural or political chord.[2] Some are issues that precede and extend beyond the platform: norms that are already contested in the broader public realm, and are coming up for public litigation because a platform is weighing in on them. Some are political movements seeking to be seen and legitimized by their presence on social media. When a platform determines that some content should be banned, its proponents can feel as if that decision settles on top of and reifies a litany of previous efforts to silence that community or marginalize that activity.

I could just as easily use as an example a community that feels it gets too little intervention from platforms, such as women enduring harassment and misogyny. Because of the scope of this problem, there is already a substantial amount of superb scholarship and journalism documenting the experience of harassment and the efforts to spur more involvement from the platforms.[3] This could tell a parallel tale about platforms having to listen to and adjust for an angry user constituency.

Instead, I want to consider a community of practice that finds itself running afoul of some edge of a platform's moderation policy, but whose members nevertheless feel they have a legitimate right to participate. Maybe it is a rule against them directly, that they feel is too restrictive— activists who reject legal prohibitions against public nudity and find their posts and images removed for precisely the same reason. Maybe it is a rule that, though not directed at them, works against them anyway—such as the drag queens suspended from platforms that require users to have just one, "real name" identity. Maybe it is a vocal political group like the "alt-right," whose adherents use provocation as a political weapon, inducing the platform to suspend them so they can use the decision itself as further ammunition. Or maybe, as in the debates around breastfeeding photos, it is a community seeking an exception to a blanket rule, and finding it must push back against social media platforms that are unaware of or unable or unwilling to carve out and adjudicate such an exception.

The dispute between Facebook moderators and breastfeeding mothers has lasted more than a decade. It has quieted in the past few years, though this does not mean it is resolved. At its peak, this disagreement powerfully shaped not only Facebook's policies, which did change in response, but also how Facebook management came to understand the job of moderation, and how users slowly came to understand how Facebook moderates. Facebook is not the only platform to struggle with the question of whether images of breastfeeding are acceptable or unacceptable; similar questions have arisen for Livejournal, YouTube, and Instagram, though not to the same degree or with the same public visibility.

The debates about breastfeeding photos on Facebook may feel like too specific an example to concentrate on, and far from other kinds of concerns that now plague social media platforms, like misogyny, terrorism, political propaganda tactics, and hate speech. But this is part of the problem for social media platforms and for how we think about them. All of the issues they police are to some degree specific to a community concerned about them, and different from one another. Yet they all coexist on the same platforms and are all policed by the same mechanisms. If the computer is a universal machine, platforms are universal media—they can be fitted for almost any communicative purpose, all at once. This is both their marvel and their hazard.

I find the debate around breastfeeding particularly illustrative. It is one of the earliest disputes about platform policies, and one of the most persistent. It has emerged on several platforms, and attained broader visibility through activism and the press. It hangs precisely on a social and legal issue that was already contested in public spaces before it was an issue on social media. And it is, not surprisingly, about women's bodies and their appropriate presentation in public, a perennial point of tension for Western debates about public propriety, for traditional broadcasting and publishing, and again for social media.

While breastfeeding was the central point of this dispute, it was woven into a larger set of questions about Facebook's comparatively strict rules against nudity: what are the reasonable exceptions to such a rule (accidental, artistic, nonrepresentational), how consistently is the rule applied, and how does a rule against nudity run up against the interests of users who find it reasonable, even empowering, to display their own bodies. While in Western culture women's exposed bodies are typically represented in media for the pleasure of men, and often for the commercial profit associated, women also expose their own bodies for a range of different reasons: as an expression of self-confidence, as a reclamation of their own sexuality, as a challenge to restrictive cultural standards of beauty (across the axes of age, race, and size), and in and around important moments in their lives that involve their bodies—not only breastfeeding but celebrating the experience of birth, expressing grief and resilience after a mastectomy, or asserting the legitimacy and beauty of their body after sexual reassignment surgery. This array of meanings does not fit neatly into the traditional, sexualized display of women's bodies as objects of desire, or the regulation of such display.

Tracking the arc of this dispute with Facebook highlights the impact that platform moderation can have when it impresses itself upon the complex terrain of social practice and meaning: the tensions between a platform's goal of simple, clear, and universal rules and the heterogeneity of its users' values and beliefs; the way platform managers find themselves having to wade into tricky, culturally contested issues; and the risk that rules can curtail the kinds of struggles for political visibility that take place on and beyond social media. Where a major social media platform sets its policy on images of breastfeeding leaves a heavy footprint on the broader social debate about breastfeeding in public, which is part of why the users irritated by the policy have continued to struggle against it instead of simply abiding by it or leaving the platform. It also highlights how, at the same time, the platform itself can become a site of contestation and activism: where the platform policies come under scrutiny, where newly politicized users can find like-minded allies and organize a collective response, both to the platform's policies and in pursuit of broader political ends.

Most important, the breastfeeding controversy shows the experience of users as they run up against platform policies, to reveal how their own understanding of and political commitments behind their practices must contend with a social media platform's efforts to impose guidelines, the real workings of its moderation efforts, and the contours of the public debate in which platforms find themselves. To this end, I interviewed several of the women who were most active in the efforts to push back against Facebook's rules, and explored discussions that took place on Facebook groups and blogs about the controversy (as well as speaking to Facebook representatives and surveying the secondary press coverage and Facebook's own public statements about it). I selected these women not because they were typical but because they were the most outspoken, the most recognized by the community that was politicized by this issue, and in some cases the ones Facebook contacted as the dispute persisted. I am not suggesting that theirs was a typical experience, if there is such a thing; rather, their experience of and insight into this dispute are particularly illuminating.

Karen Speed and her sons Quinn and Jesek; photo removed by Facebook July 2007. Used with permission of photographer and subject

In its earliest years, when Facebook was available exclusively to Ivy League college students, the site's managers probably didn't have to deal too often with photos of mothers breastfeeding their children. (It's not clear, back then, if Facebook even had "managers" responsible for content rules and removals, though as early as 2008 it had a "site integrity ops" team, and by

2009 it was touting its moderation efforts in the press.)[4] But when Facebook expanded its target membership in September 2006 from college students to anyone age thirteen or over, the influx of adults to the platform brought with it a much wider range of activities, well beyond the specific interests of well-to-do American undergraduates.

Less than a year later Facebook began removing breastfeeding photos and issuing suspensions to the users who posted them. Some of these photos were posted by new mothers to their personal profiles and shared with friends; others were posted to mothering or breastfeeding support groups on Facebook, where new mothers could get advice for the challenges involved in breastfeeding, and find some sense of communion and community with other mothers. A user would log on only to find an alert that her photo had been removed, or that she was suspended from the entire site for a specified number of days. The pro forma text from Facebook stated bluntly that her photo violated the rule against "nudity, drug use, or other obscene content"—a classification that was both vague and often insulting to these mothers.[5]

Facebook was not the first platform to run into trouble for restricting breastfeeding photos. In February 2007, a MySpace user found her breastfeeding photo removed and was threatened with account deletion if she posted it again. After the story generated some attention on a few interested "mommy blogs," and in the local press where she lived, a petition demanding that MySpace change its policy received more than eleven thousand signatures.[6] A year earlier, the blogging community LiveJournal experienced a full-blown "Nipplegate" when it clarified a rule banning nudity in "user pic" profile icons, and its volunteer abuse team requested the removal of one user's profile pic because it featured her breastfeeding. The incident garnered a great deal of heated discussion within the LiveJournal community,[7] and led to an email campaign, a one-day journal blackout, and even a (sparsely attended) "nurse-in" at the headquarters of parent company Six Apart, before an exception to the policy was made.[8] Nevertheless, it was on Facebook that breastfeeding images would become a visibly contested line of demarcation, not just between acceptable and obscene, but between the rights of a platform and the rights of users.

It is hard to know now how many women had photos removed and said nothing; this is not information Facebook makes public or is eager to share. Some women who found their images removed may have simply accepted the decision as legitimate, or were unwilling to complain about it publicly.

They may have been unaware that others were facing the same prohibitions, or were speaking out about it. But some of the mothers who had pictures removed or faced suspensions were more vocal, writing angry blog posts and in some cases turning to the local press to criticize Facebook's policy.

Having a photo removed, one that a user hadn't anticipated might violate the site's guidelines, can be an upsetting experience. This can be true for any kind of photo, but the impact may be even more palpable here. Some women spoke of feeling ashamed and humiliated that their photos, and their experiences as new mothers, were being judged obscene. Removal of a photo was literally an erasure of the woman and her accomplishment, and could easily feel like a particularly personal violation of a deeply held conviction:

> [Facebook,] I've been in quite a mood about this whole situation, honestly. I didn't just take [the photo] down because you were offended, but more because I am very disheartened and tired of the whole mess. . . . You have put me in a difficult situation because you have asked me to censor something that is very important and crucial to my life. You have asked me to put aside my personal convictions and pride in my life and my children's life and hide it. . . . I am very sad right now as I feel something dear to me has been stolen and I'm not talking about just a picture.[9]

Some angered users drew a parallel to broader efforts to prevent women from breastfeeding in public: the sidelong glances from disapproving passersby that nearly all breastfeeding mothers experience, or high-profile incidents in which breastfeeding mothers had been asked to cover up, to go the restroom, or to leave a restaurant or store—incidents that were also being publicized and discussed on Facebook and elsewhere by breastfeeding mothers. Facebook's restriction felt like an extension of the restrictions women continue to face, even in light of recent legal victories to protect and assure the right to breastfeed in public across the United States. And the contest over public breastfeeding is itself embedded in a broader debate about the merits of breastfeeding itself, in contrast to the use of baby formula; this was a culturally sensitive issue marked by judgment, conviction, and suspicion on both sides.

As more and more women faced deletions and sometimes suspensions, some were "discovering" that there was in fact content moderation at work behind the platform. But this did not mean that they clearly understood how it worked. Deletions and suspensions were generally accompanied by short, formal, and vague statements, and ways to contact the company or appeal a decision weren't easy to find. Users complained that Facebook's message to them often did not even indicate which photo was at issue; sometimes a user could discover what had been removed only by comparing her online photo album with what she had on her own computer. Some were frustrated by Facebook's inconsistency and opacity, making it difficult either to reasonably predict whether future photos would run afoul of these rules, or to generate any coherent response.

> During the time [the photo] was up, FB disabled my account several times. They gave me warnings via email, first telling me that they had removed objectionable content (without telling me what they found objectionable), then sending me pix they found obscene, warning me to removed them immediately or risk having my account permanently disabled. In each case, I immediately complied with their request. The last time they sent me two pix, one of me nursing my toddler while in labor with her sister, and the other of a baby at breast. Neither pic showed any nipple at all. I took them down as soon as I received the warning. In spite of this, FB deleted not only my [breastfeeding] page, but my [side interest] page and my personal page as well. I lost all my family pix and my friend list, and all the hard work I had put into [my breast-feeding page].[10]

All these women could do, alone or in groups, was surmise how their pictures had been identified, what criteria were being imposed and by whom, and whether these mechanisms were consistent from instance to instance. They began to develop their own theories about how their photos had been identified, how the rule was being imposed, how content moderation worked, and what motivated Facebook to handle breastfeeding images in this way. Sometimes these came close to how Facebook content moderation actually functioned, sometimes they were far off the mark. Given the opacity of Facebook's process, these presumptions were the best these women had to help them make sense of the penalties they faced. (Facebook has since made improvements in how it communicates with a user who is deemed to have violated a community guideline: identifying the photo in question, for example, and explaining somewhat more specifically which rule it violated. Still, users continue to complain about the opacity and inconsistency of this process.)

This struggle with the vagaries of Facebook's policy and its application were evident in my interviews. In this single quotation you can see the overlapping layers of speculation and uncertainty about how Facebook set and imposed rules:

> Nobody ever commented on a photo and said, "Hey, I think this is kind of inappropriate. I know my kid's on Facebook and I don't want him seeing this." You know? Nobody emailed me privately and said, "You know, I understand what you're trying to do here, but I just don't . . . I think you crossed the line." You know? There was none of that. It just . . . I'm sure someone reported it; I'm sure someone clicked the little button to report it and reported it as obscene. But yeah, there's no way of finding out why. And as far as I understand—you know, Facebook doesn't even review those, I don't think. There was a lot of speculation and of course at the time, I did a lot of research in finding out, you know, how that whole thing worked and some people said, "Well it has to be reported as obscene by two different people." And you know, everybody has a little different story. But I've heard too of people who have done tests where they put up a picture of a cat and have a friend report it as obscene just, you know, to test it. And they've had it removed too. So from what I can tell, there's not necessarily a human in the background making a judgment call either, of whether it violates the terms of service or not, you know? I can't believe that one person clicking it obscene automatically removes it. But yeah, there was some speculation as to who it would've been. You know, people ask me all the time, "Who do you think did it? Who do you think reported you?" And it's impossible to know. You know? . . . So that is frustrating too, that people can just anonymously decide what's obscene and what isn't, in their mind, and that perhaps Facebook doesn't even check it at all, they just assume that if people click it "obscene," it's really worth being called obscene.[11]

There are a number of misapprehensions in this woman's statement, a result of Facebook's opaque moderation process. But in the absence of more clarity about how this work is conducted, why, and by whom, Facebook left itself open to this kind of speculation. One user may suspect a covert cultural value judgment made by a rogue reviewer, while another might presume an insensitive identification made by an algorithm, and still another might suspect persistent trolls aggressively flagging photos from their Facebook

Anne Hinze and her son; photo removed by Facebook December 2008.
Photo by Anne Hinze, used with permission

group.[12] The opacity of the process made it difficult in practice to anticipate the rules. And it bred suspicion among otherwise healthy communities and networks of friends, as users wondered who might have flagged a photo they felt was beautiful, personal, legitimate.

It also bred suspicion about Facebook and its motivations. It was easy to imagine, especially as these women found their way into breastfeeding discussion groups and encountered others who faced similar penalties, that Facebook was deliberately targeting breastfeeding women, and these groups in particular. What did Facebook have against breastfeeding? News of each removal or suspension seemed to suggest a concerted effort whether one existed or not. At the same time, being in a group that circulates breastfeeding images, these users saw clearly how inconsistent the sanctions were, as they watched photo after photo similar to their own *not* being taken down. In these groups, women debated why one photo crossed a line and the next one in the series did not, or why one photo would be removed from a breastfeeding group where countless other similar photos remained. This perceived inconsistency undercut the legitimacy of Facebook's efforts, as they did not seem to represent a comprehensible standard.

Over the course of the next eighteen months, on their personal blogs and on Facebook, some of the affected women began to articulate a fuller criticism of Facebook's policy. Several Facebook groups emerged—the most prominent of which, Hey Facebook, Breastfeeding Is Not Obscene! grew to hundreds of thousands of members over the course of the next year. In these spaces, women began to sharpen a set of counterarguments to Facebook's policy.

Breastfeeding is physically taxing and emotionally draining. Despite idyllic media portrayals, it can be difficult, painful, and exhausting. For new mothers especially, unsure of exactly how to do it and accosted by unwanted opinions and conflicting advice, it can be an enormous triumph when it works. Many women talked about posting their photos as a marker of this hard-fought accomplishment:

> Breastfeeding isn't easy for everyone. A lot of women struggle through bad latches, poor milk supply, sore nipples, and other breastfeeding challenges and if they persevere, they want to share their success with others. Other people like to post pictures of themselves getting their university degree. Well, honestly, that was a walk in the park compared to the effort I put into breastfeeding my son.[13]

The act of taking the photo in the first place, sharing it with friends, and publicly posting it to a supportive Facebook group was a way to celebrate what they had achieved. Though most of the photos removed by Facebook were amateur shots, some were professionally done and carefully composed. Many felt that breastfeeding was aesthetically beautiful, a powerful representation of the bond between mother and child, and that this further argued against Facebook's deletions (though the site's policies do not weigh in on aesthetic quality). Though many of those who decried the policy were mothers of multiple children and were more experienced with breastfeeding, they often spoke on behalf of new mothers, noting what a challenging experience breastfeeding can be at first. Sharing photos can also be an important way to get medical advice and emotional support. For many women, breastfeeding is something that they usually do alone and have received very little instruction about; a new mother might post a photo in search of advice from more experienced women.

More often, a breastfeeding photo is a symbolic token, a badge of belonging to a community that would rally around a new mother. Facebook, and particularly the pro-breastfeeding groups in which many of these women congregated, provided an important source of advice and support and a strong sense of community. For some, social media provided a vital substitute for the kinds of support, both familial and communal, that were less and less available to new mothers. In Western settings especially, because the case for breastfeeding itself remains contentious, many women feel they have few places to turn to for practical advice or emotional camaraderie. By disrupting this community of women, Facebook might be making it less likely for women to try breastfeeding or to persist when it proved difficult:

> So I have so many moms that I've worked with that have been up against the world that tells them that they can't do it. . . . When women stopped breastfeeding and started formula feeding, we lost that wealth of knowledge, of how to meet your baby's needs at the breast, and how to respond with mothering instincts. And I see so many moms that, they have those mothering instincts, but they don't know how to trust them or listen to them because they're looking on Google, or they're looking in a book, or they're listening to their pediatrician's recommendations, and somewhere along the line, something is missing.[14]

The communities forming online provided, in their eyes, a kind of knowledge repository missing from modern culture. For Facebook to extend its "no nudity" policy into that community, and thereby disrupt its ability to embrace new mothers and circulate that knowledge, was for some a distinct failing of what social media promised to be.

For some, the value of these breastfeeding photos went beyond the women who posted them or the new mothers who saw them. Many felt that the public visibility of breastfeeding was vital to normalize it as available and legitimate; efforts to hide breastfeeding, whether that meant being asked to cover up in public or take down photos from Facebook, worked against this normalization. Seeing breastfeeding as inappropriate, dirty, or obscene—or not seeing it at all—would make it less and less acceptable for women and for the culture at large. As one interviewee put it, "What you permit, you promote."[15] In the notes from Hey Facebook, Breastfeeding Is Not Obscene! the group framed the issue in similar terms:

> When corporations and social groups (like Facebook) create and uphold policies that label breastfeeding as obscene or objectionable, the myths that breastfeeding is private, socially inappropriate or sexually explicit are perpetuated and this has a detrimental effect on societal perception and attitudes surrounding breastfeeding. This in turn has a detrimental impact on breastfeeding initiation and duration rates and stigmatizes and demeans women who are doing nothing wrong.[16]

On the Hey Facebook, Breastfeeding Is Not Obscene! group, it was common to see discussion not only about Facebook removals but about incidents in the news in which stores, airlines, and restaurants had asked a breastfeeding mother to cover up or go elsewhere. The argument about breastfeeding in public and about posting breastfeeding photos to Facebook regularly intermingled, as both were seen as working toward greater normalization for breastfeeding as a practice. "I think that breastfeeding photos do just as much good to normalize nursing as going out and nursing in public would. I think you'll almost experience more hostility from a photo than you will from just going out and nursing."[17] The support available on Facebook, both in the sense of community and in the circulation of photographic evidence, might offer a woman a stronger defense when she faced social sanctions herself:

> You know, if you're kind of a breastfeeder but not necessarily an activist—you know, maybe just knowing that there are other people out there that share the same views makes you a little bit more bold when you go into a restaurant and are asked, you know, to not nurse your infant. You know, maybe you go, "You know what? I have a right to breastfeed my child in this restaurant and I know that there's people backing me. I've got that group of—I don't know—33K on the 'Leaky Boob.' " Or whatever group that they're on on Facebook. And, you know, it gives you more boldness . . . you know, more information to stand behind, so that it does affect your life a little bit more even outside of Facebook.[18]

Some linked their critique of the policy all the way to scientific evidence of the relative merit of breast milk over formula. It was common to cite recent reports by the World Health Organization (WHO) and the Centers for Disease Control (CDC), both of which made a strong case for the health benefits of breastfeeding.

> On one hand, it is a public health issue. For many years, the World Health Organization has emphasized the need for mothers to breastfeed and has set minimum standards that many countries, including the United States, still have yet to meet. They have set these standards to help prevent the significant number of deaths of infants in our world. By removing pictures of breastfeeding, the message is sent that it is something shameful, something that should be hidden and not seen.

This can undermine the confidence and desire of future mothers to breastfeed their children, to the detriment of their children's health.[19]

If the diminished visibility of breastfeeding in public meant fewer women would attempt to breastfeed then, in the eyes of these women, Facebook's policy amounts to a public health concern.[20]

Though not all the breastfeeding photos that Facebook removed exposed the bodies of the mothers, commonly they did include exposed nipples, or breasts covered only by an infant. This was, according to Facebook, what made them unacceptable. But some found it frustrating that images of maternal care were being lumped in with images that were about the sexualized display of women's bodies. Calling these photos "obscenity" seemed to sexualize a moment that was distinctly not sexual, but rather a natural and essential part of mothering. "If the baby's in the picture and they're in the moment of feeding the baby, or about to feed the baby, or maybe the baby let go and is smiling and reaching for the mom's face, but the nipple's exposed, that's not a sexual moment. That's not a pornographic moment."[21]

For some, breastfeeding should be an exception, the same kind of exception represented by state laws that allowed for public breastfeeding where nudity is otherwise prohibited. Others connected Facebook's strictures to a long-standing, feminist critique of Western culture, that women's bodies, and breasts in particular, have been hypersexualized, treated exclusively as objects of male desire at the expense of all of their other aspects, including nutrition. "When you get down to the nitty gritty of it, it's because breasts are sexual. That's the problem. It's not about posting what you want on Facebook, it's because breasts in North American culture are intrinsically sexual here."[22] Most pointedly, some of the women whose breastfeeding photos were removed railed against the double standards they saw in what Facebook did allow. A quick search on Facebook turned up many, many other photos of women's breasts that they felt were more exposed and more salacious than their own:

> So I put into the search bar: common, different names for breasts. And immediately found all these different pages and fan pages. Like you know . . . large breasts . . . you know, all different sorts of—very much from a male perspective of oversexualizing breasts and there's thousands of fans of these pages. It wasn't just an individual posting one picture; it was—it was like pages with thousands of people. And absolutely offensively profane breasts. Posting pictures of breasts that were, you know,

distorted. Either graphic distortion from the computer (like computer generated) or just sort of from plastic surgery and . . . I was just amazed at how easily I found all these pages and all these pictures. So I reported all of them . . . I never got any response from Facebook.[23]

Several posts to the Facebook protest groups mentioned how easy it was to find hypersexualized images of cleavage, and even linked to those pages, to highlight what was apparently acceptable on Facebook. Some urged their fellow users to flag these images, and commented later on whether they were taken down quickly, or at all.

Because Facebook management was reticent to respond in the early days of this emerging controversy, aggrieved Facebook users were left to wonder why this double standard existed. Some saw it as an extension of the same double standard in American culture, where the sight of a woman breastfeeding causes anxiety in a society inured to sexualized images of breasts in media and advertising. Others noted the gender inequity both on Facebook and in Western culture, that women's nipples are taboo but men's are not, as in this comment from one of the organizers of the Facebook group, offered to the *New York Times:*

> Stephanie Knapp Muir . . . said the company's policy was unfair and discriminatory towards women. "If they were removing all photos of any exposed chest—male or female—in any context, at least that would be fair," Ms. Muir said. "But they're targeting women with these rules. They've deemed women's breasts obscene and dangerous for children and it's preposterous."[24]

Others linked it to Facebook's economic priorities:

> I believe that not only is their policy lacking an obvious need for the protection of breastfeeding; but it's also lacking in credibility. Thousands of pornographic pages exist, even after we've advocated to thousands to report them; that really shows that Facebook has an agenda, and it's certainly not the "protection of minors" that they like to claim.[25]

The women facing Facebook's removal of their breastfeeding photos articulated two kinds of counterarguments: that the policy was hypocritical, and that it was consequential. While in practice these two counterarguments were often interwoven, they strike me as representing two very different orientations. In both, there is the recognition that Facebook has the power to govern visibility, with material and semiotic consequences. But the first

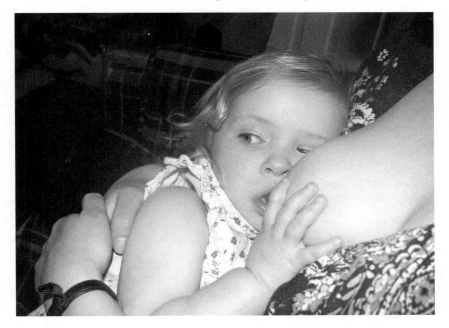

Heather Farley and her daughter; photo removed by Facebook March 2010. Photo by McKay Farley, used with permission of photographer and subject

is internal to Facebook, posed by aggrieved users to the rule makers, while the second is posed by citizens, many of whom already have a political stance on the issue, against a stakeholder who has power over what ends up in public view. What's important here is the overlap of the two, that the critique of Facebook's policy was both internalist and externalist, concerned with both the fairness of the rules and with their societal consequences.

However these decisions were framed, it was easy to see them as unreasonable and patronizing. Many of these women felt themselves subjected Facebook policies that were arbitrarily imposed—as if the women were being treated like children: "They started—I call it 'grounding.' I don't know what the official term was. But they started grounding people from being able to post pictures for a week if their offense was posting an inappropriate picture."[26]

The deletions seemed to go quiet between about November 2007 and November 2008. But in November 2008 there was another surge of removals and suspensions, once again angering some women and generating discussion in the Facebook groups devoted to the issue. By December 2008 more than eighty thousand people had joined the Hey Facebook, Breastfeeding Is Not Obscene! group, and more and more of the discussion revolved around getting Facebook to change, or at least better articulate, its position. Heather Farley, after having some of her photos removed, wrote a letter critiquing Facebook's policy that circulated widely online; in it she argued that the policy amounted to gender discrimination. The same month, Kelli Roman (cofounder and admin of the Hey Facebook group) and Stephanie Muir, both of whom had had photos deleted, organized a protest.[27] On December 27, 2008, two dozen women took part in a "nurse-in" outside Facebook's headquarters, then in Palo Alto. The next day, eleven thousand Facebook users joined in a virtual protest, replacing their profile pictures with breastfeeding images.

It would be a mistake to imagine that these women were isolated users, or that this was their first encounter with restrictions on public breastfeeding, or even that they were shocked by Facebook's efforts. Many of these women were already connected to this issue and one another—both on Facebook and beyond it, in their local and professional communities or as strangers who shared specific political goals. Many of them had found the protest communities on Facebook before ever having their own photos deleted; some were also involved in offline support groups in their own communities. The women who organized the 2008 protests, and many of the others who took part in the nurse-in or spoke to the media, were not new to these issues. As one woman put it, "Facebook, you're messing with the WRONG lactivist."[28] Farley, Muir, and Roman were all self-proclaimed "lactivists": they were already politically active promoting breastfeeding, defending the right to breastfeed in public, and criticizing companies that sold and promoted baby formula. Several were health and education professionals, others were doulas, who assist in the birthing process and advocate for women going through childbirth, and others were lactation consultants, who train new moms in the process of breastfeeding. Some posted their photos not in ignorance of Facebook's policy but as a challenge to it, and to the broader cultural taboo they saw as so problematic.

For other women who didn't already have a political or professional investment in the issue, having a photo deleted led them to these communities and helped to radicalize them. Some found their way to Hey Facebook, Breastfeeding Is Not Obscene! or other breastfeeding support pages, to discover both that they were not alone and that there was a well-established case for seeing Facebook's restrictions as aligned with other forms of public restriction of women and their bodies. Their deleted photos suddenly gained a political valence they may not have had when they were posted:

> One of my birth clients had started some sort of a Facebook group—I can't remember what it was called now, but kind of like a Bring Back [Her Name] or something page on Facebook. And that was gaining a lot of momentum, you know? People were joining that and that's when I started finding out that there was a ton of people out there that had been affected by very similar situations, you know? That they've had their accounts deactivated because of breastfeeding photos or because of maternity photos or whatever. It seemed like perhaps Facebook was kind of picking on breastfeeding photos and that kind of thing. So there was a pretty large community of support that started building pretty quickly after it happened. I think that gave me a little bit of the courage that I needed to, you know, step forward and contact media.[29]

Not only did these women find their way to this community; urged by that community to poke around to see whether Facebook allowed more sexualized images of breasts, they might also come to experience Facebook as internally contradictory: "full of boobs" and at war with lactivists.

At the same time, add yet another contradiction: the women who pushed back on Facebook's interventions used Facebook to find one another. This helped bring newly aggrieved users into the community, and provided a space in which to discuss additional incidents and sharpen their arguments. "That's how they found each other, that's how they galvanized, 'Hey, I'm having this issue.' And 'Yeah, I heard about so and so, I should put you guys in touch.' And then a movement is born, and it's basically born on the very channel that is taking the stand against them."[30] It is a curious fact of the participatory web that social media platforms sometimes find themselves hosting their own critics. And when it came time to protest, Facebook itself became a means to do so, both for organizing real-space political actions and as a virtual venue for activism. These lactivists used Facebook to circulate their critiques of Facebook's policies and, by extension, its legitimacy as an intermediary.

Emboldened by the Palo Alto protest and the support they found online, these women began to flex their political muscles: calling for a class-action lawsuit, talking of a boycott against Facebook advertisers, and demanding that Facebook change its policy. Some drafted "open letters" addressed to Facebook and CEO Mark Zuckerberg, and shared them online. Their efforts began to draw more attention from the press. And they began to connect to other organizations with related political aims—most notably TERA, the Topfree Equal Rights Association, a women's advocacy group committed to ensuring the right of women to be topless in public. TERA set up a website to host some of the breastfeeding photos that Facebook had deleted, as evidence of a concerted push against women. Some of the women I spoke with were ambivalent about the link to the topless movement, while others saw it as aligned with their concerns about the gendered inequity of Facebook's policy. Others drew comparisons to other contemporary consumer activism, like the 2012 boycott of Chick-fil-A, and to broader political mobilization efforts like the fight for gay marriage.

As Facebook began to respond to these growing criticisms, it tried a number of tactical responses, including standing firm on the rule as articulated, apologizing for errors made by individual moderators, and noting the difficulty in scale of the task involved. Eventually it attempted to further clarify its nudity policy, as a gesture both to the communities affected and to the socially progressive value of breastfeeding.

In statements in 2009, in response to press coverage of specific incidents and to the efforts of the Hey Facebook group, Facebook made its first public statement specifically about breastfeeding photos. This was not a change in policy, but an attempt to clarify. The statement appeared in a few different versions, but went something like this:

> Breastfeeding is a natural and beautiful act and we're very glad to know that it is so important to some mothers to share this experience with others on Facebook. We take no action on the vast majority of breastfeeding photos because they follow the site's Terms of Use. Photos containing a fully exposed breast do violate those Terms and may be removed. These policies are designed to ensure Facebook remains a safe, secure and trusted environment for all users, including the many children (over the age of 13) who use the site. The photos we act upon are almost exclusively brought to our attention by other users who complain.[31]

Here Facebook was attempting to shift the issue back to a more defensible distinction, that it was not the breastfeeding that Facebook objected to but the nudity that sometimes went along with it. Nudity is a cleaner and more defensible line to draw, as a Facebook representative acknowledged in a comment less than a month later: "'We think it's a consistent policy. . . . Certainly

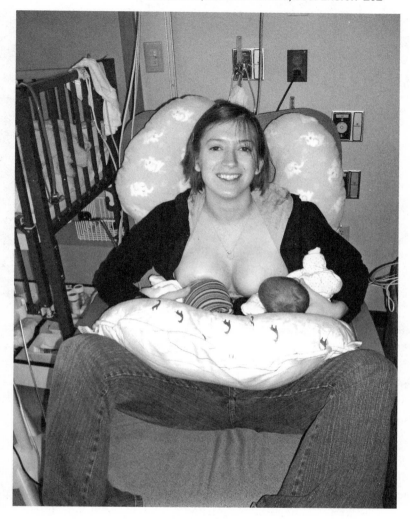

April Purinton, tandem nursing her sons, born prematurely, for the first time; photo removed by Facebook February 2010. Photo by Kyle Purinton, used with permission of photographer and subject

we can agree that there is context where nudity is not obscene, but we are reviewing thousands of complaints a day. Whether it's obscene, art or a natural act—we'd rather just leave it at nudity and draw the line there."[32] The clarification was sandwiched between an olive branch to breastfeeding women and an affirmation of Facebook's obligation to moderate the site, justified in terms of protecting children and being responsive to users. But

Emma Kwasnica and her daughter Sophie; photo removed by Facebook January 2012. Photo by Emma Kwasnica, used with permission of photographer and subject

parsing publicly what is or is not acceptable leads to skirmishes around the particular line being drawn. And for the breastfeeding community, Facebook had drawn its line precisely around the female nipple.

Perhaps Facebook management did not want to start establishing exceptions to the rule based on the social importance or aesthetic quality of the image, as other platforms have done. Basing the rule on the nipple offered Facebook a logical and more actionable distinction. But as one woman put it, "I don't know if they understand the territory they're wandering in."[33] Settling on this distinction merely shifted and focused the debate; lactivists responded by pointing out that many of the photos that had been removed (many still on the TERA website and easily reviewed) did not include exposed nipples, and that plenty of images that had not been removed did. At the same time, the discursive simplicity of the rule—no nipples!—made Facebook's efforts to police nudity even easier to criticize and ridicule.

Over the next few years, the imposition of this policy became increasingly commonplace, a fact of life for the women in these communities. Some women never ran into the policy again, while others faced dozens of removals and multiple suspensions. The groups established around the first removals persisted and grew, a place to report users who faced removals and suspensions, to trade tips for how to respond, and so forth.[34] One woman would disappear from Facebook, and news of her suspension would spread among the breastfeeding networks. When she reappeared, she would be welcomed like a returning traveler. The press would regularly highlight when Facebook's no-nudity policy was poorly implemented, including photos of nude paintings, sculptures, and baby dolls.[35]

But soon the community found a new cause célèbre. Emma Kwasnica had her first photo removed from Facebook in January 2009, and was an early and regular participant in the Hey Facebook group. After her first suspension, she wrote a powerful and widely circulated appeal to women to join the fight against Facebook.[36] In 2010, after several more photos were removed and she endured a series of lengthy suspensions,[37] she wrote a second piece arguing why breastfeeding must be more publicly visible, which also circulated widely.[38] She was joined by a handful of other women who were also outspoken about this issue, not only participating in Facebook groups but documenting the ups and downs of the issue on their own blogs, writing "open letter to Facebook"–style calls-to-arms, and organizing additional political actions.

Like many of her outspoken colleagues, Emma was not new to the tensions around public breastfeeding. She arguably fell to the left of most of the women supporting her: not only was she vocal about the right to breastfeed in public and share breastfeeding photos on Facebook, she advocated for less mainstream issues such as milk-sharing networks. Her critique of Facebook was animated not just by a sense of individual or community rights but by a distinctly feminist critique that saw Facebook's handling of this issue as fundamentally linked to male fears about women's bodies and patriarchal systems of control. In addition, she was practiced in techniques of public relations and political activism, and knew how to drive this issue into the public spotlight.

By 2012, her account had been suspended on four different occasions. In January, during yet another suspension, a new Facebook group was begun on Emma's behalf. The group, Stop Harassing Emma Kwasnica over Her Breastfeeding Pics, quickly grew as well. This was just one part of an array of political actions organized to protest Facebook's policy. A second wave of nurse-ins was held in February 2012 at Facebook headquarters and in thirteen other cities. In March 2012 the Stop Harassing Emma Kwasnica group held a "24 hours of Facebook censorship" online protest, during which they posted a breastfeeding photo every hour to see how many would be removed (two were removed, and two suspensions issued). In May 2012 a petition, "Facebook—amend breastfeeding-photo guidelines!" was circulated, gathering more than ten thousand signatures.[39] After enduring a three-day suspension, Gina Crosley-Corcoran (known through her blog as the Feminist Breeder) initiated her own "72-Hour Campaign to Normalize Breastfeeding on Facebook," in which she posted seventy-two breastfeeding photos in seventy-two hours; she was blocked again, for a week.[40]

By this time, the breastfeeding controversy had expanded in important ways. Many more women on Facebook were aware of the issue. Membership in the Hey Facebook group alone had passed 250,000, before some change in Facebook's workings cut it to 9,000; many in the group suspected that the reduction was in fact deliberate. Moreover, the frustration with Facebook's policy was increasingly being linked to other frustrations about how social media treated women. Concerns about the harassment of women, include misogynistic humor, unwanted advances, and violent threats, were growing more urgent. The resurgence of the breastfeeding issue around Emma Kwasnica was not just solidarity with one member of a community, it was part of an expanding critique of Facebook and social media more generally, along gender lines.[41]

From the breastfeeding community again came charges that Facebook itself was misogynistic, insensitive to women's issues.[42] In tandem with technology journalists and feminist bloggers, they drew parallels to Facebook's removal of birth photos, images of placentas, and photos of women showing their mastectomy scars, as well as those of tattoo artists who shared photos of their artwork for postmastectomy patients. Each removal pushed a similar button: not just that the images should be granted exemption from a rule against nudity, but that each is an all-powerful, nonsexual representation of a woman's body that had once again run afoul of Facebook's review. Note the use of the word "harassing" in the name of the group defending Emma Kwasnica: from the protestors' perspective, Facebook was not just being unfair or inconsiderate but was—especially as multiple penalties against the same women piled up—the aggressor.

Charges of hypocrisy regarding what Facebook did *not* take down grew as well. In November 2011, a Change.org petition demanding that Facebook remove several rape joke groups gathered more than 200,000 signatures, and many of the groups identified were removed.[43] The fact that Facebook moderates content, and particularly that it had been so intrusive around breastfeeding, offered a rhetorical counterpoint: as one contributor to the *Utne Reader* argued, "If Facebook were an unpoliced free-for-all, I would shrug my shoulders defeatedly at the stupid rape joke and move on. But it's a policed community. Facebook regularly monitors and removes content it deems inappropriate to a public forum, including anti-Semitic, anti-Muslim, and even I-hate-my-teacher pages. The site is particularly vigilant in removing any promotion of cutting, eating disorders, or drug use. Facebook even yanks photos of breastfeeding mothers."[44] A year later, when Women Action and the Media led a group of women's organizations to again call out Facebook groups dedicated to humor that denigrated women and celebrated sexual violence, the effort was circulated and supported by the breastfeeding community.[45]

This sense that the breastfeeding issue was now part of Facebook's larger perspective on women was strongly felt in the community:

I think it absolutely challenges our notion of neutrality, because [Facebook] has been sold to us, albeit free, but we have embraced it as something that is our forum, that lets us express ourselves as we want, when we want. And this is I think the first big challenge to that assumption. They may have—they may take down certain things that are offensive that may speak out against a group or may have hate speech or may—but this is the first time that they have organized against an entire—and they certainly wouldn't see it this way and not every person would see it this way. But to those who are on the other side of it, they feel that Facebook is essentially mobilized against an entire sex.[46]

The tech press was also increasingly aware of the now-five-year-old dispute. New controversies were often framed as the latest in a growing list of offenses, which meant that the breastfeeding issue was brought up again and again, as part of a critique that went beyond isolated incidents to be about platform moderation as a whole.[47] The Facebook guidelines for moderators leaked in 2012 began to shine light on the labor behind moderation, helping bring the whole apparatus into greater scrutiny. As the breastfeeding issue reemerged in 2012, some of the press coverage began to explicitly call on Facebook to change its policies. The *Guardian* posted a critique of the policy in its user content section Comment Is Free, even inviting users to send in their breastfeeding photos, which the *Guardian* promised to post to its Facebook page to see whether they would be removed. (After receiving hundreds of photos, the paper backed away from its promise, and produced a Tumblr gallery of them instead. This move was roundly criticized in the breastfeeding community on Facebook. Tumblr does not prohibit nudity, breastfeeding or otherwise.)

Once again, it was through Facebook that these critiques of Facebook could circulate. Inside the protest groups, and the groups merely dedicated to breastfeeding, participants circulated press coverage of the issue, concerns about related women's issues, and criticisms of Facebook more generally; women would report their photos deleted, or resurface after a suspension: "I plan to regularly, methodically, and insistently expose Facebook's misogyny and lackluster corporate responsibility. I plan to blog, Tweet, and yes, use Facebook, to reach as many people as possible to work together to ask them to change."[48] And they supported one another in other ways, celebrating new babies or commiserating about the challenges of motherhood.

Around this time, several clever challenges to Facebook's policy enjoyed viral success, including on Facebook. The most widely seen was a photo of a woman in a bath, whose oddly positioned elbows could be mistaken for exposed breasts; web magazine Theories of the Deep Understanding of Things posted the photo as a test of Facebook's removal process—and reported with glee that Facebook removed it within twenty-four hours.[49] Others highlighted the hypocrisy of Facebook's policy by posting men's nipples alongside women's.[50] One breast cancer awareness group posted a video of a woman demonstrating breast exam techniques on a topless man.[51]

The Facebook breastfeeding controversy also became further intertwined with political movements regarding the rights of women to be topless in public. As noted, this link had already been forged in 2009, when TERA offered to host deleted breastfeeding photos in order to document the controversy. But the issue of public nudity expanded greatly in 2012, with the emergence of the Free the Nipple campaign. Begun by Lina Esco as she worked on an independent film of the same name, Free the Nipple challenged public indecency laws that prohibited female nudity in public, where similar male nudity was deemed acceptable.[52] During the same time, the Ukrainian feminist group Femen staged topless protests in Europe and in the United States.[53] The #freethenipple hashtag grew in prominence over the next few years, picked up in the feminist blogosphere and the mainstream press, and spurred by high-profile celebrity support from Scout Willis, Chelsea Handler, and Miley Cyrus. All three had photos removed from Instagram.

THIS IS A MALE NIPPLE:

If you are going to post pictures of topless women, please use this acceptable male nipple template to to cover over the unacceptable female nipples.

(Simply Cut, Resize and Paste)

THANK YOU FOR HELPING TO MAKE
THE WORLD A SAFER PLACE.

"This Is a Male Nipple," circulated online in 2014. Used under CC-share-alike Creative Commons license (with gratitude to the earlier work on which it was based, by artist Micol Hebron)

The nudity policies of Facebook and Instagram, and their perceived hypocrisy about gender, became a recurring point of contention in the Free the Nipple movement, and a useful opportunity to press the larger issue. Free the Nipple, like the Facebook breastfeeding groups, circulated reports of images being removed from social media platforms.[54] In 2014, artist Micol Hebron circulated an image of a male nipple, suggesting that it be digitally added to cover women's exposed nipples in images;[55] her image went viral in 2015 and generated Instagram accounts full of these cut-and-pasted pasties.[56] (Hebron has been suspended from Facebook on several occasions.) This led to the Instagram account Genderless Nipples, which regularly posts user-submitted photos of nipples, some male and some female, so close up that they are difficult to distinguish.[57] That account was, at least in early 2018, still accessible.

It became increasingly apparent that challenging Facebook's and Instagram's rules—not just as unfair or incorrectly applied, but as unjust to women—was a powerful strategy. Facebook now had a "women problem" that united multiple communities around a common critique. The challenges also seemed to have an effect on the specific policies in question. In May 2013, after the WAM campaign against rape humor, Facebook added to its policy a clear statement condemning misogyny and threats of sexual assault veiled as humor, and indicated that it would more aggressively remove groups that trafficked in such discourse.[58] In June 2013, in response to public pressure, Facebook added a clear exception to its nudity policy to allow postmastectomy photos.[59] And in July 2013, in response to the broader critique of the opacity of their moderation process, Facebook debuted its Support Dashboard, which tracks any content a user has flagged, any complaints filed against the user's own content, and any actions taken by Facebook.

Finally, as reported in June 2014 but apparently implemented the previous month, Facebook changed its policy on breastfeeding images.[60] The relevant part of the policy on nudity—which is still prohibited categorically—now included the following caveats: "We remove photographs of people displaying genitals or focusing in on fully exposed buttocks. We also restrict some images of female breasts if they include the nipple, but our intent is to allow images that are shared for medical or health purposes. We also allow photos of women actively engaged in breastfeeding or showing breasts with postmastectomy scarring. We also allow photographs of paintings, sculptures, and other art that depicts nude figures."[61]

Many in the Facebook breastfeeding communities celebrated the policy change as a hard-fought victory. Some noted, though, that the policy had not changed in substance, only in emphasis. And some noted that the removals continued. It is possible that Facebook's new policy statement was an empty gesture—or, more likely, that these ongoing removals were a consequence of the slippage in Facebook's division of labor. It is hard to calibrate the work of hundreds of clickwork reviewers to apply an exception immediately and consistently. And a policy change doesn't necessarily affect which photos get flagged. Still, the issue certainly has cooled since the change.

Discussion has continued around Free the Nipple, surging again around a few high-profile Instagram deletions; clever memes poking at Western squeamishness about women's nipples continue to circulate. But a fascinating new wrinkle in this saga popped up in 2015, when the press noted a Twitter campaign begun by Courtney Demone, a transgender woman, asking #DoIHaveBoobsNow?[62] She uploaded topless photos of herself before and after the transition surgery, and wrote an article daring Facebook and Instagram to remove her photos. "At what point in my breast development do I need to start covering my nipples?"

Breastfeeding in public was already a publicly contested issue. Facebook did not invent this controversy, but in establishing moderation rules, it drew a line across it. This made Facebook and its moderation process a flashpoint for that same contestation, in new terms. So it's no surprise that, just as U.S. culture is in the throes of a debate about transgenderism, a community making a bid for greater cultural visibility again sees Facebook's moderation as a venue in which to test the existing boundaries of that visibility. Demone's article, of course, circulated widely on Facebook.

MODERATION AS A SPACE OF POLITICAL CONTENTION

The nearly decadelong struggle between Facebook and the breastfeeding community highlights what it really takes to moderate a platform that is being used, inhabited, by thriving communities. There are users who find that they must live with platform moderation. The interventions platforms make to police user activity intrude on existing communities, disrupt them, and rearrange them. At the same time, these communities can reorient themselves to face the moderation, whether to cope with it, evade it, or challenge it. After a great deal of effort and heartache, the Facebook breastfeeding community was able to provoke a change in the rules that acknowledged them and their values.

Nearly all aspects of the process of content moderation—setting the rules, fielding complaints, making decisions, and addressing appeals—are kept entirely hidden from users. Decisions are made behind closed doors, and built into the closed code of the platform itself. This opacity is a deep and abiding problem for content moderation and the workings of platforms. But even so, the last step, the removal of content and the suspension of users, is public—and can therefore become a public concern. And content or behavior that users find reprehensible, but that remains on a platform, is public too, and is therefore available as critical ammunition against the platform itself.

User pushback comes in a variety of forms: single users flagging content they dislike, groups of users coordinating their efforts to flag content they disapprove of, individuals complaining about a deletion or suspension (on the platform itself, on other platforms, on their own blogs, or to the press), users appealing decisions through formal channels, and groups of users turning to activism to express their outrage, about one decision or an entire policy. Furthermore, the platform itself can become a public venue for its own contestation: where policies are up for scrutiny, where support can be gathered, and where both the rule and its imposition can be challenged—in order not only to change it but to advance a broader political aim. The breastfeeding community was able to organize, sharpen its arguments, and find political allies against Facebook, on Facebook.

These are contestations around political visibility. Social media platforms can grant visibility and they can withhold it. For groups for which visibility is politically significant, the power of Facebook to render them invisible is threatening. At the same time, challenging Facebook's moderation as part of the unfair effort to hide and shame breastfeeding mothers turns out to be a way to win that visibility, on the platform and beyond.[63]

Contests around the rules imposed by social media platforms are not merely disputes about particular uses and where the line between appropriate and prohibited should be drawn. And they are not just attempts by users to claim the right to set the terms within which they participate online. As public expression has moved increasingly to these platforms, and as attention to the fact of moderation has grown, contesting the platform, its rules, and its right to intervene is becoming part of this political strategy around the issues themselves. Critics used Facebook's restriction of breastfeeding photos as a way to comment on the cultural hypocrisy of sexual mores and to connect their rule to the broader issues of breastfeeding in public and women's rights generally; critics also used Facebook's permissiveness toward rape humor and idle threats as a way to draw attention to the misogyny of online culture.

Social media platforms have become the terrain of political and cultural contest; that is apparent. But for political issues whose partisans seek visibility, access to social media platforms and the manner in which they are governed matter a great deal. The women aggrieved by Facebook's rule about breastfeeding photos were not calling for a social media platform that would allow all nudity: given their critique of the sexualized images of women's bodies they felt were all too available on Facebook, their concerns were clearly more nuanced. They believed that a blanket rule against nudity that included images of breastfeeding had implications both for the women who circulate these images and for the cultural understanding of breastfeeding.

These activists want breastfeeding to be seen, for a variety of personal, social, and political reasons. This makes them similar in aim and tactics to the performers and drag queens thwarted by Facebook's real-name policy, to protesters seeking attention and legitimacy on Twitter, to artists turning to social media to spread their political message. And it also makes them similar to the terrorists, the trolls, and the fake news opportunists, who in their own way want their visibility on social media to translate into increased political legitimacy. This is not to say that these groups are all equally deserving of visibility or recognition—just to note that each is turning to social media platforms in order to be seen. Distinguishing among them is necessarily a matter that platforms cannot avoid.

Questions of visibility extend beyond what can be seen, to what is even able to appear.[64] I mean "visibility" in the sense that some groups seeking legitimacy struggle to simply be seen against the wishes of those who would marginalize and silence them, such as proponents of gay rights or public breastfeeding; visibility in the sense that some kinds of antagonism between groups go unnoticed or uncommented on, such as the culture of violence against women; visibility in the sense that one group's speech is silenced as potentially dangerous to others, as in fundamentalist Islamic propaganda; and visibility in the sense that some kinds of images are seen as potentially dangerous to those who choose to consume them, such as "self-harm" images that may support anorexic, cutting, or suicidal behavior. Again, I do not mean to equate these efforts just because they all seek visibility. But they all, in some form or another and for different ends, seek to be rendered visible, in places where visibility can be a step toward legibility and legitimacy. This is one power of media: being visible on television, or in the news, or on social media, suggests that you count. Sometimes visibility is not just a political accomplishment but a triumph over the mechanics and governance of the medium.[65]

This case should also remind that moderation is not static: it is not the assertion of *a priori* rules and the subsequent enforcement of them. In this case, the practice emerged before the rule, the rule came under scrutiny, and the rule was eventually changed under pressure. Platform moderation is an ongoing negotiation—often an internal one, among the policy team, but sometimes with politically active user communities and sometimes on the public stage. It is both an internalist concern—what should the platform's rules be, how will they be enforced, what is a fair way to govern users?—and an externalist concern: how does what the platform allows or prohibits affect broader public knowledge and value?

Disagreements about the standards regarding breastfeeding in public coalesced around Facebook's decisions to prohibit similar kinds of exposure. That frustration moved from an online discussion of the perceived injustice, especially using Facebook itself, to find its way eventually to the front steps of Facebook's corporate headquarters. Disputing the rules set by platforms like Facebook provides an opening for political action online and in real spaces. And in the eyes of those newly motivated by this perceived injustice, the shift in Facebook's policy was a victory in the broader dispute.

The focus of this chapter has been Facebook, its policies, and its inconsistent enforcement of them, but this issue is not solely on Facebook's shoulders: there are undoubtedly users who are flagging these photos. If no one complained about breastfeeding photos, Facebook might not have had a conservative policy about them: Facebook has few policies that risk restricting and annoying users that do not also either honor a legal obligation, make Facebook more amenable to advertisers, or appease some broader swath of the user community. So while breastfeeding advocates and the tech press applauded Facebook's policy change, it is worth remembering that someone else's values were disregarded at the same time. Some gained in this particular negotiation over visibility, but some also lost. When the moderation tactics are about deletion, suspension, and removal, and changes to the rules can render a whole category acceptable that was not before, every decision will be political; every decision will have winners and losers.

It is worth noting that while Facebook and its moderation policies offered an opportunity for a public debate over values, and even provided a space to organize politically, it took political action, negative press, and a decade of "platform disobedience" to get Facebook to move (slightly) on this issue. There may be no way to satisfy the concerns of all users, to honor all ideological perspectives. But there are better ways for users to speak *to* platforms, as well as on them. If political visibility is at stake, then some form of political representation of the public in the governance of platforms is in order—not just as users, or eyeballs, or data points but as the voice of the governed.

7

to remove or to filter

More control over what you see and what you don't. *What's Safe Mode?* Safe Mode filters sensitive content in your dashboard and your search results. *Who's it for?* You, if you want it! Maybe you're happy to see sensitive content when you're scrolling through Tumblr, maybe you're not. Safe Mode puts that choice in your hands. . . . (If you're under 18: You're not able to turn off Safe Mode until you're older. You'll just have to use your imagination.)
Tumblr, "Safe Mode Is Here, Tumblr," June 2017

After Yahoo acquired Tumblr in 2013, Yahoo CEO Marissa Mayer promised "not to screw it up."[1] Still, devoted Tumblr users worried that their cool, web 2.0 image blogging platform would be domesticated by the nearly twenty-year-old search giant. One group, in particular, worried a great deal: those who used Tumblr to collect and share porn. This was and is a sizable slice of Tumblr's users: at the time, somewhere near or above 10 percent of Tumblr was "adult fare,"[2] including both fans curating their favorite professionally produced porn and amateurs sharing their own, self-produced explicit imagery.[3]

Tumblr has a more permissive policy about pornography than most social media platforms. Instead of prohibiting it, Tumblr asks users to self-rate: blogs with "occasional" nudity should be rated "NSFW." Blogs with "substantial" nudity should be rated "adult." In its community guidelines Tumblr explains this policy: "Tumblr is home to millions of readers and bloggers from a variety of locations, cultures, and backgrounds with different points of view concerning adult-oriented content. If you regularly post sexual or adult-oriented content, respect the choices of people in our community who would rather not see such content by flagging your blog . . . as Not Suitable for Work ('NSFW'). This action does not prevent you and your readers from using any of Tumblr's social features, but rather allows Tumblr users who don't want to see NSFW content to avoid seeing it."[4] Allowing pornography is uncommon but not unique among platforms; Blogger and Flickr take similarly permissive stances toward explicit content, and also ask users to rate their collections accordingly.

In May 2013, some Tumblr users noticed that blogs rated "adult" were no longer findable through the major search engines. A month later, Tumblr began using the ratings to selectively exclude posts from its own search tool. Posts from "NSFW" or "adult" blogs no longer appeared in Tumblr's search results, even if the post itself was not explicit, and regardless of whether the search was explicit. Actually, it was even more complicated than that: if the searcher already followed the explicit blog, that blog's posts would appear— if it was "NSFW." If it was "adult," the more explicit rating, those posts would not appear in the search results, even if the searcher already followed that blog.

Clear? No? It was an intricate and confusing arrangement, one that users had a hard time following and the company had a hard time explaining. The principle behind this intricate policy is not an unreasonable one: let users continue to post explicit pornography, while using the self-rating to shield users who do not want to encounter it. But enacting this principle meant codifying it in a series of if/then conditions that could be automated in Tumblr's search algorithm. And what the policy meant in practice was that while an explicit blog's existing followers could more or less still get to it, it would now be much more difficult for anyone new ever to find it, given that its posts would not appear in any search results. In addition, there were other assumptions hiding in the new policy: that the rules should be different for mobile users than for users on their computers; that "logged-out" users (which includes users who have not yet signed up for Tumblr) should not encounter explicit blogs at all; and that explicit Tumblr blogs shouldn't be appearing in search results on Google or Bing—or Yahoo. These represent somewhat different priorities, but get folded in with Tumblr's apparent concern for balancing the right to share pornography and the right not to encounter it if you choose not to.

From a public relations standpoint, Tumblr certainly could have been more transparent about the details of its original policy, or the changes it was making. David Karp, founder and CEO of Tumblr, dodged questions about it on *The Colbert Report,* saying only that Tumblr didn't want to be responsible for drawing the lines between artistic nudity, casual nudity, and hardcore porn.[5] Of course, Tumblr's rating system already asked users to make a different but equally murky distinction, between "occasional" and "substantial" nudity. And it is worth noting that Tumblr reserves the right to dispute or change users' ratings, suspend users for failing to rate their blogs accurately, and change the policy or the way it is implemented.

Certainly, there must have been some delicate conversations going on at Yahoo/Tumblr headquarters, for some time before these changes, on how both to "let Tumblr be Tumblr" (Mayer's words) and also to deal with all this porn, as "it may not be as brand safe as what's on our site" (also Mayer).[6] These are questions with real economic implications. Tumblr places ads only in its Dashboard, where only logged-in users see them, so arguably the ads are never "with" the porn, even on adult blogs—but they would appear alongside search results.[7] Yahoo may have wanted to prevent pornographic search results from turning up alongside that advertising, and its management also may have hoped eventually to pair ads with the blogs themselves—so that the "two companies will also work together to create advertising opportunities that are seamless and enhance the user experience" (Mayer again).[8]

What's ironic is that, I suspect, Tumblr and Yahoo were probably trying to find ways to remain permissive with regard to porn. They certainly were remaining more permissive than some of their competitors (so far), including Instagram,[9] Blogger,[10] Vine,[11] and Pinterest,[12] all of which made similar moves in 2013 and 2014 to remove adult content, make it systematically less visible to their users, or prevent users from pairing advertising with it. But to some Tumblr users, this felt like structural censorship, and broke the site's earlier promise to be an open publishing platform. As outspoken sex blogger Violet Blue warned, "Removal from search in every way possible is the closest thing Tumblr could do to deleting the blogs altogether."[13]

A semi-apology from Tumblr seemed to make amends, as did some changes following the uproar.[14] Tumblr subsumed the "adult" category under "NSFW" (since renamed "Explicit"). Blogs marked as such were again available in Tumblr's internal search and in the major search engines. And Tumblr promised to work on a more intelligent filtering system.[15]

CENSORS AND CHECKPOINTS

Media companies, be they broadcast or social, have just two basic things they can do with content that some but not all of their users find inappropriate. They can remove it, or they can hide it. Removal is the approach taken by most social media platforms, and by most traditional media, including broadcast radio and television, magazines, and recorded music. The advantages are numerous. There is the sense of assuredness and clarity that the problem is gone, the judgment rendered. Content that offends one user is likely to offend more, so removing it addresses multiple instances of offense; if it's gone, it cannot offend again. It demonstrates a decisive commitment to protecting the public, allows the platform to signal that it does not tolerate such content or behavior, and avoids associating the company brand with something offensive. And removal saves human resources later, having to adjudicate the same content or user again and again.

On the other hand, as we have already seen, removal comes with challenges. It is the harshest approach, in terms of its consequences. It renders the content or the user invisible on the platform. Removal is a blunt instrument, an all-or-nothing determination, removing that content for everyone, not just for those who were offended. And it runs counter to the principles of so many platforms: open participation, unencumbered interaction, and the protection of speech. Content policy managers are aware of this irony; several commented on how odd it is that, on a platform committed to open participation, their job is to kick some people off.

Disgruntled users who have had content removed or been banned from a social media platform sometimes cry "censorship." It is a powerful claim, but it is not entirely accurate. Users suspended by a platform, or even banned permanently, are not entirely shut out, as they can continue to participate on other platforms and on the broader web. This makes it hard to call this censorship in the strict sense. Moreover, "censorship" presumes a right to speak, and usually the kind of legal speech rights enshrined in the U.S. First Amendment and in similar protections around the world. But the First Amendment, and its corollaries elsewhere, are protections against restrictions by the state, not private companies. While some have argued that information intermediaries can have some of the same distorting or chilling effects that the First Amendment prevents the state from inflicting, there is currently no legal obligation on private providers to allow their users to speak, or to refrain from restricting users' speech, even if those restrictions are political, capricious, or unfair.

On most platforms, a suspended user can simply create a new profile and post again, turning platform governance into an endless game of whack-a-mole, where content reappears in slight variation, under new names, or from dummy accounts that can be identified only in hindsight. And while this whack-a-mole is a resource-intensive approach, it may be in platforms' economic best interest: while platforms do not want to host truly disruptive users, they do want as many users as possible, which means erring on the side of rehabilitation and second chances. They are vastly more willing to suspend than to ban.

Still, removal from a social media platform matters. For a user, being suspended or banned from a social media platform can have real consequences—detaching her from her social circle and loved ones, inter-rupting her professional life, and impeding her access to other platforms.[16] There may be other platforms available, but the banned user cannot take with her an entire network of people, an accumulated history of interactions, or a personal archive of content. And being excluded from the highest-profile platforms, where the most valuable audiences can be built, matters espe-cially. It's why the common admonition "If you don't like it here, just leave" is an insufficient defense of clumsy policies and toxic environments.[17] The longer a user stays on a platform and the larger it gets, the more she is com-pelled to stick with it, and the higher the cost to leave.

This means that even a perceived threat of removal has real effects. Creators adjust what they make, in an effort to stay within the rules or in response to having run afoul of them. This is, of course, the point: punitive measures like deleting a post or suspending a user for a day may deter the harasser going forward. But it also risks curtailing or chilling important speech. We cannot know how much never gets posted because users censor themselves, what adjustments they make in anticipation of the rules, and what conversations or perspectives are pushed into hiding or off the platform altogether.

In fact, to the extent that content moderation is somewhat akin to censorship, removing content or users is akin to the most profound kind of censorship. U.S. First Amendment jurisprudence has long treated interven-tions that preempt speech entirely as more problematic than ones that impose penalties after the fact, because preemption silences speech in the process.[18] Removing users from platforms not only limits their speech, it interrupts their ability to participate on that platform, and can interrupt their future speech as well.

Tumblr opted for the second, softer form of moderation: retain the content in question, but circumscribe its delivery. The same software architecture that serves up content can be used to hide content from those who might be offended, sometimes without their knowledge. Such *moderation by design* is not unique to platforms. It is the digital version of how adult content has always been handled: putting the X-rated movies in the back room at the video store, scheduling the softcore stuff on Cinemax after bedtime, scrambling the adult cable channels, wrapping the magazines in brown paper and keeping them on the shelf behind the counter.

Similar strategies emerged in the earliest efforts to deal with porn on the open web. The first attempts to regulate online pornography came in the form of either wholesale prohibitions on adult content or restrictions on access to it, usually by age. But such prohibitions found little support in a U.S. legal environment that had previously defined obscenity based on the judgment of a community, and a technical environment where information seemed to flow so promiscuously. More palatable was filtering software, which allowed individuals to block, on behalf of themselves or their children, a list of sites that offered adult material. Filtering is arguably a less invasive approach than removal. If the right balance is struck, the platform enjoys the traffic and revenue generated by both users seeking illicit content and those who prefer a "clean" experience.[19] Allowing sexual content for those who wanted it and handing responsibility to the individual appeals to American liberal values. On the other hand, critics challenged these tools for blocking too little and for blocking too much, especially when some of the blocked sites provided socially relevant material, such as sexual health advice. Others worried that filtering software was being installed by school administrators and office managers, allowing them to filter the web traffic of an entire school body or all their employees, often without the users' consent.

Social media platforms can incorporate the logic of filtering to a much more sophisticated degree. Platforms are intricate, algorithmically managed visibility machines.[20] They grant and organize visibility, not just by policy but by design: sorting and delivering information in the form of profiles, news feeds, threads, channels, categories, updates, notifications. Some content stays where you first posted it, some content is vaulted to the front page, some is delivered to your followers or friends—as you direct it, or as algorithms determine. Some content disappears, or falls away as it ages. Some users and groups are rendered visible to the public, others only to trusted users, others only in a response to a search query. Trending algorithms list what's popular according to some calculation of interest, over some period of time, across some population of users; different results are shown to different users based on who and where they are.[21] As Taina Bucher reminds us, social media platforms are about not only the promise of visibility but also the threat of invisibility.[22] If an algorithm doesn't recognize you or your content as valuable, to others it's as if you simply aren't there at all.

Platforms have many ways to direct the flow of information, structuring participation such that some actions are possible and others are simply unavailable. All aspects of a platform's material design can be understood, together, as a kind of architectural regulation.[23] A technology that facilitates some uses can do so only by inhibiting others. Software that offers a menu of options, logically, leaves off all others. And every contour of a tool can leave a subtle mark on what its users make with it. The video formats and coding protocols that YouTube requires determine how accessible the site is to content producers and to viewers equipped with different kinds of tools, and may subtly shape the videos themselves. Technical limits like the length of posted videos, and the rules dictating who gets to exceed these limits and who does not, establish a tiered hierarchy for content producers.

But the implicit constraints that follow from design can also be exploited as a deliberate form of architectural regulation.[24] YouTube makes it technically difficult to download its videos; this is not incidental to how the site was designed, it was a deliberate attempt to prevent users from copying, circulating, and reusing content, and an economic choice about how to sustain a business around these limitations. When it comes to moderating content, there are ways to use design deliberately to channel contentious content toward some users and away from others. But even more, any platform mechanism, however neutral it may appear, can also enforce moral judgments: how information is categorized, how users are verified, and how content is recommended. Each structural feature of a platform is a complex combination of technical design and human judgment, and each makes value assessments of some kind or another—not just what counts, but what should count.

When the design features of the platform are used to moderate, human judgment is transformed into a highly codified value system that's then built into the structure of the platform itself, materialized, automatically imposed, in many ways rendered invisible to the user, and thereby harder to call into question. In addition, these technical measures are never only in the service of balancing broad speech with a healthy and sustainable community; these tools are overdetermined by the competing impulses the platform faces, which usually means balancing moderation with commercial imperatives.

Most moderation by design takes a "checkpoint approach"—hide the content some people want from others who shouldn't have it. As it turns out, this is not a simple task:

First, the provider needs to know which content to hide. Those difficult distinctions—what to do with nudity that's artistic, casual, educational— never go away. But the provider can, as Tumblr does, shift the burden of making those distinctions to someone else—not just to dodge responsibility and avoid liability but to pass the decision to someone more capable of making it. Adult movie producers or magazine publishers can self-rate their content as pornographic, which many of them see as preferable to having the government do it. The MPAA sponsors its own board to rate all major films (G, PG, PG-13, R, NC-17), not only to avoid government regulation but also to offer parents guidance and to assist theater owners and advertisers who want to avoid explicit content. There are problems, of course: first, the "who are these people?" problem, as in the exclusive and secretive MPAA ratings board; second, the "aren't these people self-interested?" problem, as when TV production companies rate their own programs for broadcast. Still, self-interest is not necessarily incongruent with the interests of the provider: X-rated movie producers know that their options are the back room or nowhere; they gain little in pretending that their product is not pornographic, and gain more by clearly signaling its character to consenting adult customers.

Second, the provider needs to know who should not be given access to that content. It may seem a simple thing for a magazine seller to check a customer's ID as proof of age. But for that to work depends on a vast identity architecture already in place. A seller can verify a buyer's age because the buyer can offer a driver's license or other officially sanctioned identification: an institutional mechanism that, for its own reasons, is deeply interested in reliable age verification. That mechanism includes a massive infrastructure for record keeping, offices throughout the country, staff, bureaucracy, printing services, government authorization, and legal consequences for fraud.

Finally, there needs to be a defensible barrier between the content and the customer. The magazine stand has two such barriers, one architectural, the other financial: the upper shelf and the cash register. Adult books are placed safely behind the counter, pornographic magazines are wrapped in brown paper, adult videos are in the back room. The kids can't reach them, and will receive judgmental stares for trying. Even the tall ones can't slip away unchecked, unless they're also willing to engage in theft. The point of purchase acts as a compulsory checkpoint moment, and without proof of age there is no sale. In broadcast, the barriers were either temporal (adult content could be scheduled late at night) or technical (scrambled cable channels). Again, this requires more infrastructure than one might think: the signal is scrambled unless the cable company authorizes it to be unscrambled, which requires a technical adjustment to the receiver. The descrambler used to be in the cable box itself, making it vulnerable to those with the knowhow, tools, and desire to solder the right tab and get that channel unscrambled—thus the need for laws against tampering, another external apparatus necessary to make this moderation tactic robust.[25]

Social media platforms can engage in this kind of architectural regulation, in much more intricate ways than before, by designing moderation into the algorithms that structure them. Algorithms may not yet be sophisticated enough to identify inappropriate content automatically, but they excel at making real time determinations of whether to deliver content to a particular user, based on information they have about that user and that content. User ratings indicate which content is adult—with all the caveats that go with self-rating: user attrition and error, self-interest, and competing interpretations of the criteria. While platforms generally do not have access to government-issued identification, they do have access to information users have offered about themselves, in profiles, preferences, settings, queries, and the data traces they leave behind. And while Tumblr has no top shelf or cash register to serve as its barrier, their defensible barrier is at the point of search, the moment when platforms determine visibility, of what and to whom. Able to make instantaneous comparisons of content rating and user preference, across a vast number of information queries, the platform can deliver adult content only to a select few, at a speed and scope that a magazine seller could not imagine.

As a strategy, moderation by design has some distinct advantages. For platforms that have developed a sturdy and consenting community around adult interests, or pride themselves on allowing unfettered debate, or are determinedly hands-off when it comes to what users do, moderation by design is a mode of governance more aligned with these aims. While removal is all-or-nothing, this way the content that might offend some but not others can be retained, adding value to the archive for those untroubled by it. It allows the platform to proclaim its commitment to protecting the speech of its users, though it also opens the platform to being criticized as too permissive, and to losing advertisers skittish about a site that appears to be "full of porn." And platforms have flexibility in choosing their default position: one platform could start in an unrestricted search mode and let users opt in to a filtered mode; another platform could begin with restrictions in place as a default, and let users opt out of them.

Despite the advantages, moderation by design is politically fraught, raising questions about the regulation of public discourse that never came up for traditional media. In many cases, the moderation is invisible, and whether users are aware of moderation is important. Moderation by design is also a preemptive measure. Content that is restricted simply does not appear; users are not faced with even the indication of content that might offend them, or lure them to go looking for more. This radically complicates the offer of visibility made by these platforms: by whom and under what conditions are you visible, and how do you know whether you're visible, and under what terms?

Moderators can sequester users and even entire perspectives, while avoiding the appearance of censorship. Because they are technically there, it can be hard to identify and challenge the ways in which their visibility is hampered. This matters a great deal for those who are being partially hidden and don't know it. It especially matters for members of marginalized groups, who may have already struggled to attain visibility and legitimacy through more traditional media, and are hoping to more effectively make their case online, beyond the control of gatekeepers. And it should matter to everyone, when information on the platforms has been filtered, channeled, and choreographed in ways that make it appear that you and I are encountering the same world of available discourse, while in fact, unawares, we may be navigating overlapping but subtly different worlds of discourse, superimposed on the same platform.

SEARCHING FOR SOMETHING AND GETTING NOTHING

These hiding tactics produce one of two outcomes. With the first, a user searches for something and gets nothing; the content is withheld, but the intervention itself is apparent. With the second, a user searches for something and gets what appears to be everything relevant. This hides not only the filtered content but any sign of intervention; the results are sutured back together, leaving no evidence that anything is missing. The first may appear more egregious, but the second is arguably more dangerous.

Along with the adjustments governing how adult blogs could be found, Tumblr made a second change, specific to the mobile version of the platform.

Tumblr app, showing zero results for the search query #gay. Screen capture by Tumblr user icin2, July 18, 2013

Some search terms began to turn up no results at all—obviously sexual terms, like "porn," but also some terms that were not so narrowly porno- graphic, like #gay.[26] Tumblr issued a quasi-explanation on its blog, which some commentators and users found frustratingly vague and unapologetic.[27] Other platforms have experimented with this approach; Instagram explored hashtag blocking as a response to the availability of pro-anorexia materials, blocking terms like #proana, #thinspo, and #thighgap.

Tumblr's decision to block hashtags that might turn up porn was likely intended to satisfy requirements imposed by Apple, which sets its own rules about explicit content for the apps it is willing to provide on iOS through its app store.[28] Apple can reject apps it deems explicit, and can assign an age rating on those that may facilitate access to porn, a rating Tumblr may have wanted to avoid. It's moderators, all the way down.[29]

By blocking specific hashtags from its search results, Tumblr ensures that no (tagged) porn accidentally makes it through its app to the eyes of its gentle user. However, it also hides adult content from those who actually want it. But more troublingly, returning zero content tagged with the word "gay" hides an enormous amount of nonpornographic content as well. If I search for the word "gay," I may be looking for images of people celebrating the DOMA decision on the steps of the Supreme Court, or I may be looking for explicit pornography. It is extremely difficult for Tumblr to know which I meant.

(Occasionally, term and intent line up by design: when Instagram users began tagging pornographic images #pornstagram, the made-up word probably means little else. Yet even here, user creativity may lead discussions around this hashtag in nonpornographic directions—like this discussion of the strategy itself. This search term no longer returns any results— although, curiously, it does on Tumblr.)

Blocking #gay in order to hide porn reduces a term with multiple meanings, some deeply felt and some deeply political, to only its pornographic usage. To treat "gay" exclusively in its sexual meaning undercuts the political efforts of the LGBTQ community to identify itself as people not simply defined by their sexual preferences, and to make discussion of gay and lesbian issues more commonplace in public discourse. In doing so, Tumblr singled out a community that is already silenced and marginalized in countless other ways. Needless to say, "straight" was not blocked.

It is worth noting that blocking the word "gay" may not have been intentionally homophobic, though it came across that way to critics. A data analytic approach may have spurred this decision, without anyone thinking carefully about the social ramifications. There probably were many explicit Tumblr blogs using that keyword to identify gay porn; if Tumblr ran an analysis to identify the terms most commonly associated with porn, it might have identified #gay as a term commonly used to tag porn. A different analysis could have identified how often it's used as a slur in harassing conversations. And blocking it as a search query or excising it from comments might be a positive intervention in some of these interactions. But in specific instances—when a user is in fact seeking out sexual health resources, or speaking to his political community, or saying something genuine about himself—Tumblr was unacceptably "overblocking" legitimate expression.

Back in 2008, Google added an autocomplete feature to its search tool, after experimenting with it for nearly four years.[30] You've used it: as you begin to type your search query, Google attempts to finish it before you do, to save you a moment or two of extra typing. Its guesses are drawn both from your own past searches and in larger part from the searches of all users. While this is often a helpful and uncontroversial feature, it can sometimes produce some surprising results. While reporters in the tech press enjoyed pointing out amusing examples, it was not long before the human appetite for the sexual and the violent, already present in the corpus of past search queries, began to be reflected in the autocompletions. Google found that it had to block some of the offensive suggestions that were turning up as suggestions in response to innocuous queries, and disable the autocomplete feature altogether for queries that were likely to lead to obscene or otherwise problematic phrases.[31]

What is telling here is that Google, which has historically been adamant in refusing to censor the search tool itself, is much more willing to censor the autocomplete function. Since becoming the most dominant search engine, Google has run into the occasional controversy when a particularly offensive result has come up prominently in searches.[32] Google was criticized when users discovered that the first result to a search for the word "Jew" was a rabidly anti-Semitic site called Jewwatch. Despite the criticism, and cofounder Sergey Brin's admitted displeasure about this particular result, Google refused to censor it. Instead it inserted an explanation that emphasized the neutrality of the search tool and Google's strict policy not to intervene, explaining that search results reflect the politics of the web and the vagaries of language, not Google's opinion. Five years later, its position changed when outraged users noticed that, in response to a query of (then-first lady) "Michelle Obama," the Google Image search returned a troublingly racist image of Obama photoshopped with the face of a baboon. Google initially took the same position as with the Jewwatch controversy, arguing that as racist as the image was, it was the top result not because of Google but because people were linking to it. But criticism intensified, and Google finally decided to remove the image from the search results and replace the normal banner ad with an explanation for altering the index.

What makes autocomplete different? I suspect that it's the nature of what is being delivered. Google, both generally and specifically in its responses to controversies like Jewwatch, presents itself as merely an index— not responsible for unsavory content and, in fact, more valuable to the extent that it does not censor. This is a somewhat fanciful claim, as search engines leave off all sorts of content—criminal sites, pornographic sites, download sites that can be used for piracy, spam sites, and sites that violate Google's technical requirements. And the search engine algorithmically sorts its results in complicated and opaque ways, rendering some results so far down the list that, in practical terms, they are unavailable. But the stance Google maintains is that the search engine provides an unflinching index to all websites, regardless of their content. When Google autocompletes your half-typed search query, it is drawing from user-generated content and user data (other queries) to predict the most relevant choices. But unlike an index, here Google is in effect putting words in your mouth—did you mean *this?* The suggestion—whether it is on-point or disturbingly obscene—seems to come from Google as a recommendation, and is then fitted onto your half-query, as if you were about to say it yourself.

This pertains not just to autocomplete. The front page of YouTube, populated by algorithms assessing popularity, is also carefully managed so that salacious videos don't end up there. In 2010, users of Google's new Nexus One phone found that the speech-to-text recognition tool refused to transcribe many expletives. Google's Translate app similarly refuse to translate familiar "dirty words," in any language. And Google is not the only such censor. The Apple iPhone will not autocorrect misspelled profanity, including sensitive but not obscene words like "abortion."[33] A TripAdvisor user discovered that she could not use the words "feminism" or "misogyny" in a review (she was describing an incident at a restaurant)—but the restaurant manager could use "feminist" without a problem.[34]

In all of these cases, the absence was noticeable. Tumblr was roundly criticized for blocking #gay.[35] Women criticized Instagram in 2015 for blocking #curvy,[36] and again for blocking #goddess (but not #god).[37] Plenty of press coverage followed the introduction of Google's autocomplete function. Tech reporters noticed Instagram's blocked hashtags in 2013, and tried to identify as many as they could;[38] researchers noticed the absences in Apple spellcheck and designed an experiment to identify the entire blocked vocabulary.[39] By and large such interventions are difficult to spot, but at least the evidence that something has been moderated away remains, and that scar is a clue that critics can follow.

SEARCHING FOR SOMETHING AND GETTING WHAT APPEARS TO BE EVERYTHING

When platforms refuse to serve up results, or offer a blank page where users expect something to be, the intervention is made visible. At least the traditional checkpoint approach reminds all possible users that this provider does allow the dirty stuff, even if it is hidden away. The new customer who walks into the video store and sees that there is a back room, even if he never goes in, may reject the establishment for having even offered porn. But when Tumblr delisted its adult blogs from the major search engines, it wanted to keep Google users from even being reminded that Tumblr has porn. It wanted to hide not just the porn but even the existence of the back room. This may be a fundamental tension at the Yahoo/Tumblr partnership: management may want to allow porn, but not want to be known for allowing porn.

Much more difficult to spot, and thus much more appealing to the platform, is quietly withholding specific content from what appears to be on offer, but otherwise giving the user what appears to be everything, seemingly unfiltered. When the search results arrive, and look thorough and reasonable and relevant, it is harder to know that something has been withheld. This, more than any other aspect of platform moderation, raises questions about public knowledge and provider responsibility that have little precedent in traditional media.

Consider what, in the field of search, is known as the "accidental porn" problem. All the major search engines offer users a "safesearch" mode—if I don't want to see pornographic results, I tick a box and the search engine filters them out. You might expect the opposite to be true: if I have turned safesearch off, I have consented to and indicated my comfort with receiving adult content among my search results. But all the major search engines also go one step farther: even for users who have safesearch off, the search engine nevertheless filters out adult results—your search query is assumed to be an innocuous one, one that is not seeking adult content. In other words, even if I have safesearch off, if I search for "movies," I will not see links to adult movie sites; the search engine will deliver only nonexplicit results, using the very same algorithmic moderation as if I had safesearch turned on. If I search for "porn movies," then I get the adult content.[40]

To be safe, search engines treat all users as not wanting accidental porn: better to make the user looking for porn refine her query and ask again, than to deliver porn to users who did not expect or wish to receive it. Reasonable, perhaps; but the intervention is a hidden one, and in fact runs counter to my stated preferences. Search engines not only guess the meaning and intent of my search, based on the little they know about me, they must in fact defy the one bit of agency I have asserted here, in turning safesearch off.[41]

Because platforms use algorithms to deliver their content in a variety of ways, there are many points at which platforms can selectively withhold content. Search results are presented as measures of relevance, but the criteria that drive them are opaque, which helps hide moderation like this. But even metrics that appear to be straightforward reporting of data—activity, sales, popularity—can provide the opportunity to hide away offensive content.[42]

Twitter Trends is a rough calculation of the topics that are suddenly enjoying a great deal of activity, either regionally or across the entire platform, at a given moment. Usually these terms are hashtags that users include to link their tweets to an ongoing conversation. However, hashtags that include profanity or obscenity do not appear in the Trends list. To be clear, users can include obscene hashtags in the tweets themselves, and those tweets will not blocked or removed; other users can come across them in a public feed or because they searched for them or because they follow that user. But if, according to Twitter's calculations, a particular term that includes profanity "Trends," it will be excluded from that measure of popularity. This can sometimes lead to profanity arms races, as when 4chan pranksters began to push chosen terms, dirty but not traditionally profane, into the Twitter Trends lists, leading Twitter to add #gorillapenis and #gooddick to its list of blocked terms.[43] Google also offers a Trends function, designed to indicate the popularity of specific search queries over time and location. In 2008, once again thanks to 4chan, the Nazi swastika topped the Google Trends list; Google removed it manually, but in doing so, publicly acknowledged that their Trends service already included a porn filter for terms that are profane themselves or otherwise would clearly direct users toward pornographic content.

Amazon revealed a similar intervention, by accident, in 2009. Authors and users began to notice that specific books had dropped off the best-seller list; these books no longer even displayed a "sales rank," a regular feature indicating how much that book is selling relative to all other Amazon offerings. After some investigation it became clear that all of the books in question, more than fifty-seven thousand of them, were gay- and lesbian-themed. In a community traditionally sensitive to being rendered invisible, word began to spread, much of the debate taking place on Twitter under the hashtag #amazonfail. Theories emerged: some believed that Amazon had been hacked, perhaps as a form of punishment for selling LGBT-friendly books; others took it as evidence Amazon's own politics, under the assumption that it was trying to erase books aimed at the gay and lesbian community from its best-seller list.[44]

Amazon did not help perceptions when, in its first responses to authors whose books were suddenly unranked, it explained that "adult" content gets excluded from Amazon's search tool and sales ranking. But the response revealed Amazon's mistake: an Amazon employee had mistakenly marked these fifty-seven thousand books as "adult," a misclassification that automatically removed them from the calculation of sales rank. Amazon quickly corrected the mistake.

The incident revealed that Amazon's sales rank algorithm is a moderated one. Books that Amazon classifies as adult can be searched for and purchased, but they do not qualify for a sales rank, whether that rank is high or low. There is a mismatch between what the algorithm is claimed to measure and what it actually measures. What users cannot see reflected in the sales rank is not only that Amazon sells adult books but, perhaps more important, how popular that adult content is among Amazon customers. Seemingly quantitative metrics like "best sellers" can in fact be infused with value judgments about propriety, and can be used to obscure some content from some users.

From the platform's perspective, these subtle, algorithmic checkpoints can be extremely appealing and convenient solutions, as is apparent in an early, controversial decision by Flickr. Like Tumblr, Flickr has a relatively loose set of criteria for what can and cannot appear on its site; if you know how to look, you can find pornography, and not just the artistic nudes common to the pro-amateur and artistic photography the site catered to. Rather than prohibiting adult content, Flickr requires users to rate their photos "safe," "moderate," or "restricted." Flickr's search tool has a safesearch filter, defaulting at the start in the "moderate" position, meaning that unless the searcher adjusts that setting, he will not find images rated "restricted." Flickr hoped this would wall off the pornographic and anything else obscene.

In 2007, Flickr received complaints from the governments of Germany, South Korea, Hong Kong, and Singapore. A motley crew, but each had a similar concern; their national laws preventing minors from accessing obscene content were stricter than those in the United States, and each country felt that Flickr should do more to keep X-rated content from the nation's curious teenagers. Flickr designers could have instituted a checkpoint requiring users to confirm their ages. Instead, Flickr simply designed the system so that users who are visiting Flickr from, say, a German Internet Protocol (IP) address, cannot turn safesearch off. They will only ever see photos rated "moderate" or "safe," no matter their age.[45]

From Flickr's perspective, problem solved. Germany wants to prevent teens from encountering adult content, and with Flickr's adjustment they will not. But the decision stepped well beyond what the law required. While German teens will not find adult content on Flickr, neither will German adults, to whom this law does not apply. In other words, a law protecting minors became a technical measure restricting adults as well. (The episode also revealed a curious second problem: Flickr does not, or has failed to, prevent availability in Germany of images of swastikas, which are also illegal under German law—presumably because the images are not rated as "restricted" by Flickr users or moderators.)

Flickr's decision treads, not so carefully, on long-standing debates about how to regulate speech and culture. U.S. law has long wrestled with how to keep adult content away from children without also keeping it away from adults. On television, because it is difficult to selectively filter content for some viewers and not others, TV programming is largely restricted to "acceptable for children" (for example, no nudity), with some networks stretching what that includes (violence or sexually suggestive scenes, for example) and using the time of day as a rough barometer for when the audience is likely to include children. For film, the MPAA rating system allows films to include adult material, and depends on theater operators to serve as the checkpoints that keep children from it. American concerns about protecting children regularly run up against the First Amendment notion that adults should be able to consume the content they want. Solutions that restrict children without deeply limiting what adults can access are preferable.

In Flickr's case, however, the existing algorithmic checkpoints already in place were too convenient, too tempting. The ratings and safesearch mechanisms were already there, and the means to distinguish users by country was so simple and cheap, compared with installing and overseeing an age-identification mechanism. Whatever implications the decision had for adult users in these countries, to Flickr that cost was acceptable. But the decision is troubling for its implicit approach to public discourse and how it should be moderated.

Flickr depended on both its existing safesearch function and IP blocking, a common tool that helps websites deliver different materials depending on a user's nation of origin. IP blocking has long been available for web servers like Apache; the server compares the IP address from which the request is made, and if the address matches any from a list of prohibited users, organizations, or entire nations, refuses to deliver the requested page. The same technology has been implemented by a number of social media platforms, so that content requests emanating from particular nations will similarly go unfulfilled. This kind of moderation by nation is an emerging and appealing response to the problem of competing cultural norms.[46] Global sites can pick and choose what they deliver to whom, "out of respect for local rules." Platforms regularly use IP blocking to comply with requests from governments, particularly in the Middle East and Asia, that actively restrict the online activity of their citizens; Facebook would much prefer to block specific pages just from users in that country than find their entire platform banned.[47]

This is precisely what happened in 2010, when the High Court of Pakistan ordered a ban be imposed on all of Facebook for Pakistani users, after street protests took issue with a particular Facebook group. Titled Everybody Draw Mohammed Day, the group was one American's snarky challenge to the Muslim law prohibiting the visual representation of the Prophet. As his thinking went, if enough people drew Mohammed, there would be no way to threaten everyone with jihad or prevent this flood of images; the prohibition would collapse, or at least be exposed as absurd. As attention to the controversial group grew, among Muslims both in Pakistan and in neighboring countries, as well as among Western bloggers and journalists adamant about freedom of expression, the group swelled to 100,000 followers and spawned several related discussion groups. As the proposed day, May 20, 2010, approached, the High Court ordered the Pakistan Telecommunications Authority to block the entirety of Facebook for Pakistani users—as well as YouTube and relevant pages of Wikipedia and Flickr.

Facebook then faced a dilemma. It could, as Google famously did with China, defend the expressive freedom of the Everybody Draw Mohammed Day creators, and refuse to remove the group, enduring the Pakistani ban or even pulling out of Pakistan. It could also have deleted the group, though it would have been difficult to make the case that the page amounted to hate speech, and thus prohibited by Facebook's community guidelines. Instead, Facebook chose a third option: it removed the group only from the search results of users located in Pakistan (as well as Bangladesh and India, which also had leveled complaints about the group). For Pakistani users, the offending page was simply not there; even its removal was invisible. A search for the relevant terms would simply not return it among the results. But the group remained on the site, available in other nations, its members unaware that it had been filtered. The Pakistani secretary of IT and Telecommunications was apparently satisfied, and lifted the sitewide ban.

Of course, there was no politically safe option for Facebook in this case, nor is there ever when a social media platform receives demands from countries to remove content it would not have removed otherwise. The decision to IP-block this page for users based in Pakistan was a convenient and cautious solution, but Facebook was still criticized for it. The strategy is increasingly commonplace, though. Microsoft's Bing search engine does not respond to searches deemed "adult" if they emanate from China or several Middle Eastern nations.[48] YouTube can put content warnings on specific videos that trigger only for users from certain countries; it has also blocked specific videos from particular nations of users, including the infamous "Innocence of Muslims" video that helped spark the attack on the U.S. Embassy in Benghazi, Libya.[49] Most stunningly, this kind of nation-specific display can happen with maps: on Google Maps, Crimea is represented as part of Russia since being annexed, but only for Russian users.[50]

The distinctly global nature of these platforms raises difficult challenges for moderation. Laws that protect free expression, and that either assign responsibility to delivery platforms or insulate them from it, differ widely around the world. The kinds of content deemed offensive differ as well. And many nations have, over the past decade, asserted their right and willingness to control national Internet service and impose sitewide bans, which can be financially and publicly damaging to a platform. Traditional media did not face this challenge, or not in the same way. Most didn't reach that far, not because of regulation but because of practical limitations. A community newspaper in Bangor didn't make it all the way to Bangalore. For the kinds of content providers that did have this reach—major movie studios, satellite broadcasters, national newspapers, and book publishers—national regulations and cultural norms could be accommodated "at the border," figuratively and sometimes literally. Sanitized copies of a movie could be printed for a particular national market, or a different version of the newspaper could be printed. This might not even have felt like a great imposition, given that these media texts were redesigned anyway for an audience with different interests, reading in a different language, holding different cultural values.

Other platforms have responded differently to the dilemma posed by takedown requests, threatened sitewide bans, and other forms of political pressure from foreign nations. Twitter made a point in 2012 of articulating its stance: in response to a legal request from a foreign government to remove a tweet, Twitter will comply; but it removes the tweet only from users based in that country, via IP blocking, not sitewide, and it substitutes an alert identifying who had requested the tweet's removal. Given the growing number of these nation-specific requests and the increasing willingness of platforms to honor them, the only alternative would be to remove the tweets globally. Twitter's aim is to make the intervention visible, even as the content is absent.[51] Twitter weathered a great deal of criticism at the time for this position, but many platforms, including Facebook, have since followed Twitter's lead. YouTube indicates not just that a video has been removed, but also which of its policies it had violated and who had made the request to remove it, if the entity was an institution or a government. Google has solved the problem differently with its Blogger service; Blogger has been redesigned so that its entire corpus of blogs has been duplicated for every country. If I try to access whatever.blogger.com while I'm in France, I will be redirected to whatever.blogger.fr. This allows Google to make nation-specific interventions and alterations for anything that violates local law: if French law requires some content to be removed, Google can remove it from the .fr version, and only users in France will ever encounter this custom-moderated version.

Still, hiding the intervention as well as the content remains a tempting tactic, especially for a platform eager to be all things to all people, under competing pressures, and in possession of a great deal of data about its users. A television network couldn't show nudity to some viewers while shielding others from it; a magazine couldn't include hate speech only for those readers who hate. But social media platforms, and other digital media services, can do essentially that. Their ability to serve content to some and withhold it from others is automatic and precise.

The data that can be used to make this distinction are also much richer, and the number of assessments that can be made is vastly expanded, nearly limitless. Most platforms already collect much more data about their users than just their age and nation, as part of their service to advertisers. A platform might be tempted to use all the data at hand to anticipate what might offend—a radical expansion of the "accidental porn" problem. Platforms could try to predict, based on the data they've collected, what is or is not likely to offend a particular user, and could algorithmically keep the most contentious content away from the easily offended. If I "liked" my local evangelical church, is that reason enough to assume that I should not be shown artistic nudity? If my social network is overwhelmingly liberal, is that enough reason not to highlight a link to a rancorous Breitbart article?

If my activity data suggest that I rarely choose violent movies, would it be best not to recommend a violent news report? Algorithmic determinations often depend on the fuzzy boundaries of statistical analytics that combine all these data points. What are the implications for public discourse if Facebook could determine that an image is 60 percent likely to offend and I am 45 percent likely to be modest in my preferences, and decided based on these calculations to leave that image out of my news feed?[52] This kind of social sorting, fine-grained, fuzzy, and, predictive, is already technically available.

These kinds of precise, architectural moderation imposed by the platform may just be the tip of the iceberg. Many social media platforms already provide social sorting tools to their individual users. The manager of a Facebook page can already choose whether users from selected countries can or cannot access the page. So selectively offering content by nation or other criteria can be spooled out infinitely, allowing groups and even individual users to cherry-pick their preferred membership.

INCONSPICUOUS INTERVENTIONS INTO A PUBLIC SPHERE

Technical measures that keep some users away from some content, while continuing to display it to others, provide a convenient solution to the problems of porn, obscenity, hate, and harassment. But they also raise troubling questions about the power of social media platforms to offer different materials to different publics, in ways that are hard to discern or criticize. This strategy raises a new challenge to the dynamics of public contestation and free speech: the obscured obscuring of contentious material from the public realm for some, not for others.

Invisible interventions like Facebook hiding Everybody Draw Mohammed Day are unprecedented in traditional media. In the past, the withholding of content for reasons of propriety was always about its complete absence—a curse bleeped, a scene deleted, a topic unspoken. It was there or not, for everyone. Checkpoints like the back room in the video store and the high shelf at the magazine stand did create a way of dividing the public into two groups, adults and children, allowing some contentious material to be selectively withheld from this perceived "vulnerable audience."[53] And we do provide tools like Internet-filtering software to parents, to impose such selective restrictions on their own children. But we had no way, or the political will, to distinguish any other subcategories of people who should be prevented from seeing some things, while granting it to others, within a public communication venue.

That social media platforms can deliver and withhold with such precision, and embed that moderation into an algorithmic mechanism that seems to deliver unfiltered results, poses a new public challenge. The moment Everybody Draw Mohammed Day was selectively hidden, Facebook was no longer one site but two, one with the page and one without—two Facebooks existing simultaneously and superimposed, but only one accessible to a given user. When the next moderation decision is made, around a different piece of questionable content and a different national audience, Facebook becomes fourfold. Facebook is really a multitude of Facebooks, appearing to be one public venue but in fact spun out in slightly different versions, theoretically in as many versions as there are users. And instead of the traditional moderation problem—an entire community confronted with a contentious piece of material that is offensive to some and is perceived as valuable to others—we have the curious new problem of being led to believe that we all have access to the same things when we do not. We are left unaware that others are seeing what we are not, and that others are not seeing what we are.

Of course, given the sheer scale of social media platforms, the algorithmic sorting and personalization they engage in, the way they are adjusted according to users' preferences and social networks, and the A/B testing many engage in beneath the surface—perhaps we already have not one Facebook but millions, no two of which are the same. This is consistent with concerns raised about the personalization of news and the algorithmic tailoring of search results: we are left unsure of whether what you and I see in response to the same query or at the top of our news feeds are the same, and that the manner in which they differ may shape what we know and what we think everyone else knows.[54] Even so, it is important to note that moderation fits this logic, and takes advantage of it. The selections made for us by platforms are driven by more than just boosting user engagement and advertising revenue. Even the parts designed for all (search results, trending topics, headline news, shared moments, front pages) are selectively moderated. The sensation of a shared platform may be an illusion.

These selective interventions fracture the public, who may believe that they are all using Facebook together, as promised. If we are unaware of the criteria behind what platforms show and to whom, and we cannot see the scars left behind when platforms render content unavailable, we are left with no stable object to encounter, no common corpus of public discourse to share. Public discourse depends on contests over meaning, conducted on public stages, among groups of people who must make themselves recognizable to one another to be heard and found persuasive. Selective moderation can undercut the potential for and faith in a shared space of contestation.

Moderation by design expands beyond concern for how to best remove offending content and users while protecting speech, participation, and community. It is part of a much more complex question about the many reasons why some content is delivered and other content is not, some users are seen and others are obscured. Platforms are not flat: not only can some content be removed, but other content can be featured, highlighted, and promoted. Sometimes this curation is driven by sponsorship, with featured content enjoying a prominent place on the front page; sometimes it is through various "cream of the crop" algorithmic measures, reporting back to us what is "most read" or "most emailed" or "trending." Most of the time, it is the product of a judgment of relevance: the most relevant search result in response to your query, the "top story" in your news feed. Decisions about propriety are not separate from other decisions about which content to serve up, which to bury, and which to discard; they are inextricably entangled. And while traditional media often split the tasks of deciding what to produce and what to remove, on social media platforms the tools and the calculations are often one and the same.

These intermingled criteria not only shape what we can access or not, they dictate our entire experience of the platform. Facebook's news feed is powerfully shaped by its ranking algorithms. We have few ways to access "all" of our friends' status updates, photos, and likes except as they are presented algorithmically. Facebook itself is the result of this aggregate work of selection and moderation. In both, these commercial platforms act as speech keepers, and the criteria on which both depend help to shape what counts as appropriate cultural discourse.

These entangled judgments of relevance, value, and propriety, at least when they are recognized as such, do offer opportunity to contest the power of platforms. Interventions by the platform, real or apparent, can spark critical examination of the proper bounds of cultural discourse and the proper role of platforms. But when these interventions are made obliquely, embedded in algorithms, and buried in a mountain of search results or a flood of tweets, they can be harder to challenge.[55] In the face of ambiguous search results that could also be explained away as the result of circumstance, error, or bias, users are left with only folk theories as to why what's there is there, and what might be missing.

8

what platforms are, and what they should be

Facebook is not just technology or media, but a community of people. That means we need Community Standards that reflect our collective values for what should and should not be allowed. In the last year, the complexity of the issues we've seen has outstripped our existing processes for governing the community.

Mark Zuckerberg, chairman and CEO of Facebook,
"Building Global Community," February 2017

Content moderation is such a complex sociotechnical undertaking that, all things considered, it's amazing that it works at all, and as well as it does. Even so, as a society we have once again handed over to private companies the power to set and enforce the boundaries of appropriate public speech for us. That is enormous cultural power held by a few deeply invested stakeholders, and it is being done behind closed doors, making it difficult for anyone else to inspect or challenge. Platforms frequently, and conspicuously, fail to live up to our expectations; in fact, given the sheer enormity of the undertaking, most platforms' definition of success includes failing users on a regular basis.

And while we sometimes decry the intrusion of platform moderation, at other moments we decry its absence. We are partly to blame for having put platforms in this untenable situation, by asking way too much of them. Users cannot continue to expect platforms to be hands-off *and* expect them to solve problems perfectly *and* expect them to get with the times *and* expect them to be impartial and automatic.

We must recognize that moderation is hard work, that we are asking platforms to intervene, and that they have responded by enlisting us in the labor. What is important, then, is that we understand the ways in which platforms are moderated, by whom, and to what ends. But more than that, the discussion about content moderation needs to shift, away from a focus on the harms users face and the missteps platforms sometimes make in response, to a more expansive examination of the responsibilities of platforms, that moves beyond their legal liability to consider their greater obligations to the public.

IMPROVING MODERATION

There are many things social media companies could do to improve their content moderation: More human moderators. More expert human moderators. More diverse human moderators. More transparency in the process. Better tools for users to block bad actors. Better detection software. More empathetic engagement with victims. Consulting experts with training on hatred and sexual violence. Externally imposed monitors, public liaisons, auditors, and standards. And we could imagine how we might compel those changes: Social pressure. Premium fees for a more protected experience. Stronger legal obligations.

But these are all are just tweaks—more of the same, just more of it. And some of them are likely to happen, in the short term, as the pressure and scrutiny social media platforms face increase, and they look for steps to take that moderately address the concerns while preserving their ability to conduct business as usual. But it is clearer now than ever that the fundamental arrangement itself is flawed.

If social media platforms wanted to do more, to come at the problem in a fundamentally different way, I have suggestions that more substantively rethink not only their approach but how platforms conceive of themselves and their users. I fully acknowledge that some are politically untenable and economically outlandish, and are almost certain never to happen. I spell them out in more detail in a separate document, but in brief:

Design for Deliberate and Actionable Transparency

Calls for greater transparency in the critique of social media are so common as to be nearly vacant. But the workings of content moderation at most social media platforms are shockingly opaque, and not by accident.[1] The labor, the criteria, and the outcomes are almost entirely kept from the public. On some platforms, content disappears without explanation and rules change with notification; when platforms do respond publicly regarding controversial decisions, their statements are often short on detail and rarely articulate a larger philosophy.

Platform moderation should be much more transparent. Full stop. But transparency is not merely the absence of opacity. It requires designing new ways to make processual information visible but unobtrusive. If one of my tweets is receiving lots of responses from "egg" accounts—often the ones dedicated to trolling—that I have already blocked, how could this fact, and their number and velocity, still be made visible to me?[2] Tiny eggs, swarming like angry bees below my tweet? A pop-up histogram that indicates the intensity of the responses, algorithmically estimated? The imperative for platforms to smooth and sanitize the user experience must be tempered with an obligation to make the moderation visible. Platforms should make a radical commitment to turning the data they already have back to me in a legible and actionable form, everything they could tell me contextually about why a post is there and how I should assess it. We have already paid for this transparency, with our data.

Distribute the Agency of Moderation, Not Just the Work

When social media platforms task users with the work of moderation, overwhelmingly it is as individuals. Flagging is individual, rating content is individual, muting and blocking are by an individual and of an individual. With few exceptions, there is little support for any of this work to accumulate into something of collective value, not just for the platform but for other users. As Danielle Citron and Ben Wittes have noted, platforms have been slow to embrace even the simplest version of this, shared block lists. They also propose an easy but ingenious addition, that users be able to share lists of those they follow as well.[3]

Platforms should also let flagging accumulate into actionable data for users. Heavily flagged content, especially if by multiple, unconnected users, could be labeled as such, or put behind a clickthrough warning, even before it is reviewed. But this could be taken farther, to what I'll call *collective lenses*. Flagging a video on YouTube brings down a menu for categorizing the offense, to streamline the review process. But what if the site offered a similar tool for tagging videos as sexual, violent, spammy, false, or obscene? These would not be complaints per se, nor would they be taken as requests for their removal (as the flag currently is), though they would help YouTube find the truly reprehensible and illegal. Instead, these tags would produce aggregate data by which users could filter their viewing experience. I could subscribe to an array of these collective lenses: I don't want to see videos that more than X users have categorized as violent.[4] Trusted organizations could develop and manage their own collective lenses: imagine a lens run by the Southern Poverty Law Center to avoid content that allied users have marked as "racist," or one from Factcheck.org filtering out "disputed" news articles. This would not help the "filter bubble" problem; it might in fact exacerbate it. Then again, users would be choosing what not to see, rather than having it deleted on their behalf. It would prioritize those who want a curated experience over those who take advantage of an uncurated one.

Protect Users as They Move across Platforms

Little of what a user does to curate and defend her experience on one platform can easily be exported to others. Given that, in reality, most users use several platforms, all of these preferences should be portable. If I have flagged a video as offensive on Tumblr, I presumably don't want to see it on YouTube either; if I have marked an advertisement as misleading on Google, I presumably don't want it delivered to me again on Facebook; if I have been harassed by someone on Twitter, I presumably don't want him also harassing me on Snapchat.[5] Given that users are already being asked to rate, flag, and block, and that this labor is almost exclusively for the benefit of the platform, it is reasonable to suggest that users should also enjoy the fruits of that labor, in their interactions on this platform and elsewhere.

Social media platforms have been resistant to making users profiles and preferences interoperable. At least publicly, platform managers say that doing so would make it too easy for users to decamp to a hot, new service, if their interest in this one cooled. The accumulated history users have with a platform—established social networks, a legacy of interactions, an archive of photos, an accumulated matrix of preferences—does in fact discourage them from abandoning it, even when they are dissatisfied with how it governs their use, even when they are fed up, even when they must endure harassment to stay. This means that making it difficult to export your preferences keeps some people in unsatisfactory and even abusive conditions. The fact that this is not yet possible is a cold reminder that what users need from platforms is constrained by what platforms need in the market.[6]

Reject the Economics of Popularity

For platforms, popularity is one of the most fundamental metrics, often serving as proxy to every other: relevance, merit, newsworthiness. Platforms amplify the popular by returning it to users in the form of recommendations, cued-up videos, trends, and feeds. Harassment and hate take advantage of this: cruel insults that classmates will pass around, slurs aimed at women that fellow misogynists will applaud, nonconsensual porn that appeals to prurient interests. These are not just attacks, they generate likes, views, comments, and retweets, making it hard for platforms to discern their toxicity or pass up their popularity. With business models that use popularity as the core proxy for engagement, too often platforms err on the side of encouraging as many people to stay as possible, imposing rules with the least consequences, keeping troublesome users if they can, and bringing them back quickly if they can't.

Under a different business model, platforms might be more willing to uphold a higher standard of compassionate and just participation, and forgo users who prove unwilling to consent to the new rules of the game. Where is the platform that prioritizes the longer-term goal of encouraging people to stay and helping them thrive, and sells that priority to us for a fee? Where are the platforms that gain value when fewer users produce a richer collaboration? Until those platforms appear and thrive, general-use platforms are unlikely to pursue an affirmative aspiration (what are we here to accomplish?) rather than a negative one (what shouldn't we do while we're here?).

Put Real Diversity behind the Platform

Silicon Valley engineers, managers, and entrepreneurs are by and large a privileged lot, who tend to see society as fair and meritocratic; to them, communication just needs to be more open and information more free. But harassment and hatred are not problems specific to social media; they are endemic to a culture in which the powerful maintain their position over the less powerful through tactics of intimidation, marginalization, and cruelty, all under cover of a nominally open society. Silicon Valley engineers and entrepreneurs are not the community most likely to really get this, in their bones. It turns out that what they are good at is building communication spaces designed as unforgiving economic markets, where it is necessary and even celebrated that users shout each other down to be heard; where some feel entitled to toy with others as an end in itself, rather than accomplishing something together; where the notion of structural inequity is alien, and silencing tactics take cover behind a false faith in meritocracy. They tend to build tools "for all" that continue, extend, and reify the inequities they overlook.

What would happen if social media platforms promised that for the next decade, *all* of their new hires, 100 percent, would be women, queer people, or people of color? Sounds like an outrageous exercise in affirmative action and social engineering? It sure is. Slight improvements in workplace diversity aren't going to make the difference; we've seen what corrosive environments some of these companies can be for those who do show up. But I suggest this not only for the benefit of the new employees but for the benefit of the platform and its users. It is not that women and queer people and people of color necessarily know how to solve the problems of harassment, revenge porn, or fake news—or that the job of solving these problems should fall on their shoulders. But to truly diverse teams, the landscape will look different, the problems will surface differently, the goals will sound different. Teams that are truly diverse might be able to better stand for their diverse users, might recognize how platforms are being turned against users in ways that are antithetical to the aims and spirit of the platform, and might have the political nerve to intervene.

THE LONG HANGOVER OF WEB 2.0

Would these suggestions solve the problem? No. When I began writing this book, the pressing questions about content moderation seemed to be whether Silicon Valley could figure out which photos to delete and which to leave, which users to suspend and which to stop suspending. The years 2014 and 2015 helped reveal just how many people were suffering while platforms tried to figure this out. But 2016 and 2017 fundamentally transformed the nature of the problem. It turns out the issue is much bigger than it first seemed.

In the run-up to the 2016 presidential election in the United States, and in elections that followed on its heels in France, Germany, the Netherlands, Myanmar, and Kenya, it became clear that misinformation was spreading too readily on social media platforms like Facebook and Twitter, and in many cases, its spread was deliberate. The clamor about "fake news" may tend to erase important distinctions between propaganda, overstatement, partisan punditry, conspiracy theories, sensationalism, clickbait, and downright lies. But even so, it has made clear that social media platforms facilitated the circulation of falsehoods, and algorithmically rewarded the most popular and outlandish over more substantive journalism. The politically motivated, including Russian operatives keen on disrupting democratic political processes, and the economically motivated, including Macedonian teens keen on turning a quick profit on the clicks of the gullible, seeded online discussions with false content masquerading as legitimate news and political debate. Though it may be impossible to prove, some worried that this flood of propaganda may have been a factor in the U.S. election, handing the presidency to Donald Trump.[7] Finding the very mechanisms of democracy in peril has dramatically raised the stakes for what platforms allow and what they can prevent.

Evidence that Russian operatives also bought advertisements on Facebook, Twitter, and Google, targeted at users in battleground U.S. states, and designed to fuel racial and economic tensions on both sides of the political spectrum, expanded the issue further. Advertising on Facebook was already moderated; it is not surprising that the platform's response to this revelation was to promise better moderation. But the Russian operatives' use of social media advertising also offers a powerful reminder that, all this time, we may have been thinking about platforms in the wrong way. Facebook is not a content platform supported by advertising. It is two intertwined networks, content and advertising, both open to all. Given that small ad buys are relatively cheap, advertisers are no longer just corporate brands and established institutional actors; they can be anyone. Persuading someone through an ad is as available to almost every user as persuading him through a post. The two networks may work according to different rules: posts go to friends and friends of friends, ads go to those targeted through Facebook's algorithmically generated microdemographics. But the two also bleed into each other, as "liking" an ad will forward it to friends, and ads can be designed to look like posts. So while platforms moderate content that users circulate and content that advertisers place, the problem of policing propaganda—or harassment, hate speech, or revenge porn, for that matter—must now trace persuasive tactics that take advantage of both networks together.

The concerns around political discourse and manipulation on social media platforms feel like the crest of a larger wave that has been breaking for a few years now, a broader reconsideration, on so many fronts, of social media platforms and their power in society: concerns about privacy and surveillance, topped by the Snowden revelations of the links between Silicon Valley companies and the National Security Administration (NSA);

vulnerability to hackers, criminal or political, made plain by high-profile attacks on retailers, credit agencies, and political parties; their impact on the economics of journalism, particularly Facebook's oversized footprint, which changes as often as Facebook's priorities do; concerns about the racial and gender biases baked into their algorithms; research conducted on users without their consent; their growing influence over policy, in places like Washington, D.C., Brussels, and Davos; the inequities in their workplaces, and the precarious labor dynamics they foster as part of the "gig economy"; their impact on San Francisco, on manufacturing zones around the world, and on the environment.

Perhaps we are now experiencing the long hangover after the ebullient high of web 2.0, the birth of social media, and the rise of a global, commercial, advertising-supported Internet culture—the bursting of a cultural bubble, if not a financial one.[8] It's possible that we've simply asked too much, or expected too much, from social media. As Virginia Heffernan quipped, about Twitter, "I think we've asked way, way too much of a little microblogging platform that was meant to talk about where to get a beer in Austin, Texas, and now is moving mountains, and is a centerpiece of geopolitics. It's like asking nodes of Rubik's Cubes to manage world history."[9] Or perhaps these are growing pains. In a 2013 interview, Ken Auletta took the mounting criticism of social media as evidence that "Silicon Valley is in the equivalent of its adolescence. And, in adolescence, is suddenly a time when you become aware of things beyond yourself, become aware the world. . . . So suddenly the people at Google, the people at Twitter, the people at Amazon, awake to the fact that, oh my God, we have to learn how the rest of the world operates and lives and what they expect of us."[10] Or maybe platforms simply are vulnerable to both unpredictable and tactical misuse, because they're designed to be. As Tom Malaby put it, thinking specifically about virtual game worlds, "Like few other products we can identify—early telephone service is one, Internet search engines may be another— . . . [a platform] depends on unanticipated uses by its consumers . . . meant to make itself." Striking a new balance between control and contingency means platforms must assure an open-endedness sufficient to produce "socially legitimate spaces for the unexpected."[11]

The dreams of the open web did not fail, exactly, nor were they empty promises to begin with. Many people put in a great deal of effort, time, resources, and dollars to pursue these dreams, and to build infrastructures to support them. But when you build a system that aspires to make possible a certain kind of social activity, even if envisioned in the most positive terms, you also make possible its inverse—activity that adopts the same shape in order to accomplish the opposite end. In embracing the Internet, the web, and especially social media platforms for public discourse and sociality, we made a Faustian bargain, or a series of them, and we are now facing the sober realities they produced. If we dreamed of free information, we found we also got free advertising. If we dreamed of participation, we also got harassment. If we dreamed of sharing, we also got piracy. If we dreamed of political activism online, we also got clicktivism, political pandering, and tweetstorms. If we dreamed of forming global, decentralized communities of interest, we also got ISIS recruitment. If we dreamed of new forms of public visibility, we also got NSA surveillance. If we dreamed of free content and crowdsourced knowledge, we also got the exploitation of free labor. If we dreamed of easy interconnection between complex technical resources, we also got hacked passwords, data breaches, and cyberwar.

The companies that have profited most from our commitment to plat-forms did so by selling the promises of participatory culture. As those promises have begun to sour and the reality of their impact on public life has become more obvious and more complicated, these companies are now grappling with how best to be stewards of public culture, a responsibility that was not evident to them at the start. The debates about content mod-eration over the past half-decade can be read as social media's slow and bumpy maturation, its gathering recognition that it is a powerful infrastruc-ture for knowledge, participation, and public expression. The adjustments that platforms have already made have not sufficiently answered the now relentless scrutiny being paid to them by policy makers, the changing ex-pectations articulated by the press, and the deep ambivalence now felt by users. Social media platforms have, in many ways, reached an untenable point. This does not mean they cannot function—clearly they can—but that the challenges they face are now so deep as to be nearly paradoxical.

Social media platforms have, to a remarkable degree, displaced tradi-tional media, and they continue to enlarge their footprint. They have indeed given all comers the opportunity to speak in public and semipublic ways, and at an unprecedented, global scale. While they are not used by all, and many parts of the world are still excluded by limited resources, infra-structure, the constraints of language, or political censorship, those who do find their way to these platforms find the tools to speak, engage, and per-suade. The general-purpose platforms, especially, aspire to host all public and semipublic communication of every form, aim, and import. At the same time, they are nearly all private companies, nearly all commercially funded, nearly all built on the economic imperatives of advertising and the data collection that targeted advertising demands. Their obligations are, like those of traditional commercial media, pulled between users, content producers, and advertisers—with only the one twist: that users and producers are one and the same.

These platforms now function at a scale and under a set of expectations that increasingly demands automation. Yet the kinds of decisions that platforms must make, especially in content moderation, are precisely the kinds of decisions that should not be automated, and perhaps cannot be. They are judgments of value, meaning, importance, and offense. They depend both on a human revulsion to the horrific and a human sensitivity to contested cultural values. There is, in many cases, no right answer for whether to allow or disallow, except in relation to specific individuals, communities, or nations that have debated and regulated standards of propriety and legality. And even then, the edges of what is considered appropriate are constantly recontested, and the values they represent are always shifting.

WHAT IT TAKES TO BE A CUSTODIAN

We desperately need a thorough, public discussion about the social responsibility of platforms. This conversation has begun, but too often it revolves around specific controversies, making it hard to ask the broader question: what would it mean for social media platforms to take on some responsibility for their role in organizing, curating, and profiting from the activity of their users? For more than a decade, social media platforms have presented themselves as mere conduits, obscuring and disavowing the content moderation they do. Their instinct has been to dodge, dissemble, or deny every time it becomes clear that they produce specific kinds of public discourse in specific ways. While we cannot hold platforms responsible for the fact that some people want to post pornography, or mislead, or be hateful to others, we are now painfully aware of the ways in which platforms can invite, facilitate, amplify, and exacerbate those tendencies: weaponized and coordinated harassment; misrepresentation and propaganda buoyed by its quantified popularity; polarization as a side effect of algorithmic personalization; bots speaking as humans, humans speaking as bots; public participation emphatically figured as individual self-promotion; the tactical gaming of algorithms in order to simulate genuine cultural value. In all of these ways, and others, platforms invoke and amplify particular forms of discourse, and they moderate away others, all under the guise of being impartial conduits of open participation. As such, platforms constitute a fundamentally new information configuration, materially, institutionally, financially, and socially. While they echo and extend traditional forms of communication and exchange, they do so by being, like computers themselves, "universal machines" for many different kinds of information exchange.

Our thinking about platforms must change. It is not just, as I hope I have shown, that all platforms moderate, or that all platforms have to moderate, or that most tend to disavow it while doing so. It is that moderation, far from being occasional or ancillary, is in fact an essential, constant, and definitional part of what platforms do. I mean this literally: moderation is the essence of platforms, it is the commodity they offer. By this point in the book, this should be plain. First, moderation is a surprisingly large part of what they do, in a practical, day-to-day sense, and in terms of the time, resources, and number of employees they devote to it. Moreover, moderation shapes how platforms conceive of their users—and not just the ones who break rules or seek help. By shifting some of the labor of moderation, through flagging, platforms deputize users as amateur editors and police. From that moment, platform managers must in part think of, address, and manage users as such. This adds another layer to how users are conceived of, along with seeing them as customers, producers, free labor, and commodity. And it would not be this way if moderation were handled differently.

But in an even more fundamental way, content moderation is precisely what platforms offer. Anyone could make a website on which any user could post anything he pleased, without rules or guidelines. Such a website would, in all likelihood, quickly become a cesspool and then be discarded. But it would not be difficult, nor would it require skill or financial backing. To produce and sustain an appealing platform requires, among other things, moderation of some form. Moderation is hiding inside every promise social media platforms make to their users, from the earliest invitations to "join a thriving community" or "broadcast yourself," to Mark Zuckerberg's 2017 manifesto quoted at the start of this chapter. Every platform promises to offer something in contrast to something else—and as such, every platform promises moderation.[12]

Content moderation is a key part of what social media platforms do that is different, that distinguishes them from the open web: they moderate (removal, filtering, suspension), they recommend (news feeds, trending lists, personalized suggestions), and they curate (featured content, front-page offerings). Platforms use these three levers together to, actively and dynamically, *tune* the unexpected participation of users, produce the "right" feed for each user, the "right" social exchanges, the "right" kind of community. ("Right" here may mean ethical, legal, and healthy; but it also means whatever will promote engagement, increase ad revenue, and facilitate data collection. And given the immense pushback from users, legislators, and the press, these platforms appear to be deeply out of tune.

If content moderation is the commodity, if it is the essence of what platforms do, then it no longer makes sense to treat it as a bandage to be applied or a mess to be swept up. Too often, social media platforms treat content moderation as a problem to be solved, and solved privately and reactively. Platform managers understand their responsibility primarily as protecting users from the offense and harm they are experiencing. But now platforms find they must answer also to users who find themselves troubled by and implicated in a system that facilitates the reprehensible—even if they never see it. Removing content is no longer enough: the offense and harm in question is not just to individuals, but to the public itself, and to the institutions on which it depends. This is, according to John Dewey, the very nature of a public: "The public consists of all those who are affected by the indirect consequences of transactions to such an extent that it is deemed necessary to have those consequences systematically cared for."[13] What makes something of concern to the public is the potential need for its inhibition.

Despite the safe harbor provided by the law and the indemnity enshrined in their terms of service contracts as private actors, social media platforms inhabit a position of responsibility—not only to individual users but to the public they powerfully affect. When an intermediary grows this large, this entwined with the institutions of public discourse, this crucial, it has an *implicit contract* with the public that, whether platform management likes it or not, can differ from the contract it required users to click through. The primary and secondary effects these platforms have on essential aspects of public life, as they become apparent, now lie at their doorstep.

Fake news is a useful example. Facebook and Twitter never promised to deliver only reliable information, nor are they legally obligated to spot and remove fraud. But the implicit contract is now such that they are held accountable for some of the harms of fake news, and must find ways to intervene. This is not a contract that will ever bind the platforms in court, but it is certain to be upheld in the court of public opinion. Even as moderation grows more complicated and costly, the expectations of users have grown not more forgiving but more demanding. That is the collective enforcement of the implicit contract, and right now it is pushing platforms away from the safe harbors they have enjoyed.[14]

Rethinking content moderation might begin with this recognition, that content moderation is the essential offer platforms make, and part of how they tune the public discourse they purport to host. Platforms could be held responsible, at least partially, for how they tend to that public discourse, and to what ends. The easy version of such an obligation would be to require platforms to moderate more, or more quickly, or more aggressively, or more thoughtfully. We have already begun to see public and legal calls for such changes. But I am suggesting something else: that their shared responsibility for the public requires that they share that responsibility *with* the public—not just the labor, but the judgment.

To their credit, the major social media platforms have been startlingly innovative in how they present, organize, recommend, and facilitate the participation of users. But that innovation has focused almost exclusively on how users participate at the level of content: how to say more, see more, find more, like more, friend more. Little innovation, by comparison, has supported users' participation at the level of governance, shared decision making, collaborative design, or the orchestration of collective values. The promise of the web was not only that everyone could speak but that everyone would have the tools to form new communities on their own terms, design new models of democratic collectivity. This second half of the promise has been largely discarded by social media platforms.

In 2012, Facebook held a vote. Starting in 2009, Facebook users could actually "veto" a policy, but it required 30 percent of users to participate to make it binding. The 2012 vote received just 0.038 percent participation.[15] Facebook went ahead and amended the policy, even though a clear majority of those who did vote were against it. And it got rid of the veto policy itself.[16] The vote was, in the eyes of the press and many users, considered a failure. But instead of considering it a failure, what if it had been treated as a clumsy first step? Hundreds of thousands of users voted on an obscure data policy, after all. What if the real failure was that Facebook was discouraged from trying again? The idea of voting on site policies could have been improved, with an eye toward expanding participation, earning the necessary legitimacy, developing more sophisticated forms of voting, and making a more open process. And mechanisms of collective governance could mean much more than voting. Platforms should be developing structures for soliciting the opinions and judgment of users in the governance of groups, in the design of new features, and in the moderation of content.[17]

Facebook has followed a well-worn path, from involving its users as skilled participants with agency to treating them as customers who prioritize ease and efficiency. Much the same happened with commercial radio and the telephone, even electricity itself.[18] It would take a miracle to imagine social media platforms voluntarily reversing course. But I am not imagining some overbuilt exercise in deliberative democracy, nor do I mean to make every user accept or reject a bunch of gruesome flagged images every time she logs on. But given how effective commercial platforms have become at gleaning from users their preferences, just to more effectively advertise to them, I can only imagine what would be possible if that same innovative engineering went to gleaning from users their civic commitments—not what they like as consumers, but what they value as citizens.

It seems reasonable to think that, given everything users already do on these platforms, the data traces they leave should already make these civic values legible. Social media platforms are not just structures filled with content. Each contribution is also a tiny value assertion from each user: this is what we should be able to say, out loud, in this place. These claims attesting to what should be acceptable are implicit in the very act of posting. These are not grand claims, typically. When someone tweets what he had for breakfast, that is a tiny claim for what should be acceptable, what platforms should be for: the mundane, the intimate, the quotidian. When a critic of Twitter moans, on Twitter, that all people do is tweet what they had for breakfast, that is a claim as well: Twitter should be of more significance, should amount to something.

Some claims, from the beginning, require consideration: does "the way we do things" include this? Sometimes we debate the question explicitly. Should Twitter be more social, or more journalistic? What does it make possible, and where does it fail? But more often, these considerations accumulate slowly, over time, in the soup of a billion assertions—each one tiny, but together, legion. The accumulated claims and responses slowly form the platform.

Content moderation is fundamental to this collective assertion of value. As it currently functions, it is where, in response to some claims of what should be acceptable, platforms will sometimes refuse. Every post is a test claim for what platforms should include, and from the start, some receive the answer "no." No, this platform is not for porn. No, you can't use this platform to threaten people. No, you mustn't mislead people for a quick buck. Because every post is a "yes" claim that something does belong, it shows in relief exactly when platform managers must, or feel they must, act counter to the wants of their users.

But what if social media platforms, instead of policing content, could glean the assertions of civic value that they represent? What if they could display that back to users in innovative ways? Given the immense amount of data they collect, platforms could use that data to make more visible the lines of contestation in public discourse and offer spaces in which they can be debated, informed by the everyday traces of billions of users and the value systems they imply. Could their AI research efforts currently under way, to improve machine-learning techniques to automate the identification and removal of pornography, instead identify what we think of pornography and where it belongs? From our activity across platforms, artificial intelligence techniques could identify clusters of civic commitments—not to then impose one value system on everyone, as they do now, but to make visible to users the range of commitments, where they overlap and collide, and to help users anticipate how their contributions fit amid the varied expectations of their audience.

This would be a very different understanding of the role of "custodian"— not where platforms quietly clean up our mess, but where they take up guardianship of the unresolvable tensions of public discourse, hand back with care the agency for addressing those tensions to users, and responsibly support that process with the necessary tools, data, and insights. I do not pretend to know how to do this. But I am struck by the absence of any efforts to do so on behalf of major social media platforms.

Platforms can no longer duck the responsibility of being custodians to the massive, heterogeneous, and contested public realm they have brought into being. But neither can we duck this responsibility. As Roger Silverstone noted, "The media are too important to be left to the media."[19] But then, to what authority can we even turn? The biggest platforms are more vast, dispersed, and technologically sophisticated than the institutions that could possibly regulate them. Who has sufficient authority to compel Facebook to be a good Facebook?

As users, we demand that they moderate, and that they not moderate too much. But as citizens, perhaps we must begin to be that authority, be the custodians of the custodians. Participation comes with its own form of responsibility. We must demand that platforms take on an expanded sense of responsibility, and that they share the tools to govern collectively.

So far, we have largely failed to accept this responsibility, too easily convinced, perhaps, that the structure of the digital network would somehow manufacture consensus for us. When users threaten and harass, when they game the system, when they log on just to break the fragile accomplishments of others for kicks, this hardly demonstrates a custodial concern for what participation is, and what it should be. But simply crying foul when you don't agree with someone, or when you don't share his normative sense of propriety, or you don't like a platform's attempt to impose some rules isn't a custodial response either. And in the current arrangement, platforms in fact urge us to go no farther: "If you don't like it, flag it, and we'll handle it from there."

If platforms circulate information publicly, bring people into closer contact, and grant some the visibility they could not have otherwise—then with that comes sex and violence, deception and manipulation, cruelty and hate. Questions about the responsibility of platforms are really just part of long-standing debates about the content and character of public discourse. It is not surprising that our dilemmas about terrorism and Islamic fundamentalism, about gay sexuality, about misogyny and violence against women, each so contentious over the past decade, should erupt here too. Just as it was not surprising that the *Terror of War* photograph was such a lightning rod when it first appeared in U.S. newspapers, in the midst of a heated debate about the morality of the Vietnam War. The hard cases that platforms grapple with become a barometer of our society's pressing concerns about public discourse itself: Which representations of sexuality are empowering and which are obscene, and according to whose judgment? What is newsworthy and what is gruesome, and who draws the line? Do words cause harm and exclude people from discussion, or must those who take part in public debate endure even caustic contributions? Can a plurality of people reach consensus, or is any consensus always an artifact of the powerful? How do we balance freedom to participate with the values of the community, with the safety of individuals, with the aspirations of art, and with the wants of commerce?

The truth is, we wish platforms could moderate away the offensive and the cruel. We wish they could answer these hard questions for us and let us get on with the fun of sharing jokes, talking politics, and keeping up with those we care about. But these are the fundamental and, perhaps, unresolvable tensions of social and public life. Platforms, along with users, should take on this greater responsibility. But it is a responsibility that requires attending to these unresolvable tensions, acknowledging and staying with them—not just trying to sweep them away.

NOTES

CHAPTER 1 ALL PLATFORMS MODERATE

1 Mark Scott and Mike Isaac, "Facebook Restores Iconic Vietnam War Photo It Censored for Nudity," *New York Times,* September 9, 2016, https://www.nytimes .com/2016/09/10/technology/facebook-vietnam-war-photo-nudity.html.

2 Olivia Blair, "The Iconic Picture Causing Huge Problems for Mark Zuckerberg," *Independent,* September 9, 2016, http://www.independent.co.uk/news/people /mark-zuckerberg-facebook-accused-abusing-power-napalm-girl-vietnam-war -image-a7233431.html.

3 Espen Egil Hansen, "Dear Mark. I Am Writing This to Inform You That I Shall Not Comply with Your Requirement to Remove This Picture," *Aftenposten,* September 8, 2016, https://www.aftenposten.no/meninger/kommentar/Dear-Mark-I-am-writing -this-to-inform-you-that-I-shall-not-comply-with-your-requirement-to-remove -this-picture-604156b.html.

4 Kelly Kiveash, "Censorship Row: Facebook Reinstates Iconic 'Napalm Girl' Photo," Ars Technica, September 9, 2016, https://arstechnica.com/tech-policy/2016/09 /facebook-napalm-girl-photo-censorship-norway/.

5 Justin Osofsky, *Facebook,* September 9, 2016, https://www.facebook.com/josofsky /posts/10157347245570231.

6 Hariman and Lucaites, "Public Identity and Collective Memory," 41.

7 A National Public Radio reporter claimed that the photo was not identified algorithmically, but I also saw reports that suggested that it was. See Aarti Shahani, "With 'Napalm Girl,' Facebook Humans (Not Algorithms) Struggle to Be Editor," NPR, September 10, 2016, http://www.npr.org/sections/alltechconsidered/2016 /09/10/493454256/with-napalm-girl-facebook-humans-not-algorithms-struggle-to -be-editor.

8 Kristina Cooke, Dan Levine, and Dustin Volz, "Facebook Executives Feel the Heat of Content Controversies," Reuters, October 28, 2016, http://www.reuters.com/article /us-facebook-content-insight-idUSKCN12S0D3.

9 Mulvin, *Proxies.*

10 Zelizer, *About to Die,* 237.

11 Miller, "The Girl in the Photograph," 271.

12 David Stenerud, "The Girl in the Picture Saddened by Facebook's Focus on Nudity,"
Dagsavisen, September 2, 2016. http://www.dagsavisen.no/verden/the-girl-in-the
-picture-saddened-by-facebook-s-focus-on-nudity-1.773232.

13 Zelizer, *About to Die,* 239.

14 Mulvin, *Proxies.*

15 Miller, "The Girl in the Photograph": 263.

16 Mike Ahlers, "Nixon's Doubts over 'Napalm Girl' Photo," CNN, February 28, 2002,
http://edition.cnn.com/2002/WORLD/asiapcf/southeast/02/28/vietnam.nixon/.

17 Even in the 2016 reporting about the Facebook controversy, some publications
struggled with how to present the *Terror of War* photo. Nearly all news outlets that
reported the controversy displayed the photo; given that they're reporting on
Facebook being arguably too conservative in their judgment, it would be difficult to
then not include the photo all. But there were signs of hesitation. The British
Broadcasting Corporation included the warning "The following report contains
some disturbing images" in its video piece. Instead of using the photo on its own,
several outlets, including *Wired,* Reuters, CNet, Engadget, the Verge, Quartz, the
Financial Times, and NBC News, used (as I did) the image of *Aftenposten's* front
page—perhaps to bolster the legitimacy of showing it, or to shift that responsibility
onto another outlet, or to reduce the size of the photo itself to obscure the details.
Some (Politico, Yahoo, Ars Technica) showed the image on an easel behind an
adult Kim Phuc, another way of affirming the right to show it while also distancing
it visually. And a few, including Mediaite, the *St. Louis Dispatch,* New England
Cable News, and the *Daily Herald,* reported the controversy without showing
Ut's photo in any form. Most interesting, in a Huffington Post UK report, two
images have been removed—one with a caption that indicates that it was the
original photo. Sara C. Nelson, "Facebook Removes Iconic Picture of Fleeing Napalm
Girl Over Nudity," HuffPost UK, September 9, 2016, http://www.huffingtonpost.co
.uk/entry/facebook-removes-iconic-picture-of-fleeing-napalm-girl-over-nudity_uk
_57d2b381e4b0ced6a09924a0.

18 See Baym and boyd, "Socially Mediated Publicness"; Burgess and Green, *YouTube;*
Cammaerts, "Critiques on the Participatory Potentials"; Clark et al., "Participations";
Deuze, "Corporate Appropriation of Participatory Culture"; Fish et al., "Birds of the
Internet"; Jenkins, *Convergence Culture;* Jenkins, Ford, and Green, *Spreadable Media;*
Kelty, "Participation"; Langlois, "Participatory Culture and the New Governance of
Communication"; Sandvig, "The Social Industry"; Tufekci, "As the Pirates Become
CEOs"; Turner, "Burning Man at Google."

19 Thompson, "The New Visibility."

20 For direct contact, see Baym, *Personal Connections in the Digital Age;* Doc Searls,
"The Giant Zero," Doc Searls Weblog, February 3, 2016, https://blogs.harvard.edu
/doc/2016/02/03/the-giant-zero-2/. For affording new opportunities to speak, see
Benkler, *The Wealth of Networks;* Bruns, *Blogs, Wikipedia, Second Life, and Beyond;*

Hunter and Lastowka, "Amateur-to-Amateur"; Shirky, *Here Comes Everybody*. For networked publics, see boyd, "Social Network Sites as Networked Publics"; Varnelis, *Networked Publics*.

21 Kelty, "The Fog of Freedom"; Streeter, *The Net Effect;* Streeter, "The Internet as a Structure of Feeling"; Turner, *From Counterculture to Cyberculture.*

22 If nothing else, spam would long since have choked an unmanaged social media platform. Removing spam is censoring content; it just happens to be content that nearly all users agree should go. Nearly all users agree that spam should be deleted—which means nearly all users agree that platforms should moderate. See Brunton, *Spam.*

23 Ingraham and Reeves, "New Media, New Panics"; Marwick, "To Catch a Predator?"; McRobbie and Thornton, "Rethinking 'Moral Panic' for Multi-Mediated Social Worlds."

24 Fiss, *Liberalism Divided;* Heins, *Not in Front of the Children;* Streeter, *Selling the Air.*

25 Giulia Segreti, "Facebook CEO Says Group Will Not Become a Media Company," Reuters, August 29, 2016. http://www.reuters.com/article/us-facebook-zuckerberg -idUSKCN1141WN.

26 Napoli and Caplan, "When Media Companies Insist They're Not Media Companies and Why It Matters for Communications Policy," 2016.

27 Pasquale, "Platform Neutrality."

28 Twitter, "The Twitter Rules," https://support.twitter.com/articles/18311.

29 Gillespie, "The Politics of 'Platforms.'"

30 McPherson, Smith-Lovin, and Cook, "Birds of a Feather."

31 In this I enjoy a privilege that some users do not. If I wanted to go in search of pornography, harassment, or hate speech, I could probably find it. But if I were a woman or a member of a racial minority, pornography, harassment, and hatred might very well find me. Being a target of abuse brings you closer to the project of moderation, whether you like it or not.

32 Youmans and York, "Social Media and the Activist Toolkit."

33 Ryan Tate, "Steve Jobs Offers World 'Freedom from Porn,'" *Gawker,* May 15, 2010, http://gawker.com/5539717/steve-jobs-offers-world-freedom-from-porn.

34 Adrian Chen, "Inside Facebook's Outsourced Anti-Porn and Gore Brigade, where 'Camel Toes' are More Offensive than 'Crushed Heads,'" Gawker, February 16, 2012, http://gawker.com/5885714/.

35 Burgess and Matamoros-Fernández, "Mapping Sociocultural Controversies across Digital Media Platforms"; Chess and Shaw, "A Conspiracy of Fishes"; Massanari, "#Gamergate and The Fappening"; Banet-Weiser and Miltner, "#MasculinitySoFragile."

36 Timothy Lee, "Why Reddit Just Banned a Community Devoted to Sharing Celebrity Nudes," Vox, September 8, 2014, https://www.vox.com/2014/9/8/6121195/reddits -ban-of-thefappening-explained.

37 Adrian Chen, "The Laborers Who Keep Dick Pics and Beheadings Out of Your Facebook Feed," *Wired,* October 23, 2014, https://www.wired.com/2014/10/content -moderation/.

38 Charlie Warzel, " 'A Honeypot For Assholes': Inside Twitter's 10-Year Failure to Stop Harassment," *Buzzfeed,* August 11, 2016, https://www.buzzfeed.com /charliewarzel/a-honeypot-for-assholes-inside-twitters-10-year-failure-to-s.

39 Julia Greenberg, "Facebook and Twitter Face Tough Choices as ISIS Exploits Social Media to Spread Its Message," *Wired,* November 21, 2015, https://www.wired .com/2015/11/facebook-and-twitter-face-tough-choices-as-isis-exploits-social -media/.

40 Farhad Manjoo, "Can Facebook Fix Its Own Worst Bug?" *New York Times,* April 25, 2017, https://mobile.nytimes.com/2017/04/25/magazine/can-facebook-fix-its-own -worst-bug.html. Craig Silverman, "Here's How Fake Election News Outperformed Real Election News on Facebook," Buzzfeed, November 16, 2016, https://www .buzzfeed.com/craigsilverman/viral-fake-election-news-outperformed-real-news-on -facebook.

41 *Wired* Staff, "Dear Internet: It's Time to Fix This Mess You Made," *Wired,* August 24, 2016, https://www.wired.com/2016/08/open-letter-to-the-internet/.

42 Personal interview.

43 Bartle, "Why Governments Aren't Gods and Gods Aren't Governments"; Boellstorff, *Coming of Age in Second Life;* Kerr, De Paoli, and Keatinge, "Human and Non-Human Aspects of Governance and Regulation of MMOGs"; Kiesler et al., "Regulating Behavior in Online Communities"; Kollock and Smith, "Managing the Virtual Commons"; Malaby, "Coding Control"; Suzor, "The Role of the Rule of Law in Virtual Communities"; Taylor, "The Social Design of Virtual Worlds"; Taylor, "Beyond Management"; Zarsky, "Social Justice, Social Norms, and the Governance of Social Media."

44 Agre, "Conceptions of the User in Computer Systems Design"; Oudshoorn and Pinch, *How Users Matter*; Woolgar, "Configuring the User."

45 Anna Weiner, "Why Can't Silicon Valley Solve Its Diversity Problem?" *New Yorker,* November 26, 2016, http://www.newyorker.com/business/currency/why-cant-silicon -valley-solve-its-diversity-problem.

46 Corn-Revere, "Caught in the Seamless Web"; Deibert and Rohozinski, "Liberation vs. Control."

47 Ammori, "The 'New' New York Times," 2278. For some, awareness that their user base is international may heighten an inclination to allow context-specific beliefs govern what should and should not be said. For others, the same awareness may fuel a political mission to knowingly impose cherished American values.

48 Julia Angwin, *Stealing MySpace,* 64–65.

49 Mathew Ingram, "Here's Why Disney and Salesforce Dropped Their Bids for Twitter," *Fortune,* http://fortune.com/2016/10/18/twitter-disney-salesforce/.

50 Burgess, "From 'Broadcast Yourself' to 'Follow Your Interests.' "

51 Lessig, *Remix.*

52 Tim O'Reilly, "What Is Web 2.0: Design Patterns and Business Models for the Next Generation of Software," O'Reilly Media, September 30, 2005, http://www.oreilly .com/pub/a/web2/archive/what-is-web-20.html.

53 boyd and Ellison, "Social Network Sites"; Beer, "Social Network(ing) Sites"; Ellison and boyd, "Sociality through Social Network Sites."

54 Gehl, *Reverse Engineering Social Media;* Baym, "Social Media and the Struggle for Society"; Hearn, "Verified"; Langlois and Elmer, "The Research Politics of Social Media Platforms."

55 Helmond, "The Platformization of the Web"; Plantin et al., "Infrastructure Studies Meet Platform Studies."

56 Alexis Madrigal, "The Perfect Technocracy: Facebook's Attempt to Create Good Government for 900 Million People," *Atlantic,* June 19, 2012, http://www.theatlantic .com/technology/archive/2012/06/the-perfect-technocracy-facebooks-attempt-to -create-good-government-for-900-million-people/258484/.

57 Vaidhyanathan, *The Googlization of Everything.*

58 Turner, *From Counterculture to Cyberculture.*

59 Dibbell, "A Rape in Cyberspace"; Kraut and Resnick, *Building Successful Online Communities.*

60 Personal interview.

61 Platforms experience what is known as "eternal September." In the days of Usenet, newsgroups tended to receive an influx of new members every September, when arriving college students got access to the web for the first time and were unfamiliar with the norms of the community. When, in 1993, AOL linked its users to the web, this problem of maintaining community norms in the face of new users became a constant. See Jason Koebler, "It's September, Forever," Motherboard, September 30, 2015, https://motherboard.vice.com/en_us/article/nze8nb/its-september-forever. Many thanks to Lana Swartz for pointing out this connection.

62 It's worth acknowledging that I settled on this list in late 2017; some sites may have since disappeared, others that belong on the list may have emerged since then. Also, I don't put a whole lot of stock in these particular subcategories—the types are in fact fluid, and the services I've listed regularly combine, blur, migrate across them. They are only to demonstrate that these platforms represent a wide range of aims and designs.

63 Gillespie, "The Politics of 'Platforms.'"

64 Burgess and Green, *YouTube;* Elkin-Koren, "User-Generated Platforms"; Hunter and Lastowka, "Amateur-to-Amateur"; van Dijck, "Users Like You?"; Malaby, "Coding Control"; Malaby, *Making Virtual Worlds;* van Dijck, *The Culture of Connectivity.*

65 Social media platforms often celebrate that fact that their content comes from amateurs, users who do what they do for reasons other than the professional. As Jean Burgess notes, most platforms now mix amateur and professional content, though platforms continue to champion the amateur. But it is worth noting the professional

content is usually there under the same terms of service license as the amateur. Burgess, "From 'Broadcast Yourself' to 'Follow Your Interests.'"

66 Gehl, "The Archive and the Processor"; Couldry and van Dijck, "Researching Social Media as if the Social Mattered."

67 Gillespie, "The Politics of 'Platforms.'"

68 Marc Andreessen, "The Three Kinds of Platforms You Meet on the Internet," Blog .Pmarca.Com, June 15, 2010, http://pmarchive.com/three_kinds_of_platforms_you _meet_on_the_internet.html; Bogost and Montfort, "Platform Studies."

69 Gawer, "The Organization of Technological Platforms"; Gawer, *Platforms, Markets, and Innovation*; Rochet and Tirole, "Platform Competition in Two-sided Markets"; van Couvering, "The Political Economy of New Media Revisited"; Mansell, "The Public's Interest in Intermediaries."

70 John Herrman, "Platform Companies Are Becoming More Powerful—but What Exactly Do They Want?" *New York Times,* March 21, 2017. https://www.nytimes .com/2017/03/21/magazine/platform-companies-are-becoming-more-powerful-but -what-exactly-do-they-want.html.

71 Ananny, "From Noxious to Public?"; Baym and boyd, "Socially Mediated Publicness"; Beer and Burrows, "Sociology and, of, and in Web 2.0"; Beer, "Power through the Algorithm?"; Boellstorff, *Coming of Age in Second Life;* Braun, "Social Media and Distribution Studies"; Burgess and Green, *YouTube;* Clark et al., "Participations"; Gehl, *Reverse Engineering Social Media;* Gerlitz and Helmond, "The Like Economy"; Gibbs et al., "#Funeral and Instagram"; Gillespie, "The Politics of 'Platforms'"; Grimmelmann, "Speech Engines"; Hands, "Politics, Power, and Platformativity"; Klang, "The Rise and Fall of Freedom of Online Expression"; Langlois, "Participatory Culture and the New Governance of Communication"; Langlois et al., "Networked Publics,"; McVeigh-Schultz and Baym, "Thinking of You"; Nahon, "Where There Is Social Media, There Is Politics"; Postigo, "Social Media"; Sandvig, "The Social Industry"; Sharma, "Black Twitter?"; Snickars and Vondereau, *The YouTube Reader;* Taylor, "The Social Design of Virtual Worlds"; Vaidhyanathan, *The Googlization of Everything;* van Dijck, *The Culture of Connectivity;* Vonderau, "The Politics of Content Aggregation"; Weltevrede et al., "The Politics of Real-time."

72 van Dijck, *The Culture of Connectivity,* 20.

73 van Dijck and Poell, "Understanding Social Media Logic."

74 Balkin, "Free Speech in the Algorithmic Society"; DeNardis and Hackl, "Internet Governance by Social Media Platforms"; Flew, "Social Media Governance"; Gillespie, "Platforms Intervene"; Grimmelmann, "The Virtues of Moderation"; Klonick, "The New Governors"; Marwick, "Are There Limits to Online Free Speech?"; Matamoros-Fernández, "Platformed Racism"; Milosevic, "Social Media Companies' Cyberbullying Policies"; Ober and Wildman, "Social Media Definition and the Governance Challenge"; Roberts, "Commercial Content Moderation"; Roth, "'No Overly Suggestive Photos of Any Kind'"; Tushnet, "Power without Responsibility."

75 Kennedy et. al., "Regulation and Social Practice Online"; Lingel, *Digital Countercultures and the Struggle for Community.*

CHAPTER 2 **THE MYTH OF THE NEUTRAL PLATFORM**

Epigraph: Nitasha Tiku and Casey Newton, "Twitter CEO: 'We Suck at Dealing with Abuse,'" Verge, February 4, 2015, https://www.theverge.com/2015/2/4/7982099 /twitter-ceo-sent-memo-taking-personal-responsibility-for-the.

1 Phillips, *This Is Why We Can't Have Nice Things.*

2 Vijaya Gadde, "Twitter Executive: Here's How We're Trying to Stop Abuse While Preserving Free Speech," *Washington Post,* April 16, 2015, https://www. washingtonpost.com/posteverything/wp/2015/04/16/twitter-executive-heres-how -were-trying-to-stop-abuse-while-preserving-free-speech/.

3 Balkin, "Digital Speech and Democratic Culture"; Godwin, *Cyber Rights;* Lessig, *Code and Other Laws of Cyberspace;* Litman, *Digital Copyright.*

4 For example, see Barlow, "A Declaration of the Independence of Cyberspace"; Johnson and Post, "Law and Borders." See also Goldsmith and Wu, *Who Controls the Internet?;* Suzor, "The Role of the Rule of Law in Virtual Communities."

5 Sterling, "Short History of the Internet."

6 Lessig, *Code and Other Laws of Cyberspace;* Lessig, "The Law of the Horse"; Zittrain, "A History of Online Gatekeeping."

7 Godwin, *Cyber Rights.*

8 Maddison, "Online Obscenity and Myths of Freedom"; Marwick, "To Catch a Predator?"

9 Lessig, *Code and Other Laws of Cyberspace;* Wagner, "Filters and the First Amendment."

10 Services such as these were not referred to as platforms at the time; I'm extending contemporary use of the term backward to draw the parallel.

11 Godwin, *Cyber Rights;* Zittrain, "Internet Points of Control"; Zuckerman, "Intermediary Censorship."

12 Ardia, "Free Speech Savior or Shield for Scoundrels"; Kreimer, "Censorship by Proxy"; Mann and Belzley, "The Promise of Internet Intermediary Liability."

13 Matthew Lasar, "Nazi Hunting: How France First 'Civilized' the Internet," Ars Technica, June 22, 2011, https://arstechnica.com/tech-policy/2011/06/how-france -proved-that-the-internet-is-not-global/. See also Goldsmith and Wu, *Who Controls the Internet?*

14 Ginsburg, "Putting Cars on the 'Information Superhighway.'" See also Chander, "How Law Made Silicon Valley."

15 *Religious Technology Center v. Netcom On-Line Communication Services, Inc.,* 907 F. Supp. 1361 (N.D. Cal. 1995).

16 *A&M Records, Inc. v. Napster, Inc.,* 239 F. 3d 1004. 9th Cir. 2001. See also Litman, *Digital Copyright;* Yu, "The Escalating Copyright Wars."

17 Pfaffenberger, "'If I Want It, It's OK.'"

18 Postigo, "America Online Volunteers."

19 Kraut and Resnick, *Building Successful Online Communities*; Herring, "The Rhetorical Dynamics of Gender Harassment On-line."

20 Mike Godwin, "Meme, Counter-meme," *Wired*, October 1, 1994, https://www.wired.com/1994/10/godwin-if-2/.

21 Zickmund, "Approaching the Radical Other."

22 MacKinnon, "Punishing the Persona."

23 Anti-Defamation League, "Fighting Anti-Semitism and Hate," n.d., http://archive.adl.org/civil_rights/newcyber.pdf.

24 Dutton, "Network Rules of Order."

25 Telecommunications Act of 1996, https://transition.fcc.gov/Reports/tcom1996.txt. See also Aufderheide, *Communications Policy and the Public Interest*; Cannon, "The Legislative History of Senator Exon's Communications Decency Act."

26 Christopher Zara, "The Most Important Law in Tech Has a Problem," *Wired*, January 3, 2017, https://www.wired.com/2017/01/the-most-important-law-in-tech-has-a-problem/; Citron, *Hate Crimes in Cyberspace*, 168–75.

27 *Reno v. American Civil Liberties Union*, 521 U.S. 844 (1997). See also Rappaport, "In the Wake of *Reno v. ACLU*."

28 47 U.S. Code § 230 (Protection for private blocking and screening of offensive material), https://www.law.cornell.edu/uscode/text/47/230.

29 Mueller, "Hyper-Transparency and Social Control."

30 Ibid., 805.

31 Citron, *Hate Crimes in Cyberspace*, 168–75.

32 Tushnet, "Power without Responsibility," 1002.

33 Suzor, "The Role of the Rule of Law in Virtual Communities," 1844.

34 Ammori, "First Amendment Architecture"; Lenert, "A Communication Theory Perspective"; Mosco, "The Mythology of Telecommunications Deregulation."

35 It is worth noting that Section 230 was for "offensive material" and explicitly excluded "cases involving federal criminal law, intellectual property law, and electronic-communications privacy law." The safe harbor it establishes for ISPs and platforms does not apply to these other concerns. This explains why the platform obligations for child pornography are very different than for other categories of harmful speech, because child pornography is a federal, criminal offense. It also explains why the arrangements are different for copyright infringement. The Digital Millennium Copyright Act, also passed in 1996, offered ISPs and search engines protection against liability for their users' copyright infringement as well, but this safe harbor comes with some obligations, the most notable being that intermediaries must comply with "notice and takedown" requests from copyright owners who have identified their work as being circulated through their service. In court cases that followed, peer-to-peer networks and other online services found they did not enjoy the DMCA safe harbor when they had "materially" contributed to the circulation of

pirated content, when they enjoyed some financial benefit from it, or even when they had "induced" it by promoting their service as designed for piracy. See Fifer and Carter, "A Tale of Two Safe Harbors."

36 This was before innovations such as digital fingerprinting and other forms of automated content identification, techniques that now make it possible for platforms and ISPs to "know" of illicit content on their service, even in real time.

37 Bankston, Sohn, and McDiarmid, "Shielding the Messengers."

38 Horwitz, "The First Amendment Meets Some New Technologies."

39 Horwitz, *The Irony of Regulatory Reform;* Streeter, *Selling the Air.*

40 Balkin, "Digital Speech and Democratic Culture," 21.

41 MacKinnon et al., "Fostering Freedom Online," 40–42.

42 Lobel, "The Law of the Platform."

43 Note: the 230 definition of "interactive computer service" includes "access software provider," which does expand the definition a bit, and there have been cases where CDA was extended to include MySpace and others. See 47 U.S. Code § 230, "Protection for private blocking and screening of offensive material," https://www.law.cornell.edu/uscode/text/47/230; also Electronic Frontier Foundation, "CDA 230: Key Legal Cases," https://www.eff.org/issues/cda230/legal.

44 Tania Branigan, "Google Angers China by Shifting Service to Hong Kong," *Guardian,* March 23, 2010, https://www.theguardian.com/technology/2010/mar/23/google-china-censorship-hong-kong.

45 Paul Mozur and Vindu Goel, "To Reach China, LinkedIn Plays by Local Rules," *New York Times,* October 5, 2014, https://www.nytimes.com/2014/10/06/technology/to-reach-china-linkedin-plays-by-local-rules.html.

46 Loretta Chao and Amir Efrati, "Twitter Can Censor by Country," *Wall Street Journal,* January 28, 2012, https://www.wsj.com/articles/SB10001424052970204573704577185873204078142.

47 Some have even included "warrant canaries" in their policy statements, a sentence stating that no government subpoenas had been served—which they would remove when it was no longer true, alerting those in the know that a subpoena had been served without violating a gag order. It is not clear, however, now that it has become apparent that many companies have received such subpoenas, how useful these canaries in fact were.

48 Palfrey, "Four Phases of Internet Regulation."

49 Archetti, "Terrorism, Communication and New Media"; Eric Geller, "Why ISIS Is Winning the Online Propaganda War," *Daily Dot,* March 29, 2016, https://www.dailydot.com/layer8/isis-terrorism-social-media-internet-countering-violent-extremism/; Kaveh Waddell, "The Government Is Secretly Huddling with Companies to Fight Extremism Online," *Atlantic,* March 9, 2016, https://www.theatlantic.com/technology/archive/2016/03/the-government-is-secretly-huddling-with-companies-to-fight-extremism-online/472848/.

50 MacKinnon, *Consent of the Networked.*

51 JISC, "Hosting Liability."

52 Daphne Keller, "Making Google the Censor," *New York Times,* June 12, 2017, https://www.nytimes.com/2017/06/12/opinion/making-google-the-censor.html.

53 Courtney Radsch, "Treating the Internet as the Enemy in the Middle East," Committee to Protect Journalists, April 27, 2015, https://cpj.org/2015/04/attacks-on-the-press-treating-internet-as-enemy-in-middle-east.php.

54 Zoe Bedell and Benjmain Wittes, "Tweeting Terrorists, Part I: Don't Look Now but a Lot of Terrorist Groups Are Using Twitter," LawFareBlog, February 14, 2016, https://www.lawfareblog.com/tweeting-terrorists-part-i-dont-look-now-lot-terrorist-groups-are-using-twitter; Benjmain Wittes and Zoe Bedell, "Tweeting Terrorists, Part II: Does It Violate the Law for Twitter to Let Terrorist Groups Have Accounts?" *LawFareBlog,* February 14, 2016, https://www.lawfareblog.com/tweeting-terrorists-part-ii-does-it-violate-law-twitter-let-terrorist-groups-have-accounts; Benjamin Wittes and Zoe Bedell, "Tweeting Terrorists, Part III: How Would Twitter Defend Itself against a Material Support Prosecution," LawFareBlog, February 14, 2016, https://www.lawfareblog.com/tweeting-terrorists-part-iii-how-would-twitter-defend-itself-against-material-support-prosecution.

55 Melissa Eddy and Mark Scott, "Facebook and Twitter Could Face Fines in Germany Over Hate Speech Posts," *New York Times,* March 14, 2017, https://www.nytimes.com/2017/03/14/technology/germany-hate-speech-facebook-tech.html.

56 Lasar, "Nazi Hunting."

57 MacKinnon et al., "Fostering Freedom Online"; Emily Greenhouse, "Twitter's Speech Problem: Hashtags and Hate" *New Yorker,* January 25, 2013. In the end, the French student union involved in the case threatened a civil lawsuit did Twitter comply with the court order. Somini Sengupta, "Twitter Yields to Pressure in Hate Case in France," *New York Times,* July 12, 2013, http://www.nytimes.com/2013/07/13/technology/twitter-yields-to-pressure-in-hate-case-in-france.html.

58 David Bogado, "No to Internet Censorship in Argentina," Electronic Frontier Foundation, August 11, 2015, https://www.eff.org/deeplinks/2015/08/no-internet-censorship-argentina.

59 Radsch, "Treating the Internet as the Enemy in the Middle East."

60 Ibid.

61 Bradley Brooks and Juliana Barbassa, "Arrest of Google Brazil Head Stirs Debate over Web," Associated Press, September 27, 2012, http://finance.yahoo.com/news/arrest-google-brazil-head-stirs-debate-over-210814484--finance.html.

62 "Zuckerberg Notes Turkey's Defamation Laws over Atatürk as Facebook Updates Rules," *Hurriyet Daily News,* March 16, 2015, http://www.hurriyetdailynews.com/zuckerberg-notes-turkeys-defamation-laws-over-ataturk-as-facebook-updates-rules.aspx?pageID=238&nID=79771&NewsCatID=359.

63 Xeni Jardin, "Vietnam Complained of 'Toxic' Anti-Government Facebook Content, Now Says Facebook Has Committed to Help Censor," Boing Boing, April 26, 2017,

https://boingboing.net/2017/04/26/vietnam-complained-of-toxic.html; Shailaja Neelakantan, "Facebook Blocks 85% 'Blasphemous' Content in Pakistan, Islamabad High Court Still Unhappy," *Times of India,* March 28, 2017, http://timesofindia .indiatimes.com/world/pakistan/facebook-blocks-85-blasphemous-content-in -pakistan-islamabad-high-court-still-unhappy/articleshow/57872857.cms; TechCrunch staff, "Facebook Is Censoring Posts in Thailand That the Government Has Deemed Unsuitable," TechCrunch, January 11, 2017, http://social.techcrunch .com/2017/01/11/facebook-censorship-thailand/.

64 Daniil Turovsky, "This Is How Russian Internet Censorship Works: A Journey into the Belly of the Beast That Is the Kremlin's Media Watchdog," Meduza, August 13, 2015, https://meduza.io/en/feature/2015/08/13/this-is-how-russian-internet -censorship-works.

65 Paul Sonne and Olga Razumovskaya, "Russia Steps Up New Law to Control Foreign Internet Companies," *Wall Street Journal,* September 24, 2014, http://www.wsj.com /articles/russia-steps-up-new-law-to-control-foreign-internet -companies-1411574920.

66 Alec Luhn, "Russia Threatens to Ban Google, Twitter, and Facebook over Extremist Content," *Guardian,* May 20, 2015, http://www.theguardian.com/world/2015 /may/20/russia-threaten-ban-google-twitter-facebook-bloggers-law.

67 Medeiros, "Platform (Non-) Intervention and the 'Marketplace' Paradigm for Speech Regulation," 2.

68 Suzor et al., "Non-consensual Porn and the Responsibilities of Online Intermediaries."

69 Eric Geller, "White House and Tech Companies Brainstorm How to Slow ISIS Propaganda," *Daily Dot,* January 8, 2016, https://www.dailydot.com/layer8/white -house-tech-companies-online-extremism-meeting/.

70 Dia Kayyali and Danny O'Brien, "Facing the Challenge of Online Harassment," Electronic Frontier Foundation, January 8, 2015, https://www.eff.org. /deeplinks/2015/01/facing-challenge-online-harassment; Matias et al., "Reporting, Reviewing, and Responding to Harassment on Twitter."

71 Turner, *From Counterculture to Cyberculture.*

72 Puppis, "Media Governance"; Verhulst, "The Regulation of Digital Content."

73 Tarleton Gillespie, "Facebook's Algorithm—Why Our Assumptions Are Wrong, and Our Concerns Are Right," *Culture Digitally,* July 4, 2014, http://culturedigitally .org/2014/07/facebooks-algorithm-why-our-assumptions-are-wrong-and-our -concerns-are-right/.

74 Adam Thierer, "Celebrating 20 Years of Internet Free Speech and Free Exchange," Medium, June 21, 2017, https://readplaintext.com/celebrating-20-years-of-internet -free-speech-free-exchange-8a10f236d0bd; Electronic Frontier Foundation, "Manila Principles on Intermediary Liability."

75 David Post, "A Bit of Internet History, or How Two Members of Congress Helped Create a Trillion or so Dollars of Value," *Washington Post,* August 27, 2015,

https://www.washingtonpost.com/news/volokh-conspiracy/wp/2015/08/27/a-bit-of
-internet-history-or-how-two-members-of-congress-helped-create-a-trillion-or-so
-dollars-of-value/.

76 An intriguing exception to how Section 230 has generally been applied in U.S. courts
is the decision Roommates.com (*Fair Housing Council of San Fernando Valley, et al. v.
Roommates.com LLC,* 489 F.3d 921, CV-03-09386-PA (9th Cir., May 15, 2007) aff'd en
banc 2008 WL 879293 (9th Cir., April 3, 2008).) Roommates.com was charged with
facilitating discrimination on the basis of race and sexual preference, in part because
the roommate preference survey required that these questions be answered, and used
that information to algorithmically show some profiles to some users. Roommates.
com argued that Section 230 offered it protection from any liability for what its users
did. But the court ruled that because the platform had asked for these personal
details, and had algorithmically selected what to show to whom, it was so involved in
the creation and distribution of that information that it could not enjoy the
immunity offered by 230. This case offers an intriguing alternative for how to think
about the responsibilities of platforms now that they algorithmically sort
and display user contributions. See http://www.internetlibrary.com/topics/comm
_decency_act.cfm.

77 Christopher Zara, "The Most Important Law in Tech Has a Problem," *Wired,* January
3, 2017, https://www.wired.com/2017/01/the-most-important-law-in-tech-has-a
-problem/.

CHAPTER 3 COMMUNITY GUIDELINES, OR THE SOUND OF NO

1 Ammori "The 'New' New York Times"; DeNicola, "EULA, Codec, API"; Heins,
"The Brave New World of Social Media Censorship"; Humphreys, "Predicting,
Securing and Shaping the Future"; Suzor, "The Role of the Rule of Law in Virtual
Communities"; Wauters, Lievens, and Valcke, "Towards a Better Protection of Social
Media Users."

2 I examined the content guidelines for more than sixty popular social networking
sites, image and video archives, app stores, and blogging platforms. For a few I looked
at how the policies have changed over time, using the older versions preserved in the
Internet Archive. Through the chapter I have tried deliberately to draw examples
from a range of platforms across scales and genres—some prominent, some niche,
some dead and gone.

3 Etsy changed this language in September or October 2013.

4 Personal interview.

5 Kickstarter changed this language in June 2014.

6 Tagged published its community guidelines as posts within a blog dedicated to
community news and support. The version that included this particular phrasing
appeared in September 2011 and remained on the site as late as 2015. http://web
.archive.org/web/20150106143145/http://help.tagged.com:80/t5/Community-News
/Community-Guidelines/ba-p/511. A "new and improved" version of Tagged's

community guidelines, using different language, was posted in July 2013. http://web
.archive.org/web/20130703044652/http://help.tagged.com:80/t5/Community
-Support/New-Improved-Guidelines/td-p/178504/.

7 Instagram changed this language in April 2015.

8 Etsy changed this in September or October 2013.

9 Heins, *Not in Front of the Children;* Hendershot, *Saturday Morning Censors.*

10 Twitter changed this language in October 2015.

11 Instagram changed this language in April 2015.

12 Dino Grandoni, "James Holmes Facebook Fan Page Apparently Taken Down,"
Huffington Post, July 30, 2010, http://www.huffingtonpost.com/2012/07/30
/james-holmes-facebook-fan-page_n_1720195.html.

13 Alexis Kleinman, "Why 'Kill George Zimmerman' Facebook Pages Still Exist,"
Huffington Post, July 17, 2013, http://www.huffingtonpost.com/2013/07/17
/kill-george-zimmerman-facebook_n_3611633.html.

14 Facebook, "Community Standards and Facebook Live," July 8, 2016, https://
newsroom.fb.com/news/h/community-standards-and-facebook-live/.

15 Citron, *Hate Crimes in Cyberspace;* Reagle, *Reading the Comments;* Shepherd et al.,
"Histories of Hating."

16 Ellen Pao, "The Trolls Are Winning the Battle for the Internet," *Washington Post,*
July 16, 2015, https://www.washingtonpost.com/opinions/we-cannot-let-the
-internet-trolls-win/2015/07/16/91b1a2d2-2b17-11e5-bd33-395c05608059_story
.html.

17 Jane, " 'Your a Ugly, Whorish, Slut' "; Jeong, *The Internet of Garbage;* Faris, et al.,
"Understanding Harmful Speech Online"; Phillips, *This Is Why We Can't Have Nice
Things;* Phillips, Beyer, and Coleman, "Trolling Scholars Debunk the Idea That the
Alt-Right's Shitposters Have Magic Powers"; Shaw, "The Internet Is Full of Jerks,
Because the World Is Full of Jerks"; York, "Solutions for Online Harassment Don't
Come Easily."

18 Lenhart et al., "Online Harassment, Digital Abuse, and Cyberstalking in America";
Milosevic, "Social Media Companies' Cyberbullying Policies."

19 Phillips, *This Is Why We Can't Have Nice Things.*

20 SoundCloud changed this language in July 2015.

21 Neff and Nagy, "Talking to Bots."

22 Susan Benesch and Rebecca Mackinnon "The Innocence of YouTube," *Foreign Policy,*
October 5, 2012, http://foreignpolicy.com/2012/10/05/the-innocence-of-youtube/;
Citron, "Cyber Civil Rights"; Citron and Norton, "Intermediaries and Hate Speech";
Daniels and Everett, "Race, Civil Rights, and Hate Speech in the Digital Era"; Daniels,
"Race and Racism in Internet Studies"; Nakamura and Chow-White, *Race after the
Internet;* Sellars, "Defining Hate Speech."

23 Daniels and Everett, "Race, Civil Rights, and Hate Speech in the Digital Era";
Matamoros-Fernández, "Platformed Racism."

24 Google AdSense allows historical examples for academic purposes.

25 Medium changed this language in January 2017.

26 Personal interview.

27 Vindu Goel and Mike Isaac, "Facebook Moves to Ban Private Gun Sales on Its Site and Instagram," January 29, 2016, https://www.nytimes.com/2016/01/30/technology /facebook-gun-sales-ban.html.

28 LinkedIn, "Reporting Inaccurate Information on Another Member's Profile," https:// www.linkedin.com/help/linkedin/answer/30200; LinkedIn, "Reporting Fake Profiles," https://www.linkedin.com/help/linkedin/answer/61664.

29 Turkle, *Life on the Screen.*

30 Kennedy, "Beyond Anonymity"; Suler, "The Online Disinhibition Effect." This conclusion has been disputed, but it persists as received wisdom. See J. Nathan Matias, "The Real Name Fallacy," Coral Project, January 3, 2017, https://blog .coralproject.net/the-real-name-fallacy/.

31 boyd, "The Politics of 'Real Names.' "

32 Lil Miss Hot Mess, "One Year Later, Facebook Still Hasn't Fixed Its Controversial 'Real Names' Policy," Daily Dot, October 6, 2015, http://www.dailydot.com/opinion /facebook-real-name-policy/.

33 Lizze Plaugic, "The Enduring Strangeness of Twitter Parody Accounts," Verge, March 14, 2016, https://www.theverge.com/2016/3/14/11208538/twitter-parody-accounts -ted-ron-burgundy. Haimson and Hoffmann, "Constructing and Enforcing 'Authentic' Identity Online." Lingel and Gillespie, "One Name to Rule Them All."

34 John, *The Age of Sharing.*

35 Marwick, *Status Update;* Thompson, "The New Visibility."

36 Andrejevic et al., "Participations"; Bakioglu, "Exposing Convergence"; David and Pinch, "Six Degrees of Reputation"; Fast, Örnebring, and Karlsson, "Metaphors of Free Labor"; Herman, "Production, Consumption, and Labor in the Social Media Mode of Communication"; Jarrett, "The Relevance of 'Women's Work' "; Postigo, "The Socio-Technical Architecture of Digital Labor"; van Doorn, "Platform Labor."

37 Melissa Zimdars, "My 'Fake News List' Went Viral. But Made-Up Stories Are Only Part of the Problem," *Washington Post,* November 18, 2016, https://www.washingtonpost .com/posteverything/wp/2016/11/18/my-fake-news-list-went-viral-but-made-up -stories-are-only-part-of-the-problem/?utm_term=.e85377696beb; Angie Drobnic Holan, "2016 Lie of the Year: Fake News," Politifact, December 13, 2016, http://www .politifact.com/truth-o-meter/article/2016/dec/13/2016-lie-year-fake-news/. For a survey of the fake news phenomenon, see also Jack, "Lexicon of Lies."

38 Associated Press, " 'Pizzagate' Shooting Suspect: 'The Intel on This Wasn't 100 Percent,' " December 8, 2016, http://www.cbsnews.com/news/pizzagate-shooting -suspect-edgar-maddison-welch-intel-wasnt-100-percent/.

39 Kaveh Waddell, "Facebook and Google Won't Let Fake News Sites Use Their Ad Networks," *Atlantic,* November 15, 2016, https://www.theatlantic.com/technology

/archive/2016/11/facebook-and-google-wont-let-fake-news-sites-use-their-ads
-platforms/507737/.

40 This has expanded: for example, Google started letting users flag when their
"snippets" when they're incorrect. See Klint Finley, "Google Wants You to Help Fix
the Fake-Fact Problem," *Wired,* April 26, 2017, https://www.wired.com/2017/04
/google-wants-crowd-solve-fake-fact-problem/.

41 danah boyd, "Turmoil in Blogland," *Salon,* January 8, 2005, http://www.salon
.com/2005/01/08/livejournal/.

42 Personal interview.

43 Personal interview.

44 Carolyn Gregoire, "The Hunger Blogs: A Secret World of Teenage 'Thinspiration,'"
Huffington Post, February 8, 2012, http://www.huffingtonpost.com/2012/02/08
/thinspiration-blogs_n_1264459.html.

45 Boero and Pascoe, "Pro-Anorexia Communities and Online Interaction."

46 Alice Marwick, "Is Blocking Pro-ED Content the Right Way to Solve Eating
Disorders?" Social Media Collective, February 24, 2012, https://socialmediacollective
.org/2012/02/24/is-blocking-pro-ed-content-the-right-way-to-solve-eating-disorders/.

47 boyd, Ryan, and Leavitt, "Pro-Self-Harm and the Visibility of Youth-Generated
Problematic Content."

48 Ibid.

49 Tina Peng, "Pro-Anorexia Groups Spread to Facebook," *Newsweek,* November 22,
2008, http://www.newsweek.com/pro-anorexia-groups-spread-facebook-85129.

50 Nate Anderson, "Psychiatrists Want Crackdown on Pro-Anorexia Websites," Ars
Technica, September 20, 2009, http://arstechnica.com/tech-policy/2009/09
/psychiatrists-crack-down-on-pro-ana-eating-disorder-sites/.

51 Lindsay Tanner, "What Should YouTube Do about Graphic Self-Harm Videos?"
Salon, February 21, 2011, http://www.salon.com/2011/02/21/youtube_self_injury
_videos/.

52 Oliver Lindberg, "Interview with David Karp: The Rise and Rise of Tumblr," .net
magazine, April 2011, https://medium.com/the-lindberg-interviews/interview-with
-david-karp-the-rise-and-rise-of-tumblr-ed51085140cd.

53 Erin Gloria Ryan, "The Scary, Weird World of Pinterest Thinspo Boards," Jezebel,
March 19, 2012, http://jezebel.com/5893382/the-scary-weird-world-of-pinterest
-thinspo-boards.

54 Ibid.

55 Amy Rose Spiegel, "Here's How Social Media 'Thinspiration' Bans Are Actually
Working Out," Buzzfeed, January 11, 2013, https://www.buzzfeed.com/verymuchso
/heres-how-social-media-thinspiration-bans-are-a.

56 Sarah Perez, "Over a Year after New Content Policies, 'Self-Harm Social Media' Still
Thrives," TechCrunch, June 20, 2013, http://social.techcrunch.com/2013/06/20
/over-a-year-after-new-content-policies-self-harm-social-media-still-thrives/.

57 Suzor, "The Role of the Rule of Law in Virtual Communities."
58 Charlie Warzel, " 'A Honeypot for Assholes': Inside Twitter's 10-Year Failure To Stop Harassment," Buzzfeed, August 11, 2016, https://www.buzzfeed.com /charliewarzel/a-honeypot-for-assholes-inside-twitters-10-year-failure-to-s.
59 Roth, " 'No Overly Suggestive Photos of Any Kind.' "
60 Balkin, "Digital Speech and Democratic Culture."
61 Suzor, "The Role of the Rule of Law in Virtual Communities."

CHAPTER 4 **THREE IMPERFECT SOLUTIONS TO THE PROBLEM OF SCALE**

1 Guins, *Edited Clean Version.*
2 Marston, "The Social Construction of Scale"; Qvortrup, "Understanding New Digital Media."
3 Personal interview.
4 See Anderson et al., "Unfriending Censorship." Mikkel Flyverbom convincingly argues that all forms of transparency guide our attention to some issues and away from others. See Flyverbom, "Digital Age Transparency."
5 Mark Zuckerberg, Facebook post, May 3, 2017, https://www.facebook.com/zuck /posts/10103695315624661. See also Mike Murphy, "Facebook Is Hiring 3,000 More People to Monitor Facebook Live for Murders, Suicides, and Other Horrific Video," Quartz, May 3, 2017, https://qz.com/974720/facebook-fb-ceo-mark-zuckerberg-is -hiring-3000-more-people-to-monitor-facebook-live-for-murders-suicides-and -other-horrific-video/.
6 "Twitter: Over Half a Million Blocked for 'Terror' Ties," Al Jazeera, March 21, 2017, http://www.aljazeera.com/news/2017/03/twitter-million-blocked-terror -ties-170321185026556.html. Keep in mind that multiple accounts certainly were operated by the same individuals or groups; this does not diminish, however, how many must be reviewed in order to figure that out.
7 Shirky, *Here Comes Everybody.*
8 Many thanks to Kevin Driscoll for this observation. See Driscoll, "Social Media's Dial-Up Ancestor."
9 Forsyth, "Forum."
10 Personal interview.
11 Bernstein, *Controlling Hollywood;* Hendershot, *Saturday Morning Censors;* Hilliard and Keith, *Dirty Discourse;* Lane, *The Decency Wars;* Lewis, *Hollywood v. Hard Core;* McCracken, "Regulating Swish"; Louis Menand, "Banned Books and Blockbusters," *New Yorker,* December 12, 2016, http://www.newyorker.com/magazine/2016/12/12 /people-of-the-book-2; Miller, *Censored Hollywood;* Vaughn, *Freedom and Entertainment.*
12 Maria Bustillos, "Curses! The Birth of the Bleep and Modern American Censorship," Verge, August 27, 2013, https://www.theverge.com/2013/8/27/4545388/curses-the -birth-of-the-bleep-and-modern-american-censorship.
13 Horwitz, "The First Amendment Meets Some New Technologies"; Lane, *The Decency Wars.*

14 Ryan Tate, "Steve Jobs Offers World 'Freedom from Porn,' " *Gawker,* May 15, 2010, http://gawker.com/5539717/steve-jobs-offers-world-freedom-from-porn.

15 Zittrain, *The Future of the Internet and How to Stop It;* Grimmelman and Ohm, "Dr. Generative"; Steven Johnson, "Everybody's Business—How Apple Has Rethought a Gospel of the Web," *New York Times,* April 10, 2010, http://www.nytimes.com/2010/04/11/technology/internet/11every.html.

16 Hestres, "App Neutrality."

17 Weber, *The Success of Open Source;* Fred von Lohmann, "All Your Apps Are Belong to Apple: The iPhone Developer Program License Agreement," *Electronic Frontier Foundation,* March 9, 2010, https://www.eff.org/deeplinks/2010/03/iphone-developer-program-license-agreement-all.

18 Rogers, "Jailbroken."

19 Nick Statt, "US Government Says It's Now Okay to Jailbreak Your Tablet and Smart TV," Verge, October 27, 2015, http://www.theverge.com/2015/10/27/9622066/jailbreak-unlocked-tablet-smart-tvs-dmca-exemption-library-of-congress.

20 Boudreau and Hagiu, "Platform Rules."

21 Morris and Elkins, "There's a History for That"; Nieborg, "Crushing Candy."

22 Elaluf-Calderwood et al., "Control as a Strategy"; Tiwana, Konsynski, and Bush, "Platform Evolution."

23 Barzilai-Nahon, "Toward a Theory of Network Gatekeeping."

24 Graham Spencer, "Developers: Apple's App Review Needs Big Improvements," MacStories, March 1, 2016, https://www.macstories.net/stories/developers-apples-app-review-needs-big-improvements/. See also "Average App Store Review Times," http://appreviewtimes.com/.

25 Laura McGann, "Mark Fiore Can Win a Pulitzer Prize, but He Can't Get his iPhone Cartoon App Past Apple's Satire Police," Nieman Lab, April 15, 2010. http://www.niemanlab.org/2010/04/mark-fiore-can-win-a-pulitzer-prize-but-he-cant-get-his-iphone-cartoon-app-past-apples-satire-police/.

26 Gabe Jacobs, "Bushisms iPhone App Rejected," Gabe Jacobs Blog, September 13, 2008, http://www.gabejacobsblog.com/2008/09/13/bushisms-iphone-app-rejected/ (no longer available online); Alec, "Freedom Time Rejected by Apple for App Store," Juggleware Dev Blog, September 21, 2008, https://www.juggleware.com/blog/2008/09/freedomtime-rejected-by-apple-for-app-store/.

27 Robin Wauters, "Apple Rejects Obama Trampoline iPhone App, Leaves Us Puzzled," TechCrunch, February 7, 2009, http://techcrunch.com/2009/02/07/apple-rejects-obama-trampoline-iphone-app-leaves-us-puzzled/; Don Bora, "Rejected App (Biden's Teeth)," Eight Bit Blog, June 6, 2009, http://blog.eightbitstudios.com/rejected-app.

28 "iSinglePayer iPhone App Censored by Apple," Lambda Jive, September 26, 2009, http://lambdajive.wordpress.com/2009/09/.

29 Alec, "Steve Jobs Responds," Juggleware Dev Blog, September 23, 2008, http://www.juggleware.com/blog/2008/09/steve-jobs-writes-back/.

30 Ryan Singel, "Jobs Rewrites History about Apple Ban on Satire," *Wired,* June 3, 2010, https://www.wired.com/2010/06/jobs-apple-satire-ban/.

31 Alexia Tsotsis, "WikiLeaks iPhone App Made $5,840 before Pulled by Apple, $1 From Each Sale Will Be Donated to WikiLeaks," TechCrunch, December 22, 2010, https://techcrunch.com/2010/12/22/wikileaks-2/.

32 Rebecca Greenfield, "Apple Rejected the Drone Tracker App Because It Could," *Atlantic,* August 30, 2012, https://www.theatlantic.com/technology/archive/2012/08/apple-rejected-drone-tracker-app-because-it-could/324120/.

33 Ryan Chittum, "Apple's Speech Policies Should Still Worry the Press," *Columbia Journalism Review,* April 20, 2010, http://www.cjr.org/the_audit/apples_speech_policies_should.php.

34 Charles Christensen, "iPad Publishing No Savior for Small Press, LGBT Comics Creators," Prism Comics, June 2010, http://prismcomics.org/display.php?id=1858 (no longer available online).

35 John Gruber, "Ninjawords: iPhone Dictionary, Censored by Apple," Daring Fireball, August 4, 2009, https://daringfireball.net/2009/08/ninjawords; John Gruber, "Phil Schiller Responds Regarding Ninjawords and the App Store," Daring Fireball, August 6, 2009, https://daringfireball.net/2009/08/phil_schiller_app_store; Ryan Chittum, "Apple's Controlling Instincts Censor Ulysses All Over Again," *Columbia Journalism Review,* June 11, 2010, http://archives.cjr.org/the_audit/apples_controlling_instincts_c.php; James Montgomerie, "Whither Eucalyptus?" James Montgomerie's World Wide Web Log, May 21, 2009, http://www.blog.montgomerie.net/whither-eucalyptus.

36 Tracey Lien, "The Apple Obstacle for Serious Games," Polygon, June 21, 2013, http://www.polygon.com/2013/6/21/4449770/the-apple-obstacle-for-serious-games.

37 Chad Sapieha, "Are Games on Apple's App Store Curated or Censored?" *Financial Post,* April 22, 2013, http://business.financialpost.com/2013/04/22/is-apples-app-store-curated-or-censored/.

38 For example, Apple approved, then removed, the game Survival Island 3: Australia Story 3D because the game depended on the player bludgeoning aboriginal Australians. Daisy Dumas, "Survival Island 3: Australia Story 3D Game That Encourages Players to Bludgeon Aboriginal Australians to Death Causes Outrage," *Sydney Morning Herald,* January 16, 2016, http://www.smh.com.au/digital-life/games/survival-island-3-australia-story-3d-game-that-encourages-players-to-bludgeon-aborigines-to-death-causes-outrage-20160115-gm76mw.html.

39 A second app criticizing Apple and FoxConn, In a Permanent Save State, imagined the afterlives of dead FoxConn workers. It too was accepted but then removed two hours later. Here, the app was rejected in part for child abuse and, more generally, for being "excessively objectionable."

40 Jason Kincaid, "The New App Store Rules: No Swimsuits, No Skin, and No Innuendo," TechCrunch, February 20, 2010, https://techcrunch.com/2010/02/20/app-store-rules-sexy/.

41 Jenna Wortham, "Apple Bans Some Apps for Sex-Tinged Content" *New York Times*, February 22, 2010, http://www.nytimes.com/2010/02/23/technology/23apps.html.

42 John Koetsier, "Google Bans Glass Porn Apps (Goodbye 'Tits and Glass' App)," Venture Beat, June 3, 2013, http://venturebeat.com/2013/06/03/google-bans-porn -apps-literally-hours-after-tits-and-glass-app-launches/.

43 Miguel Helft, "Art School Runs Afoul of Facebook's Nudity Police," *New York Times*, February 18, 2011, https://bits.blogs.nytimes.com/2011/02/18/art-school-runs-afoul -of-facebooks-nudity-policy/; Robert Mankoff, "Nipplegate: Why the New Yorker Cartoon Department Is about to Be Banned from Facebook," *New Yorker*, September 10, 2012, http://www.newyorker.com/online/blogs/cartoonists/2012/09/nipplegate -why-the-new-yorker-cartoon-department-is-about-to-be-banned-from-facebook .html.

44 Gillespie, "Exodus International."

45 Lina Harper, "Grindr Tightens Guidelines: No Underwear, No Cock Size," Xtra, April 13, 2010, https://www.dailyxtra.com/grindr-tightens-guidelines-no-underwear-no -cock-size-30220.

46 Desiree Everts DeNunzio, "Bang with Friends Back in the App Store—with a New Name," CNet, August 29, 2013, http://news.cnet.com/8301-1023_3-57600699-93 /bang-with-friends-back-in-the-app-store-with-a-new-name/.

47 Mike Isaac, "LinkedIn Shuts Down 'Bang with Professionals' Hook-Up App," All Things D, February 8, 2013, http://allthingsd.com/20130208/linkedin-shuts-down -bang-with-professionals-hook-up-app/.

48 Braun and Gillespie, "Hosting the Public Discourse"; Hermida and Thurman, "A Clash of Cultures."

49 Braun, "Going Over the Top."

50 Shirky, *Here Comes Everybody*.

51 Personal interview.

52 Catherine Buni and Soraya Chemaly, "The Unsafety Net: How Social Media Turned against Women," *Atlantic,* October 9, 2014, http://www.theatlantic.com/technology /archive/2014/10/the-unsafety-net-how-social-media-turned-against-women/381261/.

53 See, for example, an early objection to flagging on Blogger: Al S. E., "Blogger Is Not a Business Like Other Businesses," The Meaning of Blogger's Flag, September 18, 2005, http://bloggercensors.blogspot.com/2005/09/blogger-is-not-business-like-other_18 .html.

54 Feenberg and Bakardjieva, "Virtual Community"; Howard and Jones, *Society Online;* Song, *Virtual Communities*.

55 YouTube, "We Are Ecstatic . . .," YouTube Official Blog, August 11, 2005, http:// youtube-global.blogspot.com/2005/08/we-are-ecstatic-to-announce-changes-we .html.

56 YouTube, "Contact Us" (archived August 13, 2005), http://web.archive.org /web/20050813010634/http://www.youtube.com/contact.php.

57 Bowker and Star, *Sorting Things Out*.

58 Peterson, "User-Generated Censorship."

59 Fiore-Silfvast, "User-Generated Warfare."

60 This may be also a tactic of governments looking to silence political criticism: Duy Hoang, "Vietnamese Government 'Opinion Shapers' Target Activist Facebook Pages," Global Voices AdVox, July 18, 2014, https://advox.globalvoices.org/2014/07/18 /vietnamese-government-opinion-shapers-target-activist-facebook-pages/.

61 Fiore-Silfvast, "User-Generated Warfare."

62 Butler et al., "Community Effort in Online Groups"; Ford, "Infoboxes and Cleanup Tags"; Geiger and Ribes, "The Work of Sustaining Order in Wikipedia." Halavais, "Do Dugg Diggers Digg Diligently?"; Kushner, "Read Only"; Niederer and van Dijck, "Wisdom of the Crowd or Technicity of Content?"; Reagle, *Good Faith Collaboration*.

63 Greg Seals, "Facebook Tells Drag Queens to Use Their Legal Names or Risk Losing Their Profiles," Daily Dot, September 11, 2014, http://www.dailydot.com/lifestyle /facebook-demands-drag-queens-change-names/; Lingel and Gillespie, "One Name to Rule Them All."

64 Chris Cox, Facebook, October 1, 2014, https://www.facebook.com/chris.cox /posts/10101301777354543.

65 Ibid.

66 Taylor Hatmaker, "RealNamePolice and the Real Story behind Facebook's Name Policy Fumble," Daily Dot, October 3, 2014, http://www.dailydot.com/technology /realnamepolice-facebook-real-names-policy/.

67 https://twitter.com/RealNamesBack/status/514182271687852032 (account since suspended).

68 https://twitter.com/RealNamesBack/status/514167671487602689 (account since suspended).

69 This suggests that Facebook probably received more flags than just those from a single individual, contrary to its apology statement.

70 Hatmaker, "RealNamePolice."

71 Ben Quinn, "YouTube Staff Too Swamped to Filter Out All Terror-Related Content," *Guardian,* January 28, 2015, https://www.theguardian.com/technology/2015/jan/28 /youtube-too-swamped-to-filter-terror-content.

72 Sam Gustin, "How Google Beat Viacom in the Landmark YouTube Copyright Case—Again," *Time,* April 19, 2013, http://business.time.com/2013/04/19/how -google-beat-viacom-in-the-landmark-youtube-copyright-case-again/.

73 Josh Constine, "Facebook Spares Humans by Fighting Offensive Photos with AI," TechCrunch, May 31, 2016, https://techcrunch.com/2016/05/31/terminating-abuse/.

74 Brian Barrett, "This Algorithm Wants to Find Who's Naked on the Internet," *Wired,* June 24, 2915, http://www.wired.com/2015/06/nude-recognition-algorithmia/.

75 boyd, Levy, and Marwick, "The Networked Nature of Algorithmic Discrimination"; Citron and Pasquale, "The Scored Society"; O'Neil, *Weapons of Math Destruction*; Pasquale, *The Black Box Society;* Shorey and Howard, "Automation, Big Data and

Politics"; Tufekci, "Algorithmic Harms beyond Facebook and Google"; Zarsky, "The Trouble with Algorithmic Decisions"; Lauren Kirchner, "When Discrimination Is Baked into Algorithms," *Atlantic,* September 6, 2015, https://www.theatlantic.com /business/archive/2015/09/discrimination-algorithms-disparate-impact/403969/.

76 Gillespie, "Algorithm"; Ian Bogost, "The Cathedral of Computation," *Atlantic,* January 1, 2015, https://www.theatlantic.com/technology/archive/2015/01/the -cathedral-of-computation/384300/; Steve Lohr, "Algorithms Get a Human Hand in Steering Web," *New York Times,* March 10, 2013, http://www.nytimes.com/2013 /03/11/technology/computer-algorithms-rely-increasingly-on-human-helpers.html.

77 Victoria Grand (YouTube), "Making YouTube a Safer Place," Google Europe Blog, June 22, 2009, https://europe.googleblog.com/2009/06/making-youtube-safer-place .html.

78 This feature was removed once YouTube's Safety Mode was introduced, which hides all comments. Christina Warren, "YouTube Adds 'Safety Mode' to Keep Videos PG," Mashable, February 10, 2010, http://mashable.com/2010/02/10/youtube-safety -mode/#6nYc4wnlZ5qB.

79 Molly McHugh, "Slack Is Overrun with Bots. Friendly, Wonderful Bots," August 21, 2015, https://www.wired.com/2015/08/slack-overrun-bots-friendly-wonderful-bots/.

80 Kevin Systrom, "Keeping Comments Safe on Instagram," September 12, 2016, http:// blog.instagram.com/post/150312324357/160912-news.

81 Ryan Dube, "Unfortunate Truths about Child Pornography and the Internet," Make Use Of, December 7, 2012, http://www.makeuseof.com/tag/unfortunate-truths -about-child-pornography-and-the-internet-feature/.

82 Microsoft PhotoDNA: https://www.microsoft.com/en-us/photodna. See also Tracy Ith, "Microsoft's PhotoDNA: Protecting Children and Businesses in the Cloud," Microsoft News Center, July 15, 2015, https://news.microsoft.com/features /microsofts-photodna-protecting-children-and-businesses-in-the-cloud/.

83 YouTube also uses a tool called ContentID to automatically identify copyrighted music in user videos that works in much the same way, by matching the "fingerprint" of the music to a database of copyrighted works.

84 Sarah Perez, "Facebook, Microsoft, Twitter and YouTube Collaborate to Remove 'Terrorist Content' from Their Services," TechCrunch, December 5, 2016, https:// techcrunch.com/2016/12/05/facebook-microsoft-twitter-and-youtube-collaborate -to-remove-terrorist-content-from-their-services/.

85 My thanks to Sarah Myers West for this insight.

86 Ap-Apid, "An Algorithm for Nudity Detection."

87 Ibid.

88 Nude.js (https://github.com/pa7/nude.js, 2010) and Algorithmia's tool (https:// isitnude.com/, 2015) both explicitly acknowledge the Ap-Apid paper as the core of their tools.

89 Ma et al., "Human Skin Detection via Semantic Constraint."

90 Lee et al., "Naked Image Detection Based on Adaptive and Extensible Skin Color Model"; Platzer, Stuetz, and Lindorfer, "Skin Sheriff"; Sengamedu, Sanyal, and Satish, "Detection of Pornographic Content in Internet Images."

91 Lee et al., "Naked Image Detection Based on Adaptive and Extensible Skin Color Model."

92 James Sutton, "Improving Nudity Detection and NSFW Image Recognition," KD Nuggets, June 25, 2016, http://www.kdnuggets.com/2016/06/algorithmia -improving-nudity-detection-nsfw-image-recognition.html.

93 Sengamedu, Sanyal, and Satish, "Detection of Pornographic Content in Internet Images."

94 Jay Mahadeokar and Gerry Pesavento, "Open Sourcing a Deep Learning Solution for Detecting NSFW Images," Yahoo Engineering blog, September 30, 2016, https:// yahooeng.tumblr.com/post/151148689421/open-sourcing-a-deep-learning -solution-for.

95 Agarwal and Sureka, "A Focused Crawler"; Djuric et al., "Hate Speech Detection with Comment Embeddings"; Sood, Antin, and Churchill, "Profanity Use in Online Communities"; Warner and Hirschberg, "Detecting Hate Speech on the World Wide Web."

96 Brendan Maher, "Can a Video Game Company Tame Toxic Behaviour?" *Nature,* March 30, 2016, http://www.nature.com/news/can-a-video-game-company-tame -toxic-behaviour-1.19647.

97 Cheng, Danescu-Niculescu-Mizil, and Leskovec, "Antisocial Behavior in Online Discussion Communities."

98 Cade Metz, "Twitter's New AI Recognizes Porn So You Don't Have To," *Wired,* July 8, 2015, http://www.wired.com/2015/07/twitters-new-ai-recognizes-porn-dont/.

99 Dyer, "Making 'White' People White."

100 See also Roth, "Looking at Shirley, the Ultimate Norm."

101 Mulvin, *Proxies.*

102 Manovich, *The Language of New Media,* 63.

103 Platzer, Stuetz, and Lindorfer, "Skin Sheriff."

104 Personal interview with Twitter content policy representative. See also Charlie Warzel, " 'A Honeypot for Assholes': Inside Twitter's 10-Year Failure to Stop Harassment," *Buzzfeed,* August 11, 2016, https://www.buzzfeed.com/charliewarzel /a-honeypot-for-assholes-inside-twitters-10-year-failure-to-s.

105 Many thanks to Mary Gray for this insight.

106 Carmel DeAmicis, "Meet the Anonymous App Police Fighting Bullies and Porn on Whisper, Yik Yak, and Potentially Secret," Gigaom, August 8, 2014, https://gigaom .com/2014/08/08/meet-the-anonymous-app-police-fighting-bullies-and-porn-on -whisper-yik-yak-and-potentially-secret/.

107 Eric Geller, "White House and Tech Companies Brainstorm How to Slow ISIS Propaganda," Daily Dot, January 8, 2016, http://www.dailydot.com/politics /white-house-tech-companies-online-extremism-meeting/; Andy Greenberg,

"Inside Google's Internet Justice League and Its AI-Powered War on Trolls," *Wired*, September 19, 2016, https://www.wired.com/2016/09/inside-googles-internet -justice-league-ai-powered-war-trolls/.

108 Munk, "100,000 False Positives for Every Real Terrorist."

109 Cheney-Lippold, *We Are Data.*

110 Kelly Tatera, "'Faception' A.I. Claims to Detect Terrorists and Pedophiles Based on Their Facial Personality," *Science Explorer,* May 26, 2016, http://thescienceexplorer .com/technology/faception-ai-claims-detect-terrorists-and-pedophiles-based-their -facial-personality; Katherine Bailey, "Put Away Your Machine Learning Hammer, Criminality Is Not a Nail," *Wired,* November 29, 2016, https://backchannel.com /put-away-your-machine-learning-hammer-criminality-is-not-a-nail-1309c84bb899 #.7izgzahok.

CHAPTER 5 THE HUMAN LABOR OF MODERATION

1 Facebook "Community Standards," https://www.facebook.com/communitystandards.

2 Nick Hopkins, "How Facebook Flouts Holocaust Denial Laws Except Where It Fears Being Sued," *Guardian,* May 24, 2017, https://www.theguardian.com /news/2017/may/24/how-facebook-flouts-holocaust-denial-laws-except-where-it -fears-being-sued.

3 Till Krause and Hannes Grassegger, "Facebook's Secret Rule of Deletion," International, http://international.sueddeutsche.de/post/154543271930/facebooks -secret-rule-of-deletion; Adrian Chen, "Inside Facebook's Outsourced Anti-Porn and Gore Brigade, where 'Camel Toes' Are More Offensive than 'Crushed Heads,'" Gawker, February 16, 2012, http://gawker.com/5885714/inside-facebooks -outsourced-anti-porn-and-gore-brigade-where-camel-toes-are-more-offensive -than-crushed-heads.

4 Josh Constine, "Facebook Now Has 2 Billion Monthly Users . . . and Responsibility," TechCrunch, June 27, 2017, https://techcrunch.com/2017/06/27/facebook-2 -billion-users/.

5 Donna Tam, "Facebook Processes More Than 500 TB of Data Daily," CNET, August 22, 2012, https://www.cnet.com/news/facebook-processes-more-than-500-tb-of -data-daily/.

6 Twitter Usage Stats, as of July 2017, http://www.internetlivestats.com/twitter -statistics/.

7 With gratitude to Dylan Mulvin for this insight.

8 Emma Barnett and Iain Hollingshead, "The Dark Side of Facebook: Our Social Networking Pages Are Being Policed by Outsourced, Unvetted Moderators," *Telegraph,* March 2, 2012, http://www.telegraph.co.uk/technology/facebook /9118778/The-dark-side-of-Facebook.html; Katie Hunt and CY Xu, "China 'Employs 2 Million to Police Internet,'" CNN, October 7, 2013, http://www.cnn .com/2013/10/07/world/asia/china-internet-monitors/index.htm.

9 Streeter, *Selling the Air.*

10 For insight into the crowdworker labor force I rely on the journalism of Adrian Chen and Catherine Buni and the scholarship of Sarah Roberts and Sarah Myers West; for insight into community managers and authorized reporters, I lean heavily on the work of J. Nathan Matias.

11 Dale Markowiz, "How I Decide Who Gets Banned on OkCupid," *New York,* February 17, 2017, http://nymag.com/thecut/2017/02/banned-from-okcupid-sexting-moderation.html.

12 Jay Rosen, "The Delete Squad: Google, Twitter, Facebook, and the New Global Battle over the Future of Free Speech," *New Republic,* April 29, 2013, https://newrepublic.com/article/113045/free-speech-internet-silicon-valley-making-rules.

13 Kirkpatrick, *The Facebook Effect.*

14 Bilton, *Hatching Twitter.*

15 Personal interview with Facebook content policy representative; also Kirkpatrick, *The Facebook Effect.*

16 Personal interview with Facebook content policy representative.

17 Nick Summers, "Facebook's 'Porn Cops' Are Key to Its Growth," *Newsweek,* April 30, 2009, http://www.newsweek.com/facebooks-porn-cops-are-key-its-growth-77055.

18 Also: "Twitter declines to comment on how it decides which accounts to suspend and which content to remove." In Yoree Koh and Reed Albergotti, "Twitter Faces Free-Speech Dilemma," *Wall Street Journal,* August 21, 2014, http://www.wsj.com/articles/twitter-is-walking-a-fine-line-confronted-with-grisly-images-1408659519.

19 Adrian Chen, "The Laborers Who Keep Dick Pics and Beheadings Out of Your Facebook Feed," Wired, October 23, 2014, https://www.wired.com/2014/10/content-moderation/; Catherine Buni and Soraya Chemaly, "The Secret Rules of the Internet," Verge, April 13, 2016, http://www.theverge.com/2016/4/13/11387934/internet-moderator-history-youtube-facebook-reddit-censorship-free-speech; Sarah Roberts, "Social Media's Silent Filter," *Atlantic,* March 8, 2017, https://www.theatlantic.com/technology/archive/2017/03/commercial-content-moderation/518796/.

20 Aarti Shahani, "From Hate Speech to Fake News: The Content Crisis Facing Mark Zuckerberg," NPR All Tech Considered, November 17, 2016, http://www.npr.org/sections/alltechconsidered/2016/11/17/495827410/from-hate-speech-to-fake-news-the-content-crisis-facing-mark-zuckerberg.

21 Adrian Chen, "The Human Toll of Protecting the Internet from the Worst of Humanity," *New Yorker,* January 28, 2017, http://www.newyorker.com/tech/elements/the-human-toll-of-protecting-the-internet-from-the-worst-of-humanity.

22 Julia Floretti and Yn Chee, "Facebook, Twitter, YouTube, Microsoft Back EU Hate Speech Rules," Reuters, May 31, 2016, http://www.reuters.com/article/us-eu-facebook-twitter-hatecrime-idUSKCN0YM0VJ.

23 Catherine Buni and Soraya Chemaly, "The Unsafety Net: How Social Media Turned against Women," *Atlantic,* October 9, 2014, http://www.theatlantic.com/technology/archive/2014/10/the-unsafety-net-how-social-media-turned-against-women/381261/.

24 Mary Gray, "Your Job Is about to Get 'Taskified,'" *Los Angeles Times,* January 8, 2016, http://www.latimes.com/opinion/op-ed/la-oe-0110-digital-turk-work-20160110 -story.html.

25 Adrian Chen, "The Laborers Who Keep Dick Pics and Beheadings Out of Your Facebook Feed," Wired, October 23, 2014, https://www.wired.com/2014/10/content -moderation/; Quentin Hardy, "Spot Pornography on Facebook for a Quarter-Cent an Image," *New York Times,* December 5, 2011, http://bits.blogs.nytimes.com/2011 /12/05/spot-porn-on-facebook-for-a-quarter-cent-an-image/.

26 Hope Reese and Nick Heath, "Inside Amazon's Clickworker Platform: How Half a Million People Are Being Paid Pennies to Train AI," TechRepublic, 2016, http://www .techrepublic.com/article/inside-amazons-clickworker-platform-how-half-a-million -people-are-training-ai-for-pennies-per-task/.

27 Irani, "The Cultural Work of Microwork," 726.

28 Ibid., 725.

29 Roberts, "Commercial Content Moderation."

30 Brad Stone, "Concern for Those Who Screen the Web for Barbarity," *New York Times,* July 18, 2010, http://www.nytimes.com/2010/07/19/technology/19screen.html.

31 Reyhan Harmanci, "Tech Confessional: The Googler Who Looked at the Worst of the Internet," Buzzfeed, August 21, 2012, https://www.buzzfeed.com/reyhan/tech -confessional-the-googler-who-looks-at-the-wo.

32 Adrian Chen, "Facebook Releases New Content Guidelines, Now Allows Bodily Fluids," Gawker, February 16, 2012, http://gawker.com/5885836/.

33 Gray, "Your Job Is about to Get 'Taskified.'"

34 Downey, "Making Media Work."

35 Roberts, "Content Moderation."

36 Roberts, "Commercial Content Moderation."

37 Postigo, "America Online Volunteers."

38 Dibbell, "A Rape in Cyberspace."

39 Dutton, "Network Rules of Order."

40 Bergstrom, "'Don't Feed the Troll'"; Lampe and Resnick, "Slash (Dot) and Burn"; Kerr and Kelleher, "The Recruitment of Passion and Community"; Shaw and Hill, "Laboratories of Oligarchy?"

41 Postigo, "America Online Volunteers."

42 Kelty, "Geeks, Social Imaginaries, and Recursive Publics."

43 A class action lawsuit and subsequent Department of Labor investigation around the turn of the millennium looked into the work conditions of AOL volunteers who managed chatrooms and bulletin boards. The volunteers argued that they functioned as employees and should be compensated fairly. Though no immediate decision was reached, AOL shifted its use of volunteers as a result, and the incident had implications for other digital media corporations. The courts eventually awarded $15 million to volunteers in the lawsuit. See Postigo, "America Online Volunteers."

44 Jessi Hempel, "Inside Reddit's Plan to Recover from Its Epic Meltdown" *Wired,* October 6, 2015, http://www.wired.com/2015/10/reddit-survived-meltdown-can-fix/; Bryan Menegus, "Reddit Is Tearing Itself Apart," Gizmodo, November 29, 2016, http://gizmodo.com/reddit-is-tearing-itself-apart-1789406294.

45 J. Nathan Matias, "What Just Happened on Reddit? Understanding the Moderator Blackout," Social Media Collective, July 9, 2015, https://socialmediacollective .org/2015/07/09/what-just-happened-on-reddit-understanding-the-moderator -blackout/; Adrian Chen, "When the Internet's 'Moderators' Are Anything But," *New York Times,* July 21, 2015, https://www.nytimes.com/2015/07/26/magazine /when-the-internets-moderators-are-anything-but.html.

46 Matias, "What Just Happened on Reddit?"

47 Andrejevic et al., "Participations"; Bakioglu, "Exposing Convergence"; David and Pinch, "Six Degrees of Reputation"; Fast, Örnebring, and Karlsson, "Metaphors of Free Labor"; Herman, "Production, Consumption and Labor in the Social Media Mode of Communication"; Jarrett, "The Relevance of 'Women's Work'"; Postigo, "The Socio-Technical Architecture of Digital Labor"; van Doorn, "Platform Labor."

48 Matias et al., "Reporting, Reviewing, and Responding to Harassment on Twitter," 9–12.

49 Juniper Downs (YouTube), "Why Flagging Matters," YouTube Official Blog, September 15, 2016, https://youtube.googleblog.com/2016/09/why-flagging-matters.html.

50 Clay Shirky, "Power Laws, Weblogs, and Inequality," Clay Shirky's Writings about the Internet, February 8, 2003, http://www.shirky.com/writings/herecomeseverybody /powerlaw_weblog.html; Jakob Nielsen, "The 90-9-1 Rule for Participation Inequality in Social Media and Online Communities," NN/g, October 9, 2006, https://www .nngroup.com/articles/participation-inequality/.

51 Personal interview.

52 Microsoft Xbox "Enforcement United," http://enforcement.xbox.com/united/home. Dave Tach, "Why Microsoft's Enforcement United Program Wants You," Polygon, August 7, 2013, https://www.polygon.com/2013/8/7/4581044/xbox-enforcement -united-program; Jen Carter, "Growing Our Trusted Flagger Program into YouTube Heroes," Official YouTube Blog, September 22, 2016, https://youtube.googleblog .com/2016/09/growing-our-trusted-flagger-program.html; Alistair Barr and Lisa Fleisher, "YouTube Enlists 'Trusted Flaggers' to Police Videos" *Wall Street Journal,* March 17, 2014, https://blogs.wsj.com/digits/2014/03/17/youtube-enlists-trusted -flaggers-to-police-videos/.

53 Yelp Elite Squad, https://www.yelp.com/elite; Nish Rocks, "Why We Created the Yelp Elite Squad," Medium, December 21, 2015, https://medium.com/@nishrocks /why-we-created-the-yelp-elite-squad-b8fa7dd2bead. See also Askay and Gossett, "Concealing Communities within the Crowd."

54 Europol, "Counter-Terrorism Specialists Team Up to Take Down Online Terrorist Propaganda," September 5, 2016, https://www.europol.europa.eu/newsroom/news /counter-terrorism-specialists-team-to-take-down-online-terrorist-propaganda.

55 Davey Alba, "Heartmob's Volunteers Crack the Trollish Eggs of Twitter," *Wired,* November 16, 2016, https://www.wired.com/2016/11/heartmob-signing-volunteers -fight-twitter-eggs/.

56 Laura Hudson, "Gamergate Target Zoe Quinn Launches Anti-Harassment Support Network" *Wired,* January 20, 2015, https://www.wired.com/2015/01/gamergate-anti -harassment-network/; Crash Override, http://www.crashoverridenetwork.com/; Trollbusters, http://www.troll-busters.com/.

57 J. Nathan Matias, "A Toxic Web: What the Victorians Can Teach Us about Online Abuse," *Guardian,* April 18, 2016, https://www.theguardian.com/technology/2016 /apr/18/a-toxic-web-what-the-victorians-can-teach-us-about-online-abuse.

58 Geiger, "Bot-Based Collective Blocklists in Twitter."

59 Patricia Cartes, "Announcing the Twitter Trust and Safety Council," Twitter Blog, February 9, 2016, https://blog.twitter.com/2016/announcing-the-twitter-trust-safety -council.

60 It's worth noting that Hollaback is among Twitter's Trust and Safety Council partners, suggesting a tendency for platforms to partner with once-independent organizations supporting users on their platform. See Klonick, "The New Governors."

61 Terrence Russell, "How Porn and Family-Friendly Photos Coexist on Flickr," *Wired,* July 11, 2007, https://www.wired.com/2007/07/how-porn-and-family-friendly -photos-coexist-on-flickr/.

62 M. G. Siegler, "Here's How iPhone App Store Ratings Work. Hint: They Don't," Tech Crunch, June 29, 2017, http://techcrunch.com/2009/06/29/heres-how-iphone-app -store-ratings-work-hint-they-dont/.

63 Ibid.

64 Personal interview.

65 Irani, "The Cultural Work of Microwork," 730.

66 Cheney-Lippold, *We Are Data;* Mayer-Schönberger and Cukier, *Big Data.*

67 Andrejevic, *Infoglut;* Jillian C. York, "Community Standards: A Comparison of Facebook vs. Google+" June 30, 2011. http://jilliancyork.com/2011/06/30/google-vs -facebook/.

CHAPTER 6 FACEBOOK, BREASTFEEDING, AND LIVING IN SUSPENSION

1 Pratt and Rosner, "The Global and the Intimate."

2 Acker and Beaton, "Software Update Unrest"; West, "Raging against the Machine"; Lingel, *Digital Countercultures and the Struggle for Community.*

3 Catherine Buni and Soraya Chemaly, "The Secret Rules of the Internet," Verge, April 13, 2016, https://www.theverge.com/2016/4/13/11387934/internet-moderator -history-youtube-facebook-reddit-censorship-free-speech. Jaclyn Friedman, Anita Sarkeesian, and Renee Bracy Sherman, "Speak Up & Stay Safe(r): A Guide to Protecting Yourself from Online Harassment," Feminist Frequency, https:// onlinesafety.feministfrequency.com/en/; Sarah Jeong, "Why It's So Hard to Stop Online Harassment," Verge, December 8, 2014, http://www.theverge.com/2014/12

/8/7350597/why-its-so-hard-to-stop-online-harassment. J. Nathan Matias, "A Toxic Web: What the Victorians Can Teach Us about Online Abuse," *Guardian,* April 18, 2016, https://www.theguardian.com/technology/2016/apr/18/a-toxic-web-what -the-victorians-can-teach-us-about-online-abuse. Whitney Phillips, "We're the Reason We Can't Have Nice Things on the Internet," Quartz, December 29, 2015, http://qz.com/582113/were-the-reason-we-cant-have-nice-things-online/.

4 Nick Summers, "Facebook's 'Porn Cops' Are Key to Its Growth," *Newsweek,* April 30, 2009, http://www.newsweek.com/facebooks-porn-cops-are-key-its-growth-77055. Miguel Helft, "Facebook Wrestles with Free Speech and Civility," *New York Times,* December 2010, http://www.nytimes.com/2010/12/13/technology/13facebook.html.

5 JQ, "Banned from Facebook Permanently—Facebook Will Not Tolerate Breastfeeding Pictures," One Small Step for Breastfeeding . . ., August 27, 2007, http://bliss -breastfeeding.blogspot.com/2007/08/banned-from-facebook-permanently.html; Andrea Gordon, "Facebook Breastfeeding Flap," *Toronto Star,* September 12, 2007, https://www.thestar.com/life/parent/2007/09/12/facebook_breastfeeding_flap.html.

6 "Breastfeeding Pictures on Myspace Petition," February 26, 2007, http://www .petitiononline.com/Brstfeed/petition.html.

7 Carrie Patterson, "Popular Blogging Site Restricts Use of Breastfeeding Photos," Boob Nazis, May 31, 2006, http://boob-nazis.livejournal.com/1783298.html.

8 LiveJournal was, at the time, a community much more accustomed to user involvement in policy decisions; the uproar around the short-lived rule may have had more to do with how the rule had been imposed.

9 Anne Hinze, "On Breastfeeding and Obscenity," In the Midst of Motherhood, December 29, 2008, http://thehinzefamily.blogspot.com/2008/12/on-breastfeeding -and-obscenity.html.

10 Anne Smith, "Breastfeeding Basics Tries Again with a New Facebook Page," posted to Stop Harassing Emma Kwasnica Facebook group, July 24, 2012, https://www .facebook.com/notes/fb-stop-harassing-emma-kwasnica-over-her-breastfeeding -pics/breastfeeding-basics-tries-again-with-a-new-facebook-page/450694764953586/.

11 Personal interview.

12 West, "Policing the Digital Semicommons."

13 Annie Urban, "Breaking It Down for Facebook," PhD in Parenting, December 30, 2008, http://www.phdinparenting.com/blog/2008/12/30/breaking-it-down-for -facebook.html.

14 Personal interview.

15 Hinze, "On Breastfeeding and Obscenity."

16 "Hey Facebook, Breastfeeding Is Not Obscene! (official petition to Facebook)," https://www.facebook.com/groups/BreastfeedingIsNotObscene/, no longer available.

17 Interview.

18 Interview.

19 Heather Farley, "Hey, Facebook!" It's All About the Hat, December 27, 2008, http:// itsallaboutthehat.blogspot.com/2008/12/hey-facebook.html.

20 According to UNICEF, the "reinforcement of a 'breastfeeding culture' and its vigorous defense against incursions of a 'formula-feeding culture' is imperative." UNICEF, "Breastfeeding," UNICEF, July 29, 2015, https://www.unicef.org/nutrition/index_24824.html.

21 Personal interview.

22 Personal interview.

23 Personal interview.

24 Jenna Wortham, "Facebook Won't Budge on Breastfeeding Photos," Bits Blog, January 2, 2009, https://bits.blogs.nytimes.com/2009/01/02/breastfeeding-facebook-photos/.

25 Personal interview.

26 Personal interview.

27 Wortham, "Facebook Won't Budge."

28 JQ, "Banned from Facebook Permanently."

29 Personal interview.

30 Personal interview.

31 Quoted in Lisa Belkin, "Censoring Breastfeeding on Facebook," Motherlode Blog, December 19, 2008, https://parenting.blogs.nytimes.com/2008/12/19/censoring-breastfeeding-on-facebook/.

32 Quoted in Jenna Wortham, "Facebook Won't Budge on Breastfeeding photos," *New York Times*, January 2, 2009, https://bits.blogs.nytimes.com/2009/01/02/breastfeeding-facebook-photos/.

33 Personal interview.

34 "Facebook Has Contacted Me! AAARGH!" posted as a note to FB! Stop Harassing Emma Kwasnica over Her Breastfeeding Pics Facebook group, January 13, 2012, https://www.facebook.com/notes/fb-stop-harassing-emma-kwasnica-over-her-breastfeeding-pics/facebook-has-contacted-me-aaargh/326125797410484.

35 John Seed, "When Is a Nude OK on Facebook?" Huffington Post, May 24, 2010, http://www.huffingtonpost.com/john-seed/when-is-a-nude-ok-on-face_b_586356.html; Elinor Mills, "Oops! Facebook Mistakenly Censors Burning Man Art," CNET, September 15, 2010, https://www.cnet.com/news/oops-facebook-mistakenly-censors-burning-man-art/; Asher Moses, "Facebook Relents on Doll Nipples Ban," *Sydney Morning Herald,* July 12, 2010, http://www.smh.com.au/technology/technology-news/facebook-relents-on-doll-nipples-ban-20100712-106f6.html.

36 Emma Kwasnica, " 'Hello,' " One Small Step for Breastfeeding . . ., January 6, 2009, http://bliss-breastfeeding.blogspot.com/2009/01/hello-my-name-is-emma-kwasnica.html.

37 Ann Douglas, "Facebook's Attack on Breastfeeding," *Toronto Star,* January 18, 2012, https://www.thestar.com/life/parent/2012/02/01/douglas_facebooks_attack_on_breastfeeding_hurts_women.html.

38 Danielle Arnold-Mckenny, "Why Seeing Breastfeeding Is Important: My Personal Challenge to You," Informed Parenting, October 3, 2010, http://iinformedparenting.blogspot.com/2010/10/seeing-breastfeeding-is-important-my.html.

39 Ann S., "Facebook—Amend Breastfeeding-Photo Guidelines!" Avaaz, May 13, 2012, https://secure.avaaz.org/en/petition/Facebook_to_amend_breastfeedingphoto _guidelines/?pv=53.

40 Gina Crosley-Corcoran, "Facebook Strikes Again! Suspended Over an AWESOME Breastfeeding Photo," TheFeministBreeder, November 13, 2012, http:// thefeministbreeder.com/facebook-strikes-again-suspended-over-an-awesome -breastfeeding-photo/; Gina Crosley-Corcoran, "Now Blocked from Facebook for SEVEN More Days! UPDATE!" TheFeministBreeder, November 16, 2012, http:// thefeministbreeder.com/now-blocked-from-facebook-for-seven-days/.

41 West, "Raging against the Machine."

42 Dan Cairns, "Too Far for Facebook? How the Site Decides What to Ban," BBC Newsbeat, October 7, 2011, http://www.bbc.co.uk/newsbeat/article/15181075 /too-far-for-facebook-how-the-site-decides-what-to-ban.

43 Laura Hudson, "Facebook's Questionable Policy on Violent Content toward Women," *Wired,* January 4, 2013, https://www.wired.com/2013/01/facebook-violence-women/.

44 Danielle Magnuson, "What's Got 800 Million Users and Loves Rape Jokes?" *Utne Reader*, November 4, 2011, http://www.utne.com/Media/Facebook-Defends-Rape -Jokes.

45 Women, Action, and the Media, "FB Agreement," May 28, 2013, http://www .womenactionmedia.org/fbagreement/; "Controversial, Harmful and Hateful Speech on Facebook," May 28, 2013. https://www.facebook.com/notes/facebooksafety /controversial-harmful-and-hateful-speech-on-facebook/574430655911054.

46 Personal interview.

47 For example, Alex Hern, "Facebook's Changing Standards: From Beheading to Breastfeeding Images," *Guardian,* October 22, 2013, https://www.theguardian.com /technology/2013/oct/22/facebook-standards-beheading-breastfeeding-social -networking; Sophie Curtis, "From Breastfeeding to Beheadings: What Can't You Post on Facebook?" October 22, 2013, http://www.telegraph.co.uk/technology /facebook/10395979/Facebook-what-you-cant-post.html.

48 April Purinton, "Facebook . . . Apparently a Safe Harbor for Misogyny," Eclectic Effervescence, May 12, 2010, http://eclecticeffervescence.blogspot.com/2010/05 /facebookapparently-safe-harbor-for.html.

49 Eric Limer, "Facebook Took Down This Picture Because It Thinks Elbows Are Boobs," Gizmodo. November 26, 2011, http://gizmodo.com/5963326/facebook -took-down-this-picture-because-it-thinks-elbows-are-boobs.

50 Lina Esco, "Facebook Wages War on the Nipple," Huffington Post, January 7, 2014, http://www.huffingtonpost.com/lina-esco/facebook-war-on-nipples_b_4548832 .html.

51 Aron Macarow, "#ManBoobs4Boobs Nails the Serious Problem with Breast Censorship on Social Media," Attn:, April 24, 2016, https://www.attn.com/stories/7704 /manboobs4boobs-nails-serious-problem-breast-censorship-social-media.

52 Free the Nipple, n.d., http://freethenipple.com/.

53 "Breast-Beating: Young Feminists Are Reviving an Old Struggle: Rights for Women's Bodies," *Economist*, May 25, 2013, https://www.economist.com/news/international /21578381-young-feminists-are-reviving-old-struggle-rights-womens-bodies-breast -beating.

54 West, "Raging against the Machine."

55 Micol Hebron, "Nipples Articles about My Digital Pasty Designed to Fight Censorship of Female Nipples," Micol Hebron Blog, June 15, 2015, http:// micolhebron.artcodeinc.com/pages/nipples-articles-about-my-digital-pasty -designed-to-fight-censorship-of-female-nipples/.

56 Nicole Charky, "Here Is the Brilliant Way Women Are Fighting Sexist Double Standards on Social Media," Attn:, July 7, 2015, https://www.attn.com/stories/2270 /nipples-facebook-instagram-social-media.

57 Anna Cieslik, "Instagram Account Genderless Nipples Is Here to Challenge Your Thoughts on NSFW Imagery," Dailybreak.com, December 12, 2016, https:// www.dailybreak.com/break/genderless-nipples-instagram; "Genderless Nipples (@genderless_nipples)," Instagram Photos and Videos, n.d., https://www.instagram .com/genderless_nipples/.

58 Marne Levine, "Controversial, Harmful, and Hateful Speech on Facebook," Facebook Safety, May 28, 2013, https://www.facebook.com/notes/facebook-safety /controversial-harmful-and-hateful-speech-on-facebook/574430655911054/.

59 Facebook Help Center, "Does Facebook Allow Post-Mastectomy Photos?" Facebook, n.d., https://www.facebook.com/help/318612434939348/.

60 Soraya Chemaly, "#FreeTheNipple: Facebook Changes Breastfeeding Mothers Photo Policy," Huffington Post, June 9, 2014, http://www.huffingtonpost.com/soraya -chemaly/freethenipple-facebook-changes_b_5473467.html; Kate Knibbs, "Facebook Changes Its Policy on Breastfeeding, Mastectomy Photos," Daily Dot, June 13, 2014, http://www.dailydot.com/irl/facebook-breastfeeding-mastectomy-nipple-photos/.

61 Facebook, "Community Standards | Encouraging Respectful Behavior | Adult Nudity and Sexual Activity," n.d., https://www.facebook.com/communitystandards#nudity. See Svati Kirsten Narula, "Facebook Redefines Nudity to Exclude Breastfeeding Shots, but Rear Ends Are Still Off Limits," Quartz, March 16, 2015, https://qz.com/363280 /facebook-redefines-nudity-to-exclude-breastfeeding-shots-but-rear-ends-are-still -off-limits/.

62 Courtney Demone, "I Am a Trans Woman. Will Facebook Censor My Breasts?" Mashable, September 30, 2015, http://mashable.com/2015/09/30/do-i-have-boobs -now/.

63 Ibrahim, "The Breastfeeding Controversy and Facebook."

64 Bakardjieva, "Subactivism"; Couldry, "The Myth of 'Us'"; Dahlberg, "The Internet, Deliberative Democracy, and Power"; Gray, *Out in the Country*; Gross, *Up from Invisibility*; Thompson, "The New Visibility."

65 Bucher, "Want to Be on the Top?"; Milan, "When Algorithms Shape Collective Action"; Thompson, "The New Visibility."

CHAPTER 7 **TO REMOVE OR TO FILTER**

1 Yahoo, "Yahoo to Acquire Tumblr: Promises Not to Screw It Up," May 20, 2013, archived at https://web.archive.org/web/20130608061321/http://yhoo.client .shareholder.com/releasedetail.cfm?ReleaseID=765892.

2 Sarah Perez, "Tumblr's Adult Fare Accounts for 11.4% of Site's Top 200K Domains, Adult Sites Are Leading Category of Referrals" TechCrunch, May 20, 2013, http:// techcrunch.com/2013/05/20/tumblrs-adult-fare-accounts-for-11-4-of-sites-top -200k-domains-tumblrs-adult-fare-accounts-for-11-4-of-sites-top-200k-domains -adults-sites-are-leading-category-of-referrals/.

3 Tiidenberg, "Boundaries and conflict in a NSFW Community on Tumblr."

4 Tumblr.com, "Community Guidelines," as it appeared in 2013 (since modified), https://www.tumblr.com/policy/en/community.

5 Seth Fiegerman, "David Karp Tells Stephen Colbert Tumblr Won't 'Police' Porn," Mashable, July 17, 2013, http://mashable.com/2013/07/17/david-karp-stephen -colbert/#lR3INKRrnGq1.

6 Mark Molloy, "Tumblr Porn Can Stay, Insists Yahoo CEO Marissa Mayer," Metro, May 21, 2013, http://metro.co.uk/2013/05/21/tumblr-porn-can-stay-insists-yahoo -ceo-marissa-mayer-3802892/.

7 Peter Kafka, "Why Yahoo Doesn't Think Tumblr Has a Porn Problem," All Things D, May 18, 2013, http://allthingsd.com/20130518/why-yahoo-doesnt-think-tumblr-has -a-porn-problem/.

8 Yahoo, "Yahoo to Acquire Tumblr."

9 Nitasha Tiku, "Instagram Institutes Harsher Rules to Control Harassment, Porn, and Nudity" Verge, April 16, 2015, http://www.theverge.com/2015/4/16/8431317 /instagram-harassment-porn-nudity.

10 Casey Johnston, "Google Threatens to Shut Down Adult Blogs with Adult Advertisements," Ars Technica, June 27, 2013, http://arstechnica.com /business/2013/06/google-threatens-to-shut-down-adult-blogs-with-adult -advertisements/.

11 Kate Knibbs, Porn Is Now Outlawed on Vine," Daily Dot, March 7, 2014, http://www .dailydot.com/technology/vine-bans-porn/.

12 Adam Clark Estes, "Pinterest Embraces Its Porn Problem, Artistically," Gizmodo, May 30, 2013, http://gizmodo.com/pinterest-embraces-its-porn-problem -artistically-510461241.

13 Violet Blue, "Adult Tumblr Blogs Now Removed from Every Form of Search Possible," ZDNet, July 19, 2013, http://www.zdnet.com/adult-tumblr-blogs-now -removed-from-every-form-of-search-possible-7000018295/.

14 Acker and Beaton, "Software Update Unrest."

15 Tumblr Staff blog, July 19, 2013, http://staff.tumblr.com/post/55906556378 /all-weve-heard-from-a-bunch-of-you-who-are.

16 West, "Policing the Digital Semicommons"; Humphreys, "Predicting, Securing, and Shaping the Future."

17 Light, *Disconnecting with Social Networking Sites.*

18 Armijo, "Kill Switches, Forum Doctrine, and the First Amendment's Digital Future"; Balkin, "Old School/New School Speech Regulation"; Meyerson, "The Neglected History of the Prior Restraint Doctrine."

19 Guins, *Edited Clean Version.*

20 Bucher, "Want to Be on the Top?"; Gillespie, "Algorithmically Recognizable."

21 Gillespie, "Can an Algorithm be Wrong?"

22 Bucher, "Want to Be on the Top?"

23 Bivens and Haimson, "Baking Gender into Social Media Design"; Bivens, "The Gender Binary Will Not Be Deprogrammed"; Burgess, "From 'Broadcast Yourself' to 'Follow Your Interests,' "; McVeigh-Schultz and Baym, "Thinking of You"; Nagy and Neff, "Imagined Affordance."

24 Gillespie, *Wired Shut;* Guins, *Edited Clean Version;* Introna and Nissenbaum, "Shaping the Web"; Lessig, *Code and Other Laws of Cyberspace;* Samuelson, "DRM {and, or, vs.} the Law"; Schüll, *Addiction by Design;* Shilton, Koepfler, and Fleischmann, "Charting Sociotechnical Dimensions of Values for Design Research"; Silverstone and Haddon, "Design and the Domestication of Information and Communication Technologies."

25 Gillespie, *Wired Shut.*

26 Natalie Robehmed, "Tumblr's Mobile Porn Filter Bans #gay," *Forbes,* July 23, 2013, http://www.forbes.com/sites/natalierobehmed/2013/07/23/tumblrs-mobile-porn -filter-bans-gay/.

27 Gavia Baker-Whitelaw, "New NSFW Content Restrictions Enrage Tumblr Users," Daily Dot, July 18, 2013, http://www.dailydot.com/lifestyle/tumblr-nsfw-content -tags-search/.

28 A Tumblr representative hinted as much in response to press coverage of the banned hashtags. "We would strongly prefer not to limit any browsing inside our apps," a spokeswoman said in an email to the Huffington Post. "But until the app marketplaces relax their content requirements, we're on the hook to develop stringent filters for mature content before we allow search terms that frequently return said content. We're determined to get there soon." Meredith Bennett-Smith, "Tumblr Mobile Filter Anti-Gay? Why App Is Banning #Gay, #Lesbian, and #Bisexual Tags," Huffington Post, July 24, 2013, http://www.huffingtonpost .com/2013/07/24/tumblr-anti-gay-filter_n_3642103.html. Tumblr CEO David Karp gave a similar explanation in his post on the controversy: Tumblr Staff blog, July 19, 2013, http://staff.tumblr.com/post/55906556378/all-weve-heard-from-a -bunch-of-you-who-are.

29 Many thanks to Nick Seaver for this turn of phrase.

30 Kevin Gibbs, "I've Got a Suggestion," Official Google Blog, December 10, 2004, https://googleblog.blogspot.com/2004/12/ive-got-suggestion.html; Jennifer Liu, "At a Loss for Words?" Official Google Blog, August 25, 2008, https://googleblog.blogspot .com/2008/08/at-loss-for-words.html; Danny Sullivan, "How Google Instant's

Autocomplete Suggestions Work," Search Engine Land, April 6, 2011, http://searchengineland.com/how-google-instant-autocomplete-suggestions-work-62592.

31 Here is how Google explains its moderation of this feature: "The search queries that you see as part of autocomplete are a reflection of the search activity of all web users and the contents of web pages indexed by Google. Just like the web, the search queries presented may include silly or strange or surprising terms and phrases. While we always strive to algorithmically reflect the diversity of content on the web (some good, some objectionable), we also apply a narrow set of removal policies for pornography, violence, hate speech, and terms that are frequently used to find content that infringes copyrights." http://support.google.com/websearch/bin/answer.py?hl=en&answer=106230. See also 2600.com, "Google Blacklist—Words That Google Instant Doesn't Like," September 30, 2009, https://www.2600.com/googleblacklist/; Samuel Gibbs, "Google Alters Search Autocomplete to Remove 'Are Jews Evil' Suggestion," Guardian, December 5, 2016, https://www.theguardian.com/technology/2016/dec/05/google-alters-search-autocomplete-remove-are-jews-evil-suggestion.

32 Noble, "Missed Connections"; Noble, Algorithms of Oppression.

33 Michael Keller, "The Apple 'Kill List': What Your iPhone Doesn't Want You to Type," Daily Beast, July 16, 2013, http://www.thedailybeast.com/the-apple-kill-list-what-your-iphone-doesnt-want-you-to-type.

34 C. A. Pinkham, " 'Feminism' and 'Misogyny' Are Banned Words on TripAdvisor," Kitchenette, March 15, 2015, http://kitchenette.jezebel.com/feminism-and-misogyny-are-apparently-banned-words-o-1691599391.

35 Aja Romano, "29 Tags Tumblr Banned from Its Mobile App (and 10 It Didn't)," Daily Dot, July 18, 2013, https://www.dailydot.com/business/banned-tumblr-tags-mobile/.

36 Lisa Respers France, "The Skinny on Instagram Banning #curvy," CNN Living, July 16, 2015, http://www.cnn.com/2015/07/16/living/curvy-instagram-ban-feat/index.html.

37 "Instagram Users Sound Off over Blocked #goddess Hashtag," ABC7 San Francisco, July 28, 2015, http://abc7news.com/888880/.

38 "The Banned #Hashtags of Instagram," Data Pack, n.d., http://thedatapack.com/banned-hashtags-instagram/.

39 Keller, "The Apple 'Kill List.' " For how the research was done, see "Today We Published a Data Story Looking at How iOS Devices Fail to Accurately Correct Some Words such as 'Abortion' and 'Rape,' " NewsBeast Labs, July 16, 2013, http://newsbeastlabs-blog.tumblr.com/post/55590097779/today-we-published-a-data-story-looking-at-how-ios.

40 Nick Seaver (personal communication) notes that music recommenders make a similar intervention around children's music and holiday music: the assumption, again, is that users do not want to hear holiday music in response to a query that does not seem to specify that category.

41 Jemima Kiss, "YouTube Looking at Standalone 'SafeTube' Site for Families," *Guardian*, May 29, 2009, https://www.theguardian.com/media/pda/2009/may/29/youtube-google.

42 Beer and Burrows, "Popular Culture, Digital Archives, and the New Social Life of Data"; Gillespie, "Can an Algorithm Be Wrong?"; Gillespie, "#trendingistrending"; Hallinan and Striphas, "Recommended for You."

43 Harrison Hoffman, "4chan May Be behind Attack on Twitter," CNET, July 6, 2009, https://www.cnet.com/news/4chan-may-be-behind-attack-on-twitter/.

44 Mary Hodder, "Why Amazon Didn't Just Have a Glitch," TechCrunch, April 14, 2009, https://techcrunch.com/2009/04/14/guest-post-why-amazon-didnt-just-have-a-glitch/.

45 Terrence Russell, "German Users in Revolt over Flickr Image Restrictions," *Wired*, June 15, 2007, https://www.wired.com/2007/06/german_users_in/.

46 Deibert and Rohozinski, "Liberation vs. Control."

47 Deibert, et al., *Access Denied;* Deibert et al., *Access Controlled.*

48 Helmi Noman, "Sex, Social Mores, and Keyword Filtering: Microsoft Bing in the 'Arabian Countries,'" OpenNet initiative, 2010, https://opennet.net/sex-social-mores-and-keyword-filtering-microsoft-bing-arabian-countries.

49 Rebecca Rosen, "What to Make of Google's Decision to Block the 'Innocence of Muslims' Movie," *Atlantic*, September 14, 2012, https://www.theatlantic.com/technology/archive/2012/09/what-to-make-of-googles-decision-to-block-the-innocence-of-muslims-movie/262395/.

50 Bill Chappell, "Google Maps Displays Crimean Border Differently in Russia, U.S.," NPR, April 12, 2014, http://www.npr.org/blogs/thetwo-way/2014/04/12/302337754/google-maps-displays-crimean-border-differently-in-russia-u-s.

51 Twitter, "Tweets Still Must Flow," Twitter Blog, January 26, 2012, https://blog.twitter.com/official/en_us/a/2012/tweets-still-must-flow.html; Eva Galperin, "What Does Twitter's Country-by-Country Takedown System Mean for Freedom of Expression?" Electronic Frontier Foundation, January 27, 2012, https://www.eff.org/deeplinks/2012/01/what-does-twitter%E2%80%99s-country-country-takedown-system-mean-freedom-expression.

52 Many thanks to Nick Seaver for this observation.

53 Schudson, *Advertising, the Uneasy Persuasion.*

54 Pariser, *The Filter Bubble;* Sunstein, *Republic.com 2.0.*

55 Ananny, "The Curious Connection between Apps for Gay Men and Sex Offenders."

CHAPTER 8 **WHAT PLATFORMS ARE, AND WHAT THEY SHOULD BE**

1 Flyverbom, "Digital Age Transparency."

2 Twitter has since changed the "egg" icon that used to represent accounts that had not added a profile photo, because it had become associated with trolling. Sorry, it's still an egg. See Kaitlyn Tiffany, "Twitter Wants You to Stop Saying 'Twitter Eggs,'" Verge, March 31, 2017, https://www.theverge.com/tldr/2017/3/31/15139464/twitter-egg-replaced-harassment-terms-trolls-language.

3 Danielle Citron and Ben Wittes, "Follow Buddies and Block Buddies: A Simple Proposal to Improve Civility, Control, and Privacy on Twitter," Lawfareblog, January 4, 2017, https://lawfareblog.com/follow-buddies-and-block-buddies -simple-proposal-improve-civility-control-and-privacy-twitter; Geiger, "Bot-Based Collective Blocklists in Twitter."

4 If for some reason the platform wanted to make it possible, users could even seek out content that others had marked "violent."

5 According to the WAM report, "Reporters were asked if the harassment was occurring on multiple platforms. 54 reports (17%) mention harassment taking place on multiple platforms" (15).

6 Many thanks to Sharif Mowlabocus for this insight.

7 Alexis Madrigal, "What Facebook Did to American Democracy," *Atlantic,* October 12, 2017, https://www.theatlantic.com/technology/archive/2017/10/what-facebook -did/542502/.

8 Blank and Reisdorf, "The Participatory Web"; Halavais, "The Blogosphere and Its Problems"; Postigo, "Questioning the Web 2.0 Discourse"; Dahlgren, "The Internet as a Civic Space"; Levina and Hasinoff, "The Silicon Valley Ethos." For an insightful repudiation of this "discourse of versions" and the historical distortions it can introduce, see Ankerson, "Social Media and the 'Read-Only' Web."

9 Virginia Heffernan, "Trumpcast Live from the Tribeca Film Festival," Trumpcast, May 1, 2017, http://www.slate.com/articles/podcasts/trumpcast/2017/05/trumpcast _at_the_tribeca_film_festival.html.

10 George Packer and Ken Auletta, "George Packer and Ken Auletta on Silicon Valley," *New Yorker* Out Loud Podcast, May 21, 2013, http://www.newyorker.com/podcast /out-loud/george-packer-and-ken-auletta-on-silicon-valley.

11 Malaby, *Making Virtual Worlds,* 8, 14.

12 Burgess, "From 'Broadcast Yourself' to 'Follow your Interests' "; Hoffman, Proferes, and Zimmer, " 'Making the World More Open and Connected.' "

13 Dewey, *The Public and Its Problems,* 15–16.

14 Ananny, "From Noxious to Public?"

15 At the time, if a proposed policy amendment received more than three thousand comments, it had to go to the users for a vote, and required 30 percent of Facebook users' participation to make their decision binding. This, at the time, would have required 270 million people to participate. The 2012 vote regarded a new privacy policy that would allow Facebook to share user data with the newly acquired Instagram. See Casey Johnston, "Whopping. 038% of Facebook Users Vote on Data Use Policy Change," June 8, 2012, https://arstechnica.com/information-technology /2012/06/whopping-00038-of-facebook-users-vote-on-data-use-policy-change/.

16 There were reasons not to think of this as a well-executed democratic exercise. The policy itself had been written by Facebook managers and demonstrated little concern for the users, the expectation for participation was too high, and the election had little legitimacy among users. Facebook publicized the vote only the second time

around, with an email to all users, perhaps to avoid a binding decision they didn't want. Ryan Tate, "How You Killed Facebook Democracy: A Short History," *Wired*, December 10, 2012, https://www.wired.com/2012/12/you-killed-facebook-democracy/.

17 Kelty, "Geeks, Social Imaginaries, and Recursive Publics."

18 Marvin, *When Old Technologies Were New;* Douglas, *Inventing American Broadcasting;* Wu, *The Master Switch.*

19 Silverstone, *Media and Morality,* 167.

BIBLIOGRAPHY

ACKER, AMELIA, AND BRIAN BEATON. 2016. "Software Update Unrest: The Recent Happenings around Tinder and Tesla." In *Hawaii International Conference on System Sciences, Proceedings of the 49th Annual Conference,* 1891–1900. Washington, DC: IEEE Computer Society.

AGARWAL, SWATI, AND ASHISH SUREKA. 2014. "A Focused Crawler for Mining Hate and Extremism Promoting Videos on YouTube." In *Proceedings of the 25th ACM Conference on Hypertext and Social Media,* 294–96. New York: ACM Press.

AGRE, PHILIP. 1995. "Conceptions of the User in Computer Systems Design." In *The Social and Interactional Dimensions of Human-Computer Interfaces,* ed. Peter Thomas, 67–106. New York: Cambridge University Press.

AMMORI, MARVIN. 2011. "First Amendment Architecture." *Wisconsin Law Review* 2012 (1). https://papers.ssrn.com/sol3/papers.cfm?abstract_id=1791125.

———. 2014. "The 'New' New York Times: Free Speech Lawyering in the Age of Google and Twitter." *Harvard Law Review* 127 (8): 2259–95.

ANANNY, MIKE. 2011. "The Curious Connection between Apps for Gay Men and Sex Offenders." *Atlantic,* April 14. http://www.theatlantic.com/technology/archive/2011/04/the-curious-connection-between-apps-for-gay-men-and-sex-offenders/237340/.

———. 2015. "From Noxious to Public? Tracing Ethical Dynamics of Social Media Platform Conversions." *Social Media + Society* 1 (1): 2056305115578140.

ANDERSON, JESSICA, MATTHEW STENDER, SARAH MYERS WEST, AND JILLIAN C. YORK. 2016. "Unfriending Censorship: Insights from Four Months of Crowdsourced Data on Social Media Censorship." Onlinecensorship.org. http://www.tasharuk.net/resources/files/1459500033Onlinecensorship.orgReport31March2016.pdf.

ANDREJEVIC, MARK. 2013. *Infoglut: How Too Much Information Is Changing the Way We Think and Know.* New York: Routledge.

ANDREJEVIC, MARK, JOHN BANKS, JOHN EDWARD CAMPBELL, NICK COULDRY, ADAM FISH, ALISON HEARN, AND LAURIE OUELLETTE. 2014. "Participations: Dialogues on the Participatory Promise of Contemporary Culture and Politics—Part 2: Labor." *International Journal of Communication* 8: 1089–1106.

ANGWIN, JULIA. 2009. *Stealing MySpace: The Battle to Control the Most Popular Website in America.* New York: Random House.

ANKERSON, MEGAN. 2015. "Social Media and the 'Read-Only' Web: Reconfiguring Social Logics and Historical Boundaries." *Social Media + Society* 1 (2): 2056305115621935.

AP-APID, BIRGITTA. 2005. "An Algorithm for Nudity Detection." In *Proceedings of the 5th Philippine Computing Science Congress,* 201–5. Cebu City, Philippines.

ARCHETTI, CRISTINA. 2015. "Terrorism, Communication, and New Media: Explaining Radicalization in the Digital Age." *Perspectives on Terrorism* 9 (1). http://www.terrorismanalysts.com/pt/index.php/pot/article/view/401.

ARDIA, DAVID S. 2010. "Free Speech Savior or Shield for Scoundrels: An Empirical Study of Intermediary Immunity under Section 230 of the Communications Decency Act." *Loyola of Los Angeles Law Review* 43 (2): 373–506.

ARMIJO, ENRIQUE. 2013. "Kill Switches, Forum Doctrine, and the First Amendment's Digital Future." *Cardozo Arts and Entertainment L aw Journal* 32: 411–69.

ASKAY, DAVID A., AND LORIL GOSSETT. 2015. "Concealing Communities within the Crowd: Hiding Organizational Identities and Brokering Member Identifications of the Yelp Elite Squad." *Management Communication Quarterly* 29 (4): 616–41.

AUFDERHEIDE, PATRICIA. 1999. *Communications Policy and the Public Interest: The Telecommunications Act of 1996.* New York: Guilford.

BAKARDJIEVA, MARIA. 2009. "Subactivism: Lifeworld and Politics in the Age of the Internet." *Information Society* 25 (2): 91–104.

BAKIOGLU, B. S. 2016. "Exposing Convergence: YouTube, Fan Labour, and Anxiety of Cultural Production in Lonelygirl15." *Convergence: The International Journal of Research into New Media Technologies.*

BALKIN, JACK M. 2004. "Digital Speech and Democratic Culture: A Theory of Freedom of Expression for the Information Society." *New York University Law Review* 79: 1–55.

———. 2014. "Old School/New School Speech Regulation." *Harvard Law Review* 127 (8): 2296–2342.

———. 2017. "Free Speech in the Algorithmic Society: Big Data, Private Governance, and New School Speech Regulation." Unpublished manuscript. https://papers.ssrn.com/sol3/papers.cfm?abstract_id=3038939.

BANET-WEISER, SARAH, AND KATE MILTNER. 2016. "#MasculinitySoFragile: Culture, Structure, and Networked Misogyny." *Feminist Media Studies* 16 (1): 171–74.

BANKSTON, KEVIN, DAVID SOHN, AND ANDREW MCDIARMID. 2012. "Shielding the Messengers: Protecting Platforms for Expression and Innovation." Center for Democracy and Technology.

BARLOW, JOHN PERRY. 1996. "A Declaration of the Independence of Cyberspace." http://wac.colostate.edu/rhetnet/barlow/barlow_declaration.html.

BARTLE, RICHARD A. 2006. "Why Governments Aren't Gods and Gods Aren't Governments." *First Monday.* http://firstmonday.org/htbin/cgiwrap/bin/ojs /index.php/fm/article/viewArticle/1612.

BARZILAI-NAHON, KARINE. 2008. "Toward a Theory of Network Gatekeeping: A Framework for Exploring Information Control." *Journal of the American Society for Information Science and Technology* 59 (9): 1493–1512.

BAYM, NANCY K. 2010. *Personal Connections in the Digital Age.* Cambridge: Polity.

———. 2015. "Social Media and the Struggle for Society." *Social Media + Society* 1 (1): 2056305115580477.

BAYM, NANCY K., AND DANAH BOYD. 2012. "Socially Mediated Publicness: An Introduction." *Journal of Broadcasting and Electronic Media* 56 (3): 320–29.

BEER, DAVID. 2008. "Social Network(ing) Sites . . . Revisiting the Story so Far: A Response to danah boyd and Nicole Ellison." *Journal of Computer-Mediated Communication* 13 (2): 516–29.

———. 2009. "Power through the Algorithm? Participatory Web Cultures and the Technological Unconscious." *New Media and Society* 11 (6): 985–1002.

BEER, DAVID, AND ROGER BURROWS. 2007. "Sociology and, of, and in Web 2.0: Some Initial Considerations." *Sociological Research Online* 12 (5).

———. 2013. "Popular Culture, Digital Archives, and the New Social Life of Data." *Theory, Culture & Society* 30 (4): 47–71.

BENKLER, YOCHAI. 2006. *The Wealth of Networks: How Social Production Transforms Markets and Freedom.* New Haven: Yale University Press.

BERGSTROM, KELLY. 2011. " 'Don't Feed the Troll': Shutting Down Debate about Community Expectations on Reddit. Com." *First Monday* 16 (8), http:// firstmonday.org/ojs/index.php/fm/article/viewArticle/3498.

BERNSTEIN, MATTHEW, ED. 1999. *Controlling Hollywood: Censorship and Regulation in the Studio Era.* New Brunswick, NJ: Rutgers University Press.

BILTON, NICK. 2014. *Hatching Twitter: A True Story of Money, Power, Friendship, and Betrayal.* New York: Portfolio.

BIVENS, RENA. 2017. "The Gender Binary Will Not Be Deprogrammed: Ten Years of Coding Gender on Facebook." *New Media and Society* 19 (6): 880–98.

BIVENS, RENA, AND OLIVER L. HAIMSON. 2016. "Baking Gender into Social Media Design: How Platforms Shape Categories for Users and Advertisers." *Social Media + Society* 2 (4): 2056305116672486.

BLANK, GRANT, AND BIANCA C. REISDORF. 2012. "The Participatory Web: A User Perspective on Web 2.0." *Information, Communication, and Society* 15 (4): 537–54.

BOELLSTORFF, TOM. 2008. *Coming of Age in Second Life: An Anthropologist Explores the Virtually Human.* Princeton: Princeton University Press.

BOERO, NATALIE, AND C. J. PASCOE. 2012. "Pro-Anorexia Communities and Online Interaction: Bringing the Pro-Ana Body Online." *Body and Society* 18 (2): 27–57.

BOGOST, IAN, AND NICK MONTFORT. 2009. "Platform Studies: Frequently Questioned Answers." Irvine, CA. https://escholarship.org/uc/item /01r0k9br.pdf.

BOUDREAU, KEVIN J., AND ANDREI HAGIU. 2009. "Platform Rules: Multi-Sided Platforms as Regulators." In *Platforms, Markets and Innovation,* ed. Annabelle Gawer, 163–91. Cheltenham, UK: Edward Elgar. http://papers .ssrn.com/sol3/papers.cfm?abstract_id=1269966.

BOWKER, GEOFFREY, AND SUSAN LEIGH STAR. 2000. *Sorting Things Out: Classification and Its Consequences.* Cambridge: MIT Press.

BOYD, DANAH. 2011. "Social Network Sites as Networked Publics: Affordances, Dynamics, and Implications." In *A Networked Self: Identity, Community, and Culture on Social Network Sites,* ed. Zizi Papacharissi, 39–58. New York: Routledge. http://www.danah.org/papers/2010/SNSasNetworkedPublics.
———. 2012. "The Politics of 'Real Names.'" *Communications of the ACM* 55 (8): 29.

BOYD, DANAH M., AND NICOLE B. ELLISON. 2007. "Social Network Sites: Definition, History, and Scholarship." *Journal of Computer-Mediated Communication* 13 (1): 210–30.

BOYD, DANAH, KAREN LEVY, AND ALICE MARWICK. 2014. "The Networked Nature of Algorithmic Discrimination." Open Technology Institute. http://www .danah.org/papers/2014/DataDiscrimination.pdf.

BOYD, DANAH, JENNY RYAN, AND ALEX LEAVITT. 2010. "Pro-Self-Harm and the Visibility of Youth-Generated Problematic Content." *ISJLP* 7: 1.

BRAUN, JOSHUA. 2013. "Going over the Top: Online Television Distribution as Sociotechnical System: Online Television Distribution." *Communication, Culture, and Critique* 6 (3): 432–58.
———. 2015. "Social Media and Distribution Studies." *Social Media + Society* 1 (1): 2056305115580483.

BRAUN, JOSHUA, AND TARLETON GILLESPIE. 2011. "Hosting the Public Discourse, Hosting the Public: When Online News and Social Media Converge." *Journalism Practice* 5 (4): 383–98.

BRUNS, AXEL. 2008. *Blogs, Wikipedia, Second Life, and Beyond: From Production to Produsage.* New York: Peter Lang.

BRUNTON, FINN. 2013. *Spam: A Shadow History of the Internet.* Cambridge: MIT Press.

BUCHER, TAINA. 2012. "Want to Be on the Top? Algorithmic Power and the Threat of Invisibility on Facebook." *New Media and Society* 14 (7): 1164–80.

BURGESS, JEAN. 2015. "From 'Broadcast Yourself' to 'Follow Your Interests': Making Over Social Media." *International Journal of Cultural Studies* 18 (3): 281–85.

BURGESS, JEAN, AND JOSHUA GREEN. 2009. *YouTube: Online Video and Participatory Culture.* Cambridge: Polity.

BURGESS, JEAN, AND ARIADNA MATAMOROS-FERNÁNDEZ. 2016. "Mapping Sociocultural Controversies across Digital Media Platforms: One Week of #gamergate on Twitter, YouTube, and Tumblr." *Communication Research and Practice* 2 (1): 79–96.

BUTLER, BRIAN, LEE SPROULL, SARA KIESLER, AND ROBERT E. KRAUT. 2007. "Community Effort in Online Groups: Who Does the Work and Why?" In *Leadership at a Distance: Research in Technologically-Supported Work,* ed. Suzanne Weisband, 346–62. Hillsdale, NJ: Erlbaum.

CAMMAERTS, BART. 2008. "Critiques on the Participatory Potentials of Web 2.0." *Communication, Culture, and Critique* 1 (4): 358–77.

CANNON, ROBERT. 1996. "The Legislative History of Senator Exon's Communications Decency Act: Regulating Barbarians on the Information Superhighway." *Federal Communications Law Journal* 49: 51.

CHANDER, ANUPAM. 2014. "How Law Made Silicon Valley." *Emory Law Journal* 63: 639–94.

CHENEY-LIPPOLD, JOHN. 2017. *We Are Data: Algorithms and the Making of Our Digital Selves.* New York: NYU Press.

CHENG, JUSTIN, CRISTIAN DANESCU-NICULESCU-MIZIL, AND JURE LESKOVEC. 2015. "Antisocial Behavior in Online Discussion Communities." arXiv. http://arxiv.org/abs/1504.00680.

CHESS, SHIRA, AND ADRIENNE SHAW. 2015. "A Conspiracy of Fishes, or, How We Learned to Stop Worrying about #GamerGate and Embrace Hegemonic Masculinity." *Journal of Broadcasting and Electronic Media* 59 (1): 208–20.

CITRON, DANIELLE. 2009. "Cyber Civil Rights." *Boston University Law Review* 89: 61–125.

———. 2014. *Hate Crimes in Cyberspace.* Cambridge: Harvard University Press.

CITRON, DANIELLE, AND HELEN L. NORTON. 2011. "Intermediaries and Hate Speech: Fostering Digital Citizenship for Our Information Age." *Boston University Law Review* 91: 14–35.

CITRON, DANIELLE, AND FRANK A. PASQUALE. 2014. "The Scored Society: Due Process for Automated Predictions." *Washington Law Review* 89. http://papers.ssrn.com/sol3/papers.cfm?abstract_id=2376209.

CLARK, JESSICA, NICK COULDRY, ABIGAIL DE KOSNIK, TARLETON GILLESPIE, HENRY JENKINS, CHRISTOPHER KELTY, ZIZI PAPACHARISSI, ALISON POWELL, AND JOSÉ VAN DIJCK. 2014. "Participations: Dialogues on the Participatory Promise of Contemporary Culture and Politics—Part 5: Platforms." *International Journal of Communication* 8: 1446–73.

CORN-REVERE, ROBERT. 2002. "Caught in the Seamless Web: Does the Internet's Global Reach Justify Less Freedom of Speech?" 71. Cato Institute. http://issuelab.datasco.pe/results/cato_institute_45.pdf.

COULDRY, NICK. 2015. "The Myth of 'Us': Digital Networks, Political Change, and the Production of Collectivity." *Information, Communication, and Society* 18 (6): 608–26.

COULDRY, NICK, AND JOSÉ VAN DIJCK. 2015. "Researching Social Media as if the Social Mattered." *Social Media + Society* 1 (2), 2056305115604174.

CRAWFORD, KATE, AND TARLETON GILLESPIE. 2016. "What Is a Flag For? Social Media Reporting Tools and the Vocabulary of Complaint." *New Media and Society* 18 (3): 410–28.

DAHLBERG, LINCOLN. 2007. "The Internet, Deliberative Democracy, and Power: Radicalizing the Public Sphere." *International Journal of Media and Cultural Politics* 3 (1).

DAHLGREN, PETER. 2015. "The Internet as a Civic Space." In *Handbook of Digital Politics,* ed. Stephen Coleman and Deen Freelon, 17–34. Cheltenham, UK: Edward Elgar.

DANIELS, JESSE. 2013. "Race and Racism in Internet Studies: A Review and Critique." *New Media and Society* 15 (5): 695–719.

DANIELS, JESSIE, AND ANNA EVERETT. 2008. "Race, Civil Rights, and Hate Speech in the Digital Era." In *Learning Race and Ethnicity: Youth and Digital Media.* Cambridge: MIT Press. http://academicworks.cuny.edu/gc_pubs/193/.

DAVID, SHAY, AND TREVOR JOHN PINCH. 2005. "Six Degrees of Reputation: The Use and Abuse of Online Review and Recommendation Systems." *First Monday,* special issue 6: Commercial Applications of the Internet. http://firstmonday .org/ojs/index.php/fm/article/view/1590/1505.

DEIBERT, RONALD, JOHN PALFREY, RAFAL ROHOZINSKI, AND JONATHAN ZITTRAIN, EDS. 2008. *Access Denied: The Practice and Policy of Global Internet Filtering.* Cambridge: MIT Press.

———, eds. 2010. *Access Controlled: The Shaping of Power, Rights, and Rule in Cyberspace.* Cambridge: MIT Press.

DEIBERT, RONALD, AND RAFAL ROHOZINSKI. 2010. "Liberation vs. Control: The Future of Cyberspace." *Journal of Democracy* 21 (4): 43–57.

DENARDIS, LAURA, AND ANDREA HACKL. 2015. "Internet Governance by Social Media Platforms." *Telecommunications Policy* 39 (9): 761–70.

DENICOLA, LANE. 2012. "EULA, Codec, API: On the Opacity of Digital Culture." In *Moving Data: The iPhone and the Future of Media,* ed. Pelle Snickars and Patrick Vonderau, 265–77. New York: Columbia University Press.

DEUZE, MARK. 2008. "Corporate Appropriation of Participatory Culture." *Participation and Media Production: Critical Reflections on Content Creation,* ed. Nico Carpentier and Benjamin De Cleen, 27–40. Newcastle: Cambridge Scholars.

DEWEY, JOHN. 1927. *The Public and Its Problems.* Athens, OH: Swallow.

DIBBELL, JULIAN. 1993. "A Rape in Cyberspace." *Village Voice,* December 23.

DJURIC, NEMANJA, JING ZHOU, ROBIN MORRIS, MIHAJLO GRBOVIC, VLADAN RADOSAVLJEVIC, AND NARAYAN BHAMIDIPATI. 2015. "Hate Speech Detection with Comment Embeddings." In *Proceedings of the 24th International Conference on World Wide Web*, 29–30. New York: ACM Press.

DOUGLAS, SUSAN. 1987. *Inventing American Broadcasting, 1899–1922.* Baltimore: Johns Hopkins University Press.

DOWNEY, GREG. 2014. "Making Media Work: Time, Space, Identity, and Labor in the Analysis of Information and Communication Infrastructures." *Media Technologies: Essays on Communication, Materiality, and Society*, ed. Tarleton Gillespie, Pablo Boczkowski, and Kirsten Foot, 141–65. Cambridge: MIT Press.

DRISCOLL, KEVIN. 2016. "Social Media's Dial-Up Ancestor: The Bulletin Board System." *IEEE Spectrum* 53 (11): 54–60.

DUTTON, W. H. 1996. "Network Rules of Order: Regulating Speech in Public Electronic Fora." *Media, Culture, and Society* 18 (2): 269–90.

DYER, RICHARD. 1999. "Making 'White' People White." In *The Social Shaping of Technology*, ed. Donald A. MacKenzie and Judy Wajcman, 134–37. Buckingham, UK: Open University Press.

ELALUF-CALDERWOOD, S. M., B. D. EATON, CARSTEN SØRENSEN, AND YOUNGJIN YOO. 2011. "Control as a Strategy for the Development of Generativity in Business Models for Mobile Platforms." In *15th International Conference on Intelligence in Next Generation Networks*, 271–76. http://ieeexplore.ieee.org /xpls/abs_all.jsp?arnumber=6081088.

ELECTRONIC FRONTIER FOUNDATION. 2015. "Manila Principles on Intermediary Liability." https://www.manilaprinciples.org/.

ELKIN-KOREN, NIVA. 2010. "User-Generated Platforms." In *Working within the Boundaries of Intellectual Property: Innovation Policy for the Knowledge Society*, ed. Rochelle Dreyfuss, Diane Zimmerman, and Harry First, 111–30. Oxford: Oxford University Press. http://papers.ssrn.com/sol3/papers .cfm?abstract_id=1648465.

ELLISON, NICOLE, AND DANAH BOYD. 2013. "Sociality through Social Network Sites." In *The Oxford Handbook of Internet Studies*, ed. William H. Dutton, 151–72. Oxford: Oxford University Press.

FARIS, ROBERT, AMAR ASHAR, URS GASSER, AND DAISY JOO. 2016. "Understanding Harmful Speech Online." https://papers.ssrn.com/sol3/papers.cfm?abstract _id=2882824.

FAST, KARIN, HENRIK ÖRNEBRING, AND MICHAEL KARLSSON. 2016. "Metaphors of Free Labor: A Typology of Unpaid Work in the Media Sector." *Media, Culture, and Society* 38 (7): 963–78.

FEENBERG, A., AND M. BAKARDJIEVA. 2004. "Virtual Community: No 'Killer Implication.'" *New Media and Society* 6 (1): 37–43.

FIFER, SAMUEL, AND S. ROBERTS CARTER. 2004. "A Tale of Two Safe Harbors: The Scope of ISP Liability and the Values of the Internet." *Journal of Internet Law* 8 (2): 13–20.

FIORE-SILVFAST, BRITTANY. 2012. "User-Generated Warfare: A Case of Converging Wartime Information Networks and Coproductive Regulation on YouTube." *International Journal of Communication* 6: 24.

FISH, ADAM, LUIS F. R. MURILLO, LILLY NGUYEN, AARON PANOFSKY, AND CHRISTOPHER M. KELTY. 2011. "Birds of the Internet: Towards a Field Guide to the Organization and Governance of Participation." *Journal of Cultural Economy* 4 (2): 157–87.

FISS, OWEN. 1996. *Liberalism Divided: Freedom of Speech and the Many Uses of State Power.* Boulder, CO: Westview.

FLEW, TERRY. 2015. "Social Media Governance." *Social Media + Society* 1 (1): 2056305115578136.

FLYVERBOM, MIKKEL. 2016. "Digital Age Transparency: Mediation and the Management of Visibilities." *International Journal of Communication* 10: 13.

FORD, HEATHER. 2014. "Infoboxes and Cleanup Tags: Artifacts of Wikipedia Newsmaking." *Journalism,* 1464884914545739.

FORSYTH, HOPE. 2016. "Forum." In *Digital Keywords: A Vocabulary of Information Society and Culture,* ed. Ben Peters, 132–39. Princeton: Princeton University Press.

GAWER, ANNABELLE. 2010. "The Organization of Technological Platforms." In *Technology and Organization: Essays in Honour of Joan Woodward,* ed. Nelson Phillips, Graham Sewell, and Dorothy Griffiths, 287–96. Bingley, UK: Emerald Group Publishing Limited.

———, ed. 2011. *Platforms, Markets, and Innovation.* Cheltenham: Edward Elgar.

GEHL, ROBERT W. 2011. "The Archive and the Processor: The Internal Logic of Web 2.0." *New Media and Society* 13 (8): 1228–44.

———. 2014. *Reverse Engineering Social Media: Software, Culture, and Political Economy in New Media Capitalism.* Philadelphia: Temple University Press.

GEIGER, R. STUART. 2016. "Bot-Based Collective Blocklists in Twitter: The Counterpublic Moderation of Harassment in a Networked Public Space." *Information, Communication, and Society* 19 (6): 787–803.

GEIGER, R. STUART, AND DAVID RIBES. 2010. "The Work of Sustaining Order in Wikipedia: The Banning of a Vandal." In *Proceedings of the 2010 ACM Conference on Computer Supported Cooperative Work,* 117–26. New York: ACM Press. http://dl.acm.org/citation.cfm?id=1718941.

GERLITZ, C., AND A. HELMOND. 2013. "The Like Economy: Social Buttons and the Data-Intensive Web." *New Media and Society* 15 (8): 1348–65.

GIBBS, MARTIN, JAMES MEESE, MICHAEL ARNOLD, BJORN NANSEN, AND MARCUS CARTER. 2015. "#Funeral and Instagram: Death, Social Media, and Platform Vernacular." *Information, Communication, and Society* 18 (3): 255–68.

GILLESPIE, TARLETON. 2007. *Wired Shut: Copyright and the Shape of Digital Culture.* Cambridge: MIT Press.

————. 2010. "The Politics of 'Platforms.'" *New Media and Society* 12 (3): 347–64.

————. 2012. "Can an Algorithm Be Wrong?" *Limn* 1 (2). http://escholarship .org/uc/item/0jk9k4hj.

————. 2015. "Platforms Intervene." *Social Media + Society* 1 (1): 2056305115580479.

————. 2016a. "Algorithm." In *Digital Keywords: A Vocabulary of Information Society and Culture,* ed. Ben Peters, 18–30. Princeton: Princeton University Press. http://culturedigitally.org/2016/08/keyword-algorithm/.

————. 2016b. "#trendingistrending: When Algorithms Become Culture." In *Algorithmic Cultures: Essays on Meaning, Performance and New Technologies,* ed. Robert Seyfert and Jonathan Roberge, 52–75. London: Routledge. http:// culturedigitally.org/2016/02/trendingistrending/.

————. 2017. "Algorithmically Recognizable: Santorum's Google Problem, and Google's Santorum Problem." *Information, Communication, and Society* 20 (1): 63–80.

————. 2018. "Exodus International." In *Appified,* ed. Jeremy Morris and Sarah Murray. Ann Arbor: University of Michigan Press.

GINSBURG, JANE C. 1995. "Putting Cars on the 'Information Superhighway': Authors, Exploiters, and Copyright in Cyberspace." *Columbia Law Review* 95 (6): 1466–99.

GODWIN, MIKE. 2003. *Cyber Rights: Defending Free Speech in the Digital Age.* Rev. ed. Cambridge: MIT Press.

GOLDSMITH, JACK, AND TIM WU. 2008. *Who Controls the Internet? Illusions of a Borderless World.* New York: Oxford University Press.

GRAY, MARY L. 2009. *Out in the Country: Youth, Media, and Queer Visibility in Rural America.* New York: NYU Press.

GRIMMELMANN, JAMES. 2014. "Speech Engines." *Minnesota Law Review* 98 (3): 868–952.

————. 2015. "The Virtues of Moderation: Online Communities as Semicommons." *Yale Journal of Law and Technology* 17 (42).

GRIMMELMANN, JAMES, AND PAUL OHM. 2010. "Dr. Generative, or: How I Learned to Stop Worrying and Love the iPhone." *Maryland Law Review* 69: 910–53.

GROSS, LARRY. 2002. *Up from Invisibility: Lesbians, Gay Men, and the Media in America.* New York: Columbia University Press.

GUINS, RAIFORD. 2009. *Edited Clean Version: Technology and the Culture of Control.* Minneapolis: University of Minnesota Press.

HAIMSON, OLIVER L., AND ANNA LAUREN HOFFMANN. 2016. "Constructing and Enforcing 'Authentic' Identity Online: Facebook, Real Names, and Non-Normative Identities." *First Monday* 21 (6). http://ojs-prod-lib.cc.uic.edu /ojs/index.php/fm/article/view/6791.

HALAVAIS, ALEXANDER. 2009. "Do Dugg Diggers Digg Diligently? Feedback as Motivation in Collaborative Moderation Systems." *Information, Communication, and Society* 12 (3): 444–59.

———. 2016. "The Blogosphere and Its Problems: Web 2.0 Undermining Civic Webspaces." *First Monday* 21 (6). http://ojs-prod-lib.cc.uic.edu/ojs/index.php/fm/article/view/6788.

HALLINAN, BLAKE, AND TED STRIPHAS. 2016. "Recommended for You: The Netflix Prize and the Production of Algorithmic Culture." *New Media and Society* 18 (1): 117–37.

HANDS, JOSS. 2013. "Introduction: Politics, Power, and 'Platformativity.' " *Culture Machine* 14: 1–9.

HARIMAN, ROBERT, AND JOHN LOUIS LUCAITES. 2003. "Public Identity and Collective Memory in U.S. Iconic Photography: The Image of 'Accidental Napalm.' " *Critical Studies in Media Communication* 20 (1): 35–66.

HEARN, ALISON. 2017. "Verified: Self-presentation, Identity Management, and Selfhood in the Age of Big Data." *Popular Communication* 15 (2): 62–77.

HEINS, MARJORIE. 2001. *Not in Front of the Children: "Indecency," Censorship, and the Innocence of Youth.* New Brunswick, NJ: Rutgers University Press.

———. 2013. "The Brave New World of Social Media Censorship." *Harvard Law Review Forum* 127 (8): 325–30.

HELMOND, ANNE. 2015. "The Platformization of the Web: Making Web Data Platform Ready." *Social Media + Society* 1 (2): 2056305115603080.

HENDERSHOT, HEATHER. 1998. *Saturday Morning Censors: Television Regulation before the V-Chip.* Durham, NC: Duke University Press.

HERMAN, ANDREW. 2014. "Production, Consumption, and Labor in the Social Media Mode of Communication." In *The Social Media Handbook,* ed. Jeremy Hunsinger and Theresa M. Senft, 30–44. New York: Routledge.

HERMIDA, ALFRED, AND NEIL THURMAN. 2008. "A Clash of Cultures: The Integration of User-Generated Content within Professional Journalistic Frameworks at British Newspaper Websites." *Journalism Practice* 2 (3): 343–56.

HERRING, SUSAN C. 1999. "The Rhetorical Dynamics of Gender Harassment On-Line." *Information Society* 15 (3): 151–67.

HESTRES, LUIS E. 2013. "App Neutrality: Apple's App Store and Freedom of Expression Online." *International Journal of Communication* 7: 1265–80.

HILLIARD, ROBERT L., AND MICHAEL C. KEITH. 2006. *Dirty Discourse: Sex and Indecency in Broadcasting.* 2nd ed. Malden, MA: Wiley-Blackwell.

HOFFMANN, ANNA LAUREN, NICHOLAS PROFERES, AND MICHAEL ZIMMER. 2016. " 'Making the World More Open and Connected': Mark Zuckerberg and the Discursive Construction of Facebook and Its Users." *New Media and Society,* 1461444816660784.

HORWITZ, ROBERT B. 1991a. "The First Amendment Meets Some New Technologies." *Theory and Society* 20 (1): 21–72.

———. 1991b. *The Irony of Regulatory Reform: The Deregulation of American Telecommunications.* New York: Oxford University Press.

HOWARD, PHILIP N., AND STEVE JONES, EDS. 2004. *Society Online: The Internet in Context.* Thousand Oaks, CA: Sage.

HUMPHREYS, SAL. 2013. "Predicting, Securing, and Shaping the Future: Mechanisms of Governance in Online Social Environments." *International Journal of Media and Cultural Politics* 9 (3): 247–58.

HUNTER, DAN, AND GREG LASTOWKA. 2004. "Amateur-to-Amateur." *William and Mary Law Review* 46. http://papers.ssrn.com/sol3/papers.cfm?abstract _id=601808.

IBRAHIM, YASMIN. 2010. "The Breastfeeding Controversy and Facebook: Politicization of Image, Privacy and Protest." *International Journal of E-Politics* 1 (2): 16–28.

INGRAHAM, CHRIS, AND JOSHUA REEVES. 2016. "New Media, New Panics." *Critical Studies in Media Communication* 33 (5): 455–67.

INTRONA, LUCAS D., AND HELEN NISSENBAUM. 2000. "Shaping the Web: Why the Politics of Search Engines Matters." *Information Society* 16 (3): 169–85.

IRANI, LILLY. 2015. "The Cultural Work of Microwork." *New Media and Society* 17 (5): 720–39.

JACK, CAROLINE. 2017. "Lexicon of Lies: Terms for Problematic Information." Data and Society Research Institute. https://datasociety.net/output/lexicon -of-lies/.

JANE, EMMA A. 2014. " 'Your a Ugly, Whorish, Slut': Understanding E-Bile." *Feminist Media Studies* 14 (4): 531–46.

JARRETT, KYLIE. 2014. "The Relevance of 'Women's Work': Social Reproduction and Immaterial Labor in Digital Media." *Television and New Media* 15 (1): 14–29.

JENKINS, HENRY. 2006. *Convergence Culture: Where Old and New Media Collide.* New York: NYU Press.

JENKINS, HENRY, SAM FORD, AND JOSHUA GREEN. 2013. *Spreadable Media: Creating Value and Meaning in a Networked Culture.* New York: NYU Press.

JEONG, SARAH. 2015. *The Internet of Garbage.* Forbes Media. http://www.forbes .com/ebooks/the-internet-of-garbage/.

JISC (JOINT INFORMATION SYSTEMS COMMITTEE). 2007. "Hosting Liability." https:// www.jisc.ac.uk/guides/hosting-liability.

JOHN, NICHOLAS A. 2016. *The Age of Sharing.* Malden, MA: Polity.

JOHNSON, DAVID, AND DAVID G. POST. 1996. "Law and Borders: The Rise of Law in Cyberspace." *Stanford Law Review* 48: 1367–1402.

KELTY, CHRISTOPHER. 2005. "Geeks, Social Imaginaries, and Recursive Publics." *Cultural Anthropology* 20 (2): 185–214.

———. 2014. "The Fog of Freedom." In *Media Technologies: Essays on Communication, Materiality, and Society,* ed. Tarleton Gillespie, Pablo Boczkowski, and Kirsten Foot, 195–220. Cambridge: MIT Press.

———. 2016. "Participation." In *Digital Keywords: A Vocabulary of Information Society and Culture,* ed. Benjamin Peters, 227–41. http://escholarship.org /uc/item/8z13p7g9.pdf.

KENNEDY, H. 2006. "Beyond Anonymity, or Future Directions for Internet Identity Research." *New Media and Society* 8 (6): 859–76.

KENNEDY, JENNY, JAMES MEESE, AND EMILY VAN DER NAGEL. 2016. "Regulation and Social Practice Online." *Continuum* 30 (2): 146–57.

KERR, APHRA, STEFANO DE PAOLI, AND MAX KEATINGE. 2011. "Human and Non-Human Aspects of Governance and Regulation of MMOGs." Paper presented at A Decade in Internet Time: OII Symposium on the Dynamics of the Internet and Society, 21–24. University of Oxford.

KERR, APHRA, AND JOHN D. KELLEHER. 2015. "The Recruitment of Passion and Community in the Service of Capital: Community Managers in the Digital Games Industry." *Critical Studies in Media Communication* 32 (3): 177–92.

KIESLER, SARA, ROBERT KRAUT, PAUL RESNICK, AND ANIKET KITTUR. 2011. "Regulating Behavior in Online Communities." In *Building Successful Online Communities: Evidence-Based Social Design,* ed. Robert E. Kraut and Paul Resnick, 77–124. Cambridge: MIT Press.

KIRKPATRICK, DAVID. 2010. *The Facebook Effect: The Inside Story of the Company That Is Connecting the World.* New York: Simon and Schuster.

KLANG, MATHIAS. 2014. "The Rise and Fall of Freedom of Online Expression." In *The Cambridge Handbook of Human Dignity: Interdisciplinary Perspectives,* ed. Marcus Düwell, Jens Braarvig, Roger Brownsword, and Dietmar Mieth, 505–13. Cambridge: Cambridge University Press.

KLONICK, KATE. 2017. "The New Governors: The People, Rules, and Processes Governing Online Speech." https://papers.ssrn.com/sol3/papers. cfm?abstract_id=2937985.

KOLLOCK, PETER, AND MARC SMITH. 1996. "Managing the Virtual Commons." In *Computer-Mediated Communication: Linguistic, Social, and Cross-Cultural Perspectives,* ed. Susan Herring, 109–28. Amsterdam: John Benjamins.

KRAUT, ROBERT E., AND PAUL RESNICK. 2011. *Building Successful Online Communities: Evidence-Based Social Design.* Cambridge: MIT Press.

KREIMER, SETH F. 2006. "Censorship by Proxy: The First Amendment, Internet Intermediaries, and the Problem of the Weakest Link." *University of Pennsylvania Law Review* 155 (1): 11.

KUSHNER, SCOTT. 2016. "Read Only: The Persistence of Lurking in Web 2.0." *First Monday* 21 (6). http://pear.accc.uic.edu/ojs/index.php/fm/article/view/6789.

LAMPE, CLIFF, AND PAUL RESNICK. 2004. "Slash(Dot) and Burn: Distributed Moderation in a Large Online Conversation Space." In *Proceedings of the SIGCHI Conference on Human Factors in Computing Systems,* 543–50. New York: ACM Press. http://dl.acm.org/citation.cfm?id=985761.

LANE, FREDERICK S. 2006. *The Decency Wars: The Campaign to Cleanse American Culture.* Amherst, NY: Prometheus.

LANGLOIS, G. 2013. "Participatory Culture and the New Governance of Communication: The Paradox of Participatory Media." *Television and New Media* 14 (2): 91–105.

LANGLOIS, GANAELE, AND GREG ELMER. 2013. "The Research Politics of Social Media Platforms." *Culture Machine* 14: 1–17.

LANGLOIS, GANAELE, GREG ELMER, FENWICK MCKELVEY, AND ZACHARY DEVEREAUX. 2009. "Networked Publics: The Double Articulation of Code and Politics on Facebook." *Canadian Journal of Communication* 34 (3). http://www .cjc-online.ca/index.php/journal/article/viewArticle/2114.

LEE, JIANN-SHU, YUNG-MING KUO, PAU-CHOO CHUNG, AND E.-LIANG CHEN. 2007. "Naked Image Detection Based on Adaptive and Extensible Skin Color Model." *Pattern Recognition* 40 (8): 2261–70.

LENERT, EDWARD. 1998. "A Communication Theory Perspective on Telecommunications Policy." *Journal of Communication* 48 (4): 3–23.

LENHART, AMANDA, MICHELLE YBARRA, KATHRYN ZICKHUR, AND MYESHIA PRICE-FEENEY. 2016. "Online Harassment, Digital Abuse, and Cyberstalking in America." New York: Data and Society Research Institute.

LESSIG, LAWRENCE. 1999a. *Code and Other Laws of Cyberspace.* New York: Basic.

———. 1999b. "The Law of the Horse: What Cyberlaw Might Teach." *Harvard Law Review,* 501–49.

———. 2008. *Remix: Making Art and Commerce Thrive in the Hybrid Economy.* London: A and C Black.

LEVINA, MARINA, AND AMY HASINOFF. 2017. "The Silicon Valley Ethos: Tech Industry Products, Discourses, and Practices." *Television and New Media* 18 (6): 489–95.

LEWIS, JON. 2002. *Hollywood v. Hard Core: How the Struggle over Censorship Created the Modern Film Industry.* New York: NYU Press.

LIGHT, BEN. 2014. *Disconnecting with Social Networking Sites.* London: Palgrave Macmillan.

LINGEL, JESSA, AND TARLETON GILLESPIE. 2014. "One Name to Rule Them All: Facebook's Identity Problem." *Atlantic,* October 2. http://www.theatlantic .com/technology/archive/2014/10/one-name-to-rule-them-all-facebook -still-insists-on-a-single-identity/381039/.

LITMAN, JESSICA. 2001. *Digital Copyright: Protecting Intellectual Property on the Internet.* Amherst, NY: Prometheus.

LOBEL, ORLY. 2016. "The Law of the Platform." *Minnesota Law Review* 101 (1): 87–166.

MA, BINBIN, CHANGQING ZHANG, JINGJING CHEN, RI QU, JIANGJIAN XIAO, AND XIAOCHUN CAO. 2014. "Human Skin Detection via Semantic Constraint." In *Proceedings of International Conference on Internet Multimedia Computing and Service,* 181. New York: ACM Press. http://dl.acm.org/citation.cfm?id=2632885.

MACKINNON, REBECCA. 2012. *Consent of the Networked: The Worldwide Struggle for Internet Freedom.* New York: Basic.

MACKINNON, REBECCA, ELONNAI HICKOK, ALLON BAR, AND HAI-IN LIM. 2014. "Fostering Freedom Online: The Roles, Challenges and Obstacles of Internet Intermediaries." Paris: UNESCO/Internet Society. http://unesdoc .unesco.org/images/0023/002311/231162e.pdf.

MACKINNON, RICHARD C. 2002. "Punishing the Persona: Correctional Strategies for the Virtual Offender." In *Virtual Culture: Identity and Communication in Cybersociety,* ed. Steve Jones, 206–35. London: Sage.

MADDISON, STEPHEN. 2010. "Online Obscenity and Myths of Freedom: Dangerous Images, Child Porn, and Neoliberalism." In *Porn.com: Making Sense of Online Pornography,* ed. Feona Attwood, 17–33. New York: Peter Lang.

MALABY, THOMAS M. 2006. "Coding Control: Governance and Contingency in the Production of Online Worlds." *First Monday.* http://firstmonday.org/ojs /index.php/fm/article/viewArticle/1613.

———. 2009. *Making Virtual Worlds: Linden Lab and Second Life.* Ithaca: Cornell University Press.

MANN, RONALD J., AND SETH R. BELZLEY. 2005. "The Promise of Internet Intermediary Liability." *William and Mary Law Review* 47: 239–308.

MANOVICH, LEV. 2001. *The Language of New Media.* Cambridge: MIT Press.

MANSELL, ROBIN. 2015. "The Public's Interest in Intermediaries." *Info* 17 (6): 8–18.

MARSTON, SALLIE A. 2000. "The Social Construction of Scale." *Progress in Human Geography* 24 (2): 219–42.

MARVIN, CAROLYN. 1990. *When Old Technologies Were New: Thinking about Electric Communication in the Late Nineteenth Century.* New York: Oxford University Press.

MARWICK, ALICE E. 2008. "To Catch a Predator? The MySpace Moral Panic." *First Monday* 13 (6). http://firstmonday.org/htbin/cgiwrap/bin/ojs/index.php /fm/article/viewArticle/2152.

———. 2015. *Status Update: Celebrity, Publicity, and Branding in the Social Media Age.* New Haven: Yale University Press.

———. 2017. "Are There Limits to Online Free Speech?" Data and Society Research Institute. https://points.datasociety.net/are-there-limits-to-online -free-speech-14dbb7069aec.

MASSANARI, ADRIENNE. 2015. "#Gamergate and The Fappening: How Reddit's Algorithm, Governance, and Culture Support Toxic Technocultures." *New Media and Society* 19 (3): 329–46.

MATAMOROS-FERNÁNDEZ, ARIADNA. 2017. "Platformed Racism: The Mediation and Circulation of an Australian Race-based Controversy on Twitter, Facebook and YouTube." *Information, Communication, and Society* 20 (6): 930–46.

MATIAS, J. NATHAN, AMY JOHNSON, WHITNEY ERIN BOESEL, BRIAN KEEGAN, JACLYN FRIEDMAN, AND CHARLIE DETAR. 2015. "Reporting, Reviewing, and Responding to Harassment on Twitter." arXiv. http://arxiv.org/abs/1505.03359.

MAYER-SCHÖNBERGER, VIKTOR, AND KENNETH CUKIER. 2014. *Big Data: A Revolution That Will Transform How We Live, Work, And Think.* Boston: Eamon Dolan/Mariner.

MCCRACKEN, CHELSEA. 2013. "Regulating Swish: Early Television Censorship." *Media History* 19 (3): 354–68.

MCPHERSON, MILLER, LYNN SMITH-LOVIN, AND JAMES M. COOK. 2001. "Birds of a Feather: Homophily in Social Networks." *Annual Review of Sociology* 27 (1): 415–44.

MCROBBIE, ANGELA, AND SARAH L. THORNTON. 1995. "Rethinking 'Moral Panic' for Multi-Mediated Social Worlds." *British Journal of Sociology,* 559–74.

MCVEIGH-SCHULTZ, JOSHUA, AND NANCY K. BAYM. 2015. "Thinking of You: Vernacular Affordance in the Context of the Microsocial Relationship App, Couple." *Social Media + Society* 1 (2): 2056305115604649.

MEDEIROS, BEN. 2017. "Platform (Non-) Intervention and the 'Marketplace' Paradigm for Speech Regulation." *Social Media + Society* 3 (1): 2056305117691997.

MEYERSON, MICHAEL. 2001. "The Neglected History of the Prior Restraint Doctrine: Rediscovering the Link between the First Amendment and the Separation of Powers." *Indiana Law Review* 34 (2): 295–342.

MILAN, STEFANIA. 2015. "When Algorithms Shape Collective Action: Social Media and the Dynamics of Cloud Protesting." *Social Media + Society* 1 (2): 2056305115622481.

MILLER, FRANK. 1994. *Censored Hollywood: Sex, Sin, and Violence on Screen.* Atlanta: Turner.

MILLER, NANCY K. 2004. "The Girl in the Photograph: The Vietnam War and the Making of National Memory." *JAC* 24 (2): 261–90.

MILOSEVIC, TIJANA. 2016. "Social Media Companies' Cyberbullying Policies." *International Journal of Communication* 10: 5164–85.

MORRIS, JEREMY, AND EVAN ELKINS. 2015. "There's a History for That: Apps and Mundane Software as Commodity." *Fibreculture Journal,* no. 25: 63–88.

MOSCO, VINCENT. 1990. "The Mythology of Telecommunications Deregulation." *Journal of Communication* 40 (1): 36–49.

MUELLER, MILTON L. 2015. "Hyper-Transparency and Social Control: Social Media as Magnets for Regulation." *Telecommunications Policy* 39 (9): 804–10.

MULVIN, DYLAN. Forthcoming. *Proxies: Standards and Their Media.* Cambridge: MIT Press.

MUNK, TIMME BISGAARD. 2017 "100,000 False Positives for Every Real Terrorist: Why Anti-Terror Algorithms Don't Work." *First Monday* 22 (9). https://firstmonday.org/ojs/index.php/fm/article/view/7126.

NAGY, PETER, AND GINA NEFF. 2015. "Imagined Affordance: Reconstructing a Keyword for Communication Theory." *Social Media + Society* 1 (2): 2056305115603385.

NAHON, KARINE. 2016. "Where There Is Social Media, There Is Politics." *Routledge Companion to Social Media and Politics,* ed. Axel Bruns, Gunn Enli, Eli Skogerbo, Anders Olof Larsson, and Christian Christensen, 39–55. New York: Routledge.

NAKAMURA, LISA, AND PETER CHOW-WHITE, EDS. 2012. *Race after the Internet.* New York: Routledge.

NAPOLI, PHILIP M., AND ROBYN CAPLAN. 2016. "When Media Companies Insist They're Not Media Companies and Why It Matters for Communications Policy." https://papers.ssrn.com/sol3/papers.cfm?abstract_id=2750148.

NEFF, GINA, AND PETER NAGY. 2016. "Talking to Bots: Symbiotic Agency and the Case of Tay." *International Journal of Communication* 10: 4915–31.

NIEBORG, DAVID B. 2015. "Crushing Candy: The Free-to-Play Game in Its Connective Commodity Form." *Social Media + Society* 1 (2): 2056305115621932.

NIEDERER, S., AND J. VAN DIJCK. 2010. "Wisdom of the Crowd or Technicity of Content? Wikipedia as a Sociotechnical System." *New Media and Society* 12 (8): 1368–87.

NOBLE, SAFIYA UMOJA. 2012. "Missed Connections: What Search Engines Say about Women." *Bitch Magazine,* Spring.

———. 2018. *Algorithms of Oppression: How Search Engines Reinforce Racism.* New York: NYU Press.

OBAR, JONATHAN, AND STEVE WILDMAN. 2015. "Social Media Definition and the Governance Challenge: An Introduction to the Special Issue." *Telecommunications Policy* 39 (9): 745–50.

O'NEIL, CATHY. 2016. *Weapons of Math Destruction: How Big Data Increases Inequality and Threatens Democracy.* New York: Crown.

OUDSHOORN, NELLY, AND TREVOR PINCH, EDS. 2005. *How Users Matter: The Co-Construction of Users and Technology.* Cambridge: MIT Press.

PALFREY, JOHN. 2010. "Four Phases of Internet Regulation." *Social Research: An International Quarterly,* 77 (3): 981–96.

PAPACHARISSI, ZIZI. 2015. "We Have Always Been Social." *Social Media + Society* 1 (1): 2056305115581185.

PARISER, ELI. 2011. *The Filter Bubble: How the New Personalized Web Is Changing What We Read and How We Think.* New York: Penguin.

PASQUALE, FRANK. 2015. *The Black Box Society: The Secret Algorithms That Control Money and Information.* Cambridge: Harvard University Press.

———. 2016. "Platform Neutrality: Enhancing Freedom of Expression in Spheres of Private Power." *Theoretical Inquiries in Law,* forthcoming. http://papers.ssrn.com/sol3/papers.cfm?abstract_id=2779270.

PETERSON, CHRISTOPHER E. 2013. "User-Generated Censorship: Manipulating the Maps of Social Media." Massachusetts Institute of Technology. http://18.7.29.232/handle/1721.1/81132.

PFAFFENBERGER, BRYAN. 1996. "'If I Want It, It's OK': Usenet and the (Outer) Limits of Free Speech." *Information Society* 12 (4): 365–86.

PHILLIPS, WHITNEY. 2015. *This Is Why We Can't Have Nice Things: Mapping the Relationship between Online Trolling and Mainstream Culture.* Cambridge: MIT Press.

PHILLIPS, WHITNEY, JESSICA L. BEYER, AND GABRIELLA COLEMAN. 2017. "Trolling Scholars Debunk the Idea That the Alt-Right's Shitposters Have Magic Powers." Motherboard, March 22. https://motherboard.vice.com/en_us/article/z4k549/trolling-scholars-debunk-the-idea-that-the-alt-rights-trolls-have-magic-powers.

PLANTIN, JEAN-CHRISTOPHE, CARL LAGOZE, PAUL N. EDWARDS, AND CHRISTIAN SANDVIG. 2016. "Infrastructure Studies Meet Platform Studies in the Age of Google and Facebook." *New Media and Society,* 1461444816661553.

PLATZER, CHRISTIAN, MARTIN STUETZ, AND MARTINA LINDORFER. 2014. "Skin Sheriff: A Machine Learning Solution for Detecting Explicit Images." In *Proceedings of the 2nd International Workshop on Security and Forensics in Communication Systems,* 45–56. New York: ACM Press.

POSTIGO, HECTOR. 2009. "America Online Volunteers: Lessons from an Early Co-Production Community." *International Journal of Cultural Studies* 12 (5): 451–69.

———. 2011. "Questioning the Web 2.0 Discourse: Social Roles, Production, Values, and the Case of the Human Rights Portal." *Information Society* 27 (3): 181–93.

———. 2014. "The Socio-Technical Architecture of Digital Labor: Converting Play into YouTube Money." *New Media and Society* 18 (2): 332–49.

———. 2015. "Social Media: The Unbearable Lightness of Meaning." *Social Media + Society* 1 (1): 2056305115580342.

PRATT, GERALDINE, AND VICTORIA ROSNER. 2006. "Introduction: The Global and the Intimate." *Women's Studies Quarterly,* 3 (1–2): 13–24.

PUPPIS, MANUEL. 2010. "Media Governance: A New Concept for the Analysis of Media Policy and Regulation." *Communication, Culture, and Critique* 3 (2): 134–49.

QVORTRUP, LARS. 2006. "Understanding New Digital Media: Medium Theory or Complexity Theory?" *European Journal of Communication* 21 (3): 345–56.

RAPPAPORT, KIM. 1997. "In the Wake of *Reno v. ACLU:* The Continued Struggle in Western Constitutional Democracies with Internet Censorship and Freedom of Speech Online." *American University International Law Review* 13 (3): 727.

REAGLE, JOSEPH. 2010. *Good Faith Collaboration: The Culture of Wikipedia.* History and Foundations of Information Science. Cambridge: MIT Press.

————. 2015. *Reading the Comments: Likers, Haters, and Manipulators at the Bottom of the Web.* Cambridge: MIT Press.

ROBERTS, SARAH T. 2016. "Commercial Content Moderation: Digital Laborers' Dirty Work." In *Intersectional Internet: Race, Sex, Class and Culture Online,* ed. Safiya Umoja Noble and Brendesha Tynes, 147–59. New York: Peter Lang. http://ir.lib.uwo.ca/commpub/12/?utm_source =ir.lib.uwo.ca%2Fcommpub%2F12&utm_medium=PDF&utm _campaign=PDFCoverPages.

————. 2017. "Content Moderation." http://escholarship.org/uc/item/7371c1hf .pdf.

ROCHET, JEAN-CHARLES, AND JEAN TIROLE. 2003. "Platform Competition in Two-Sided Markets." *Journal of the European Economic Association* 1 (4): 990–1029.

ROGERS, KEVIN. 2013. "Jailbroken: Examining the Policy and Legal Implications of iPhone Jailbreaking." *Pittsburgh Journal of Technology Law and Policy* 13 (2).

ROTH, LORNA. 2009. "Looking at Shirley, the Ultimate Norm: Colour Balance, Image Technologies, and Cognitive Equity." *Canadian Journal of Communication* 34 (1): 111.

ROTH, YOEL. 2015. " 'No Overly Suggestive Photos of Any Kind': Content Management and the Policing of Self in Gay Digital Communities." *Communication, Culture, and Critique* 8 (3): 414–32.

SAMUELSON, PAMELA. 2003. "DRM {and, or, vs.} the Law." *Communications of the ACM* 46 (4): 41–45.

SANDVIG, CHRISTIAN. 2015. "The Social Industry." *Social Media + Society* 1 (1): 2056305115582047.

SCHUDSON, MICHAEL. 1984. *Advertising, the Uneasy Persuasion: Its Dubious Impact on American Society.* New York: Basic.

SCHÜLL, NATASHA DOW. 2012. *Addiction by Design: Machine Gambling in Las Vegas.* Princeton: Princeton University Press.

SELLARS, ANDREW. 2016. "Defining Hate Speech." https://papers.ssrn.com/sol3 /papers.cfm?abstract_id=2882244.

SENGAMEDU, SRINIVASAN H., SUBHAJIT SANYAL, AND SRIRAM SATISH. 2011. "Detection of Pornographic Content in Internet Images." In *Proceedings of the 19th ACM International Conference on Multimedia,* 1141–44. New York: ACM Press. http://dl.acm.org/citation.cfm?id=2071959.

SHARMA, SANJAY. 2013. "Black Twitter? Racial Hashtags, Networks and Contagion." *New Formations* 78 (1): 46–64.

SHAW, AARON, AND BENJAMIN M. HILL. 2014. "Laboratories of Oligarchy? How the Iron Law Extends to Peer Production." *Journal of Communication* 64 (2): 215–38.

SHAW, ADRIENNE. 2014. "The Internet Is Full of Jerks, Because the World Is Full of Jerks: What Feminist Theory Teaches Us about the Internet." *Communication and Critical/Cultural Studies* 11 (3): 273–77.

SHEPHERD, TAMARA, ALLISON HARVEY, TIM JORDAN, SAM SRAUY, AND KATE MILTNER. 2015. "Histories of Hating." *Social Media + Society* 1 (2): 2056305115603997.

SHILTON, KATIE, JES A. KOEPFLER, AND KENNETH R. FLEISCHMANN. 2013. "Charting Sociotechnical Dimensions of Values for Design Research." *Information Society* 29 (5): 259–71.

SHIRKY, CLAY. 2008. *Here Comes Everybody: How Change Happens when People Come Together.* New York: Penguin.

SHOREY, SAMANTHA, AND PHILIP N. HOWARD. 2016. "Automation, Big Data, and Politics: A Research Review." *International Journal of Communication* 10: 5032–55.

SILVERSTONE, ROGER. 2007. *Media and Morality: On the Rise of the Mediapolis.* Cambridge: Polity.

SILVERSTONE, ROGER, AND LESLIE HADDON. 1998. "Design and the Domestication of Information and Communication Technologies." In *Communication by Design: The Politics of Information and Communication Technologies,* ed. Robin Mansell and Roger Silverstone, 44–74. Oxford: Oxford University Press.

SNICKARS, PELLE, AND PATRICK VONDERAU, EDS. 2009. *The YouTube Reader.* Mediehistoriskt Arkiv 12. Stockholm: National Library of Sweden.

SONG, FELICIA WU. 2009. *Virtual Communities: Bowling Alone, Online Together.* New York: Peter Lang.

SOOD, SARA, JUDD ANTIN, AND ELIZABETH CHURCHILL. 2012. "Profanity Use in Online Communities." In *Proceedings of the SIGCHI Conference on Human Factors in Computing Systems,* 1481–90. New York: ACM Press. http://dl.acm.org/citation.cfm?id=2208610.

STERLING, BRUCE. 1992. "Short History of the Internet." https://w2.eff.org/Net_culture/internet_sterling.history.txt.

STREETER, THOMAS. 1996. *Selling the Air: A Critique of the Policy of Commercial Broadcasting in the United States.* Chicago: University of Chicago Press.

———. 2010. *The Net Effect: Romanticism, Capitalism, and the Internet.* New York: NYU Press.

———. 2017. "The Internet as a Structure of Feeling: 1992–1996." *Internet Histories* 1 (1–2): 79–89.

SULER, JOHN. 2004. "The Online Disinhibition Effect." *CyberPsychology and Behavior* 7 (3): 321–26.

SUNSTEIN, CASS R. 2009. *Republic. Com 2.0.* Princeton: Princeton University Press.

SUZOR, NICOLAS. 2010. "The Role of the Rule of Law in Virtual Communities." *Berkeley Technology Law Journal* 25 (4): 1817–86.

SUZOR, NICOLAS, BRYONY SEIGNIOR, AND JENNIFER SINGLETON. 2017. "Non-consensual Porn and the Responsibilities of Online Intermediaries." *Melbourne University Law Review* 40 (3): 1057–97.

TAYLOR, T. L. 2004. "The Social Design of Virtual Worlds: Constructing the User and Community through Code." In *Internet Research Annual,* vol. 1, *Selected Papers from the Association of Internet Researchers Conferences 2000–2002,* 260–68.

———. 2006. "Beyond Management: Considering Participatory Design and Governance in Player Culture." *First Monday.* http://journals.uic.edu/ojs/index.php/fm/article/view/1611.

THOMPSON, J. B. 2005. "The New Visibility." *Theory, Culture, and Society* 22 (6): 31–51.

TIIDENBERG, KATRIN. 2016. "Boundaries and Conflict in a NSFW Community on Tumblr: The Meanings and Uses of Selfies." *New Media and Society* 18 (8): 1563–78.

TIWANA, AMRIT, BENN KONSYNSKI, AND ASHLEY A. BUSH. 2010. "Platform Evolution: Coevolution of Platform Architecture, Governance, and Environmental Dynamics." *Information Systems Research* 21 (4): 675–87.

TUFEKCI, ZEYNEP. 2015. "Algorithmic Harms beyond Facebook and Google: Emergent Challenges of Computational Agency." *Journal on Telecommunications and High-Tech Law* 13 (2): 203–18.

———. 2016. "As the Pirates Become CEOs: The Closing of the Open Internet." *Daedalus* 145 (1): 65–78.

TURKLE, SHERRY. 1997. *Life on the Screen: Identity in the Age of the Internet.* New York: Simon and Schuster.

TURNER, FRED. 2006. *From Counterculture to Cyberculture: Stewart Brand, the Whole Earth Network, and the Rise of Digital Utopianism.* Chicago: University of Chicago Press.

———. 2009. "Burning Man at Google: A Cultural Infrastructure for New Media Production." *New Media and Society* 11 (1–2): 73–94.

TUSHNET, REBECCA. 2008. "Power without Responsibility: Intermediaries and the First Amendment." *George Washington Law Review* 76: 101.

VAIDHYANATHAN, SIVA. 2012. *The Googlization of Everything (and Why We Should Worry).* Berkeley: University of California Press.

VAN COUVERING, ELIZABETH. 2017. "The Political Economy of New Media Revisited: Platformisation, Mediatisation, and the Politics of Algorithms." In *Proceedings of the 50th Annual Conference.* University of Hawai'i at Manoa.

VAN DIJCK, JOSÉ. 2009. "Users Like You? Theorizing Agency in User-Generated Content." *Media, Culture, and Society* 31 (1): 41–58.

———. 2013. *The Culture of Connectivity: A Critical History of Social Media.* Oxford: Oxford University Press.

VAN DIJCK, JOSÉ, AND THOMAS POELL. 2013. "Understanding Social Media Logic." 2–14. http://www.librelloph.com/ojs/index.php/mediaandcommunication /article/view/37.

VAN DOORN, NIELS. 2017. "Platform Labor: On the Gendered and Racialized Exploitation of Low-Income Service Work in the 'on-Demand' Economy." *Information, Communication, and Society* 20 (6): 898–914.

VARNELIS, KAZYS, ED. 2008. *Networked Publics.* Cambridge: MIT Press.

VAUGHN, STEPHEN. 2006. *Freedom and Entertainment: Rating the Movies in an Age of New Media.* New York: Cambridge University Press.

VERHULST, S. 2006. "The Regulation of Digital Content." *The Handbook of New Media: Social Shaping and Consequences of ICTs,* ed. Leah Lievrouw and Sonia Livingstone, 329–49. London: Sage.

VICKERY, JACQUELINE RYAN, AND TRACY EVERBACH, EDS. 2018. *Mediating Misogyny: Gender, Technology, and Harassment.* London: Palgrave Macmillan.

VONDERAU, PATRICK. 2014. "The Politics of Content Aggregation." *Television and New Media,* 1527476414554402.

WAGNER, R. POLK. 1998. "Filters and the First Amendment." *Minnesota Law Review* 83: 755.

WARNER, WILLIAM, AND JULIA HIRSCHBERG. 2012. "Detecting Hate Speech on the World Wide Web." In *Proceedings of the Second Workshop on Language in Social Media,* 19–26. Association for Computational Linguistics. http://dl .acm.org/citation.cfm?id=2390377.

WAUTERS, E., E. LIEVENS, AND P. VALCKE. 2014. "Towards a Better Protection of Social Media Users: A Legal Perspective on the Terms of Use of Social Networking Sites." *International Journal of Law and Information Technology* 22 (3): 254–94.

WEBER, STEVEN. 2009. *The Success of Open Source.* Cambridge: Harvard University Press.

WELTEVREDE, ESTHER, ANNE HELMOND, AND CAROLIN GERLITZ. 2014. "The Politics of Real-Time: A Device Perspective on Social Media Platforms and Search Engines." *Theory, Culture, and Society* 31 (6): 125–50.

WEST, SARAH MYERS. 2017. "Raging against the Machine: Network Gatekeeping and Collective Action on Social Media Platforms." *Media and Communication* 5 (3): 28–36.

———. Forthcoming. "A Conceptual Framework for the (Private) Public Sphere: Surveying User Experiences of Content Moderation on Social Media Platforms." Manuscript submitted for publication.

WOOLGAR, STEVE. 1990. "Configuring the User: The Case of Usability Trials." *Sociological Review* 38 (S1).

WU, TIM. 2010. *The Master Switch: The Rise and Fall of Information Empires.* New York: Knopf.

YORK, JILLIAN C. 2015. "Solutions for Online Harassment Don't Come Easily." *Fibreculture Journal* 26: 297–301.

YOUMANS, WILLIAM, AND JILLIAN C. YORK. 2012. "Social Media and the Activist Toolkit: User Agreements, Corporate Interests, and the Information Infrastructure of Modern Social Movements." *Journal of Communication* 62 (2): 315–29.

YU, PETER K. 2003. "The Escalating Copyright Wars." *Hofstra Law Review* 32: 907–51.

ZARSKY, TAL Z. 2014. "Social Justice, Social Norms, and the Governance of Social Media." *Pace Law Review* 35: 154.

———. 2016. "The Trouble with Algorithmic Decisions: An Analytic Road Map to Examine Efficiency and Fairness in Automated and Opaque Decision Making." *Science, Technology, and Human Values* 41 (1): 118–32.

ZELIZER, BARBIE. 2010. *About to Die: How News Images Move the Public.* New York: Oxford University Press.

ZICKMUND, SUSAN. 2002. "Approaching the Radical Other: The Discursive Culture of Cyberhate." In *Virtual Culture: Identity and Communication in Cybersociety,* 185–205. London: Sage.

ZITTRAIN, JONATHAN. 2002. "Internet Points of Control." *Boston College Law Review* 44: 653.

———. 2006. "A History of Online Gatekeeping." *Harvard Journal of Law and Technology* 19 (2): 253.

———. 2008. *The Future of the Internet and How to Stop It.* New Haven: Yale University Press.

ZUCKERMAN, ETHAN. 2010. "Intermediary Censorship." In *Access Controlled: The Shaping of Power, Rights, and Rule in Cyberspace,* ed. Ronald Deibert, John Palfrey, Rafal Rohozinski, and Jonathan Zittrain, 71–85. Cambridge: MIT Press.

ACKNOWLEDGMENTS

I don't relish admitting it out loud, but this book was a long time in the making, too long. So I have many people to thank, and I am almost certainly going to overlook someone. I've been supported by so many and in so many ways, I hope I will have the chance to express my gratitude to everyone, if not here, then in some way, eventually.

I must first thank my two intellectual homes: all my friends and colleagues in the Department of Communication at Cornell University, and all my friends and colleagues in the Social Media Collective and at Microsoft Research New England. I'm so fortunate to have been able to work and thrive in two such generous, diverse, and brilliant groups. My thanks to Cornell University and Microsoft, for making these places possible and inviting me to be part of them. My particular gratitude goes to Jennifer Chayes and Christian Borgs, who lead the Microsoft Research lab in New England, for their fierce commitment to Microsoft Research's support for serious and independent scholarly work. In addition, I am deeply grateful for the fellowship at the Collegium de Lyon, generously supported by the European Institutes for Advanced Study (EURIAS) Fellowship Programme, where I was able to start thinking through the ideas in this book.

Thanks to all who listened to me jabber on about all this, perhaps ad nauseam. And when it became clear that I was the limiting factor keeping my drafts from improving any further, some of those people were kind enough to read and comment on it, at its most drafty. For this, and for everything, I am especially grateful to Mike Ananny, Nancy Baym, danah boyd, Sarah Brayne, Andre Brock, Nick Couldry, Kate Crawford, Kevin Driscoll, Stephanie Duguay, Christina Dunbar-Hester, Megan Finn, Ysabel Gerrard, Mary Gray, Dan Greene, Lee Humphreys, Steve Jackson, Henry Jenkins, Kate Klonick, Leah Lievrouw, Jessa Lingel, Annette Markham, Nathan Matias, Jeremy Morris, Sharif Mowlabocus, Dylan Mulvin, Genevieve Patterson,

Hector Postigo, Stephanie Schulte, Nick Seaver, Sarah Sobieraj, Jonathan Sterne, Nick Suzor, Lana Swartz, TL Taylor, Jose van Dijck, and Sarah Myers West.

A few Cornell undergraduate students helped me with some of early digging; my thanks to Joe D'Angelo, Allison Fischler, Mo Rahman, Julia Rizzo, and Erica Southerland. I owe a debt of gratitude to the stellar research assistants at Microsoft Research for their help: Andrea Alarcon, Sarah Hamid, Rebecca Hoffman, and Kate Miltner. And finally, several of my graduate students at Cornell helped with this research: my thanks to Josh Braun, Dima Epstein, Tony Liao—and a special thank-you to Caroline Jack, who helped in so many ways, including conducting several of the interviews that form the basis of Chapter 6.

I also want to thank Yale University Press, including Alison MacKeen, who first signed the book; Eva Skewes, who helped as editorial assistant; Dan Heaton for his superb copyediting; the anonymous reviewers who read the proposal and the finished manuscript; and most of all my editor, Joe Calamia, who patiently saw me through the process, improving the book and easing my anxiety along the way.

Finally, my deepest love and gratitude to my family—who, for reasons I can't always explain, are willing to both applaud my efforts and forgive my foolishness.

Bits and pieces of the writing appeared elsewhere in other forms. Parts of Chapter 2 appeared in Tarleton Gillespie, "Regulation of and by Platforms," in *SAGE Handbook of Social Media,* ed. Jean Burgess, Thomas Poell, and Alice Marwick (London: Sage, 2017). Bits of Chapter 3 appeared in Jessa Lingel and Tarleton Gillespie, "One Name to Rule Them All: Facebook's Identity Problem," *Atlantic,* October 2, 2014, http://www.theatlantic.com /technology/archive/2014/10/one-name-to-rule-them-all-facebook-still -insists-on-a-single-identity/381039/. Parts of Chapter 4 appeared in Kate Crawford and Tarleton Gillespie, "What Is a Flag For? Social Media Reporting Tools and the Vocabulary of Complaint," *New Media and Society* 18, no. 3 (2016; online, 2014): 410–28. Bits of Chapter 5 appeared in Tarleton Gillespie, "Facebook Can't Moderate in Secret Anymore," Culture Digitally, May 23, 2017, http://culturedigitally.org/2017/05/facebook-cant-moderate -in-secret-any-more/. Parts of Chapter 7 appeared in Tarleton Gillespie, "Tumblr, NSFW Porn Blogging, and the Challenge of Checkpoints," Culture Digitally, July 26, 2013, http://culturedigitally.org/2013/07/tumblr-nsfw

-porn-blogging-and-the-challenge-of-checkpoints/. A small part of Chapter 8 will also appear as Tarleton Gillespie, "What Platforms Should Do about Harassment," in *Mediating Misogyny: Gender, Technology, and Harassment,* ed. Jacqueline Vickery and Tracy Everbach (London: Palgrave Macmillan, 2018). A particular thank-you to my colleague Kate Crawford, who generously gave her permission for elements of our coauthored essay to be included here.